T0331255

YOUTH ENTREPRENEURSHIP AND LOCAL DEVELOPMENT IN CENTRAL AND EASTERN EUROPE

Youth Entrepreneurship and Local Development in Central and Eastern Europe

Edited by

PAUL BLOKKER
University of Sussex, UK

BRUNO DALLAGO
University of Trento, Italy

LONDON AND NEW YORK

First published 2008 by Ashgate Publishing

Reissued 2018 by Routledge
2 Park Square, Milton Park, Abingdon, Oxon OX14 4RN
605 Third Avenue, New York, NY 10017

First issued in paperback 2021

Routledge is an imprint of the Taylor & Francis Group, an informa business

A Library of Congress record exists under LC control number: 2007030991

Notice:
Product or corporate names may be trademarks or registered trademarks, and are used only for identification and explanation without intent to infringe.

Publisher's Note
The publisher has gone to great lengths to ensure the quality of this reprint but points out that some imperfections in the original copies may be apparent.

Disclaimer
The publisher has made every effort to trace copyright holders and welcomes correspondence from those they have been unable to contact.

ISBN 13: 978-0-8153-9919-3 (hbk)
ISBN 13: 978-1-3511-4264-9 (ebk)
ISBN 13: 978-1-138-35804-1 (pbk)

DOI: 10.4324/9781351142649

Contents

List of Figures

List of Tables

Notes on Contributors

Sergio Arzeni is Director of the Centre for Entrepreneurship and Local Employment and Economic Development, OECD, Paris, France. His work has focused primarily on entrepreneurship and innovation, on job creation and social cohesion, on the internationalisation of SMEs and area-based approaches to economic development. He has worked at the OECD for 23 years, previously serving as an economist for the Italian Parliament, the Italian Trade Unions and the European Commission. As an economic journalist he has contributed to several Italian and international newspapers. He holds a First Class Honours Degree in Political Science from the University of Rome and specialised in Industrial Economics at the University of Luxembourg and on International Economic Relations at the Brookings Institution in Washington D.C., USA.

Ivo Bićanić is Professor at the Faculty of Economics, University of Zagreb and Recurrent Visiting Professor at the Department of Economics, Central European University, Budapest. Following a degree from Zagreb University he completed his postgraduate studies in economics at St. Antony's College, University of Oxford and a doctorate at Zagreb University. After research in the early 1990s on the break up of Yugoslavia, his research interests shifted towards growth theory and growth prospects of Croatia and Southeast European economies. His most recent publications include "The Economic Lag of Transition Economies" in Vojmir Franicevic and Milica Uvalic eds., *Equality, Participation, Transition: Essays in honour of Branko Horvat*, St. Martins Press, London, 2000; "Poverty and Development in Southeast Europe", *Journal of Southeast European and Black Sea Studies*, vol: 1 (2001).

Paul Blokker holds a Ph.D. from the European University Institute, Florence. Currently, he is a Marie Curie Postdoctoral Fellow at the University of Sussex. He was research associate in the Joint European Master in Comparative Local Development and has taught at the faculty of Sociology, University of Trento. His research interests include: Social and Political Theory, Varieties of Modernity, Transformation in Central and Eastern Europe, and European integration. His recent publications include: 2006, 'The Post-Enlargement European Order: Europe "United in Diversity"'?, *European Diversity and Autonomy Papers – EDAP*, 2006/1, at www.eurac.edu/edap; 2005, 'Post-Communist Modernization, Transition Studies, and Diversity in Europe', *European Journal of Social Theory*, 8(4): 503–525; 2004, 'Ideas, Culture, and History in Transition Studies', Review Essay, in: *Czech Sociological Review*, vol. 40, no. 6; 2002, 'Continuity in Change: Social Consequences of Economic Reform in Romania', in: A.E. Fernández Jilberto and M. Riethof (eds), *Labour Relations in Development*, London: Routledge.

Bruno Dallago holds a Ph.D. in economics, and is Professor of Economics at the University of Trento and Academic Director of the Graduate School on Local Development. He was President of the European Association for Comparative Economic Studies, Visiting Professor at various universities including the University of California at Berkeley and Hitotsubashi University, Tokyo and consultant to various international organizations. He is author and editor of several books in Italian and English and various articles in scholarly journals. His research interests include comparative economics, transforming economies of Central and East Europe, SMEs and entrepreneurship, and corporate governance. His recent publications include: 2007, *Corporate Restructuring and Governance in Transition Economies*, with Ichiro Iwasaki (eds.), Basingstoke: Palgrave Macmillan; 2006, *Transformation and European Integration. The Local Dimension*, Basingstoke/New York: Palgrave Macmillan (ed.); 2003, *Small and Medium Enterprises in Transitional Economies*, with R.J. McIntyre (eds.) Basingstoke/New York: Palgrave Macmillan/WIDER.

Miroslav Glas studied economics at the University of Ljubljana and University of Zagreb, and defended his Ph.D. thesis on income distribution at the University of Ljubljana, where he is currently working as Professor of Economics and Entrepreneurship. His research is focused on income and wealth distribution and inequality, management issues related to business ethics, corporate social responsibility and other issues of business environment, as well as entrepreneurship policy and small business management. As an international consultant he has been involved in several Central and Eastern European countries. He is head of the Entrepreneurship Development Centre at the Faculty of Economics, University of Ljubljana, where he also initiated the foundation of Ljubljana University Incubator. He is author of a number of textbooks on economics and entrepreneurship, papers in international journals as well as papers at international conferences and workshops on entrepreneurship.

Klaus Haftendorn joined the ILO in 1995 as Senior Specialist in SME development within the Job Creation and Enterprise Department. He managed among others a large portfolio of SME projects in East-Europe and Central Asia. These projects combined local economic development through business creation and business promotion by setting up Business Development Centres. Since the UN Millennium Summit in 2000 he became involved in the Youth Employment Network (YEN) created by the UN Secretary General connecting together the World Bank, the ILO and the UN Secretariat to reduce youth unemployment. He became member of the YEN High Level Panel working groups on Employability and Entrepreneurship.

Mihály Laki obtained his Ph.D. at the Budapest University of Economics in 1996, taught at the Central European University, Department of Political Sciences, and is senior research fellow of the Institute of Economics at the Hungarian Academy of Sciences since 1989. His research field covers issues of firm behaviour, privatisation, enterpreneurship and market structures in transitional countries, especially in Hungary. He was a member of the Economics Committee of the Hungaria Academy of Sciences, and is currently a member of the editorial board of several journals.

His teaching activity includes various foreign universities (CEU, Justus Liebig Universität, University of California San Diego).

Marina Lang-Perica is Head of the Department for Entrepreneurship Infrastructure of the Croatian Ministry of Economy, Labour and Entrepreneurship. She graduated at the Faculty of Economy, Zagreb University in 1984. She has many years of experience working with governmental departments, regional/local governments, private sector firms and NGOs. She is a certified entrepreneurship trainer and lecturer in the field of SMEs, SME development policies (strategy development, policy analysis, business plans, good practice, SWOT analysis, comparative analysis, etc.). She is an expert on the present state of SMEs in Croatia, institution-building (conception of SME institutions, strategy, policy and training resources, management development).

Jay Mitra is the Founding Professor of Business Enterprise and Innovation, Director of the Centre for Entrepreneurship Research at the University of Essex, and Head of the School of Entrepreneurship and Business, at the University of Essex, UK. He is also the Director of the Scientific Committee on Entrepreneurship for the OECD (Organisation for Economic Co-operation and Development) and its LEED (Local Economic and Employment) Programme, in Paris, France, and in Trento, Italy. He is currently a Visiting Professor at the School of Management at Fudan University in China and The Centre for China Public Sector Economy Research at Jilin University. He is a Fellow of the Royal Society of Arts in the UK. Jay Mitra also leads the International Entrepreneurship Forum, a unique forum of researchers, policy makers and business practitioners concerned with entrepreneurship, innovation and regional development. Educated in India and the UK, Professor Mitra trained in the private sector in the UK, worked as a Principal Officer for local government also in the UK, specialising in economic and business development, and taught at 3 other universities before joining the University of Essex. He also set up two businesses in London. He has written and published widely on the subject of entrepreneurship, innovation and economic development and has made keynote presentations at leading academic and policy conferences around the world.

Rossitsa Rangelova is Senior Research Fellow at the Institute of Economics, Bulgarian Academy of Sciences. In the 1990s she was Visiting Professor at several universities including: Illinois State University (USA), University of Bristol (UK), University of Groningen (the Netherlands), and Central European University (Hungary). In the mid-1990s she was expert to the Bulgarian Ministry of Economic Development. Her research areas include international comparative economic performance studies, measuring economic growth, human capital, migration and gender studies.

Ken Roberts is Professor of Sociology at the University of Liverpool. He is one of the UK's senior youth researchers, and since 1991 he has coordinated a series of projects into the impact of the macro-changes among young people in former communist countries. Currently he is investigating changes, convergences and divergences in education and the labour markets in Central Asia, and in another project he is applying event history analysis and multiple sequential analysis to clarify young people's patterns of life stage transition in the South Caucasus. His books include *Surviving Post-Communism: Young People in the Former Soviet Union* (2000), *Class in Modern Britain* (2001), *The Leisure Industries* (2004), and *Leisure in Contemporary Society* (2006).

Aleksander Surdej is a Professor of European Public Policies at the Cracow University of Economics. His research interests focus on the methods of public policy analysis and on the political economy of post-communist transformations in Central Europe. He is the author and co-author of many articles, book chapters and policy reports published in English, Italian and Polish in academic publications and the publications of policy research centers like the World Bank or UNU WIDER. He was a fellow of the Royal Institute of Advance Social Studies in the Netherlands, Jean Monet Fellow at the EUI, Florence and a grant holder of the CEU. Recently he has published a book in Polish on "The Determinants of Efficiency of Administrative Instruments in Regulatory Policies".

Péter Szirmai is Associate Professor at the Corvinus University of Budapest and Director of the Small Business Development Center. He has been working as a university professor for 35 years. In 1982 he established his private consulting firm, the ERGONORG Ltd. and besides teaching, he works as an entrepreneur and as a researcher. In 1990 he founded the SBDC at the University of Economic Sciences. Since 1988 he is the co-president of the National Association of Entrepreneurs and Employers, deputy member of the Governing Body of the ILO, member of the National ILO Council. He was the organizer of the Hungarian LiveWire Foundation that supports young entrepreneurs and he is the president of the Foundation's Board.

Blaž Zupan studied business and economics at the University of Ljubljana, Slovenia, and entrepreneurship at Wilfried Laurier University, Canada. Shortly, he will obtain his masters degree in entrepreneurship. He is currently working as an assistant to Miroslav Glas at the department of Entrepreneurship, Faculty of Economics, University of Ljubljana. He is a teaching assistant on the courses 'Business and its Environment', 'Family business', 'Entrepreneurship', and 'Management of SMEs' among others. His interests are in the areas of business harvest, family business and new venture creation.

Preface

This book deals with a topical but undeveloped argument: the opportunities and barriers for youth entrepreneurship amid systemic change in Central and Eastern Europe. Youth entrepreneurship is a critical policy issue all over the world for two reasons. First, unemployment is especially high among young people, particularly in backward and disadvantaged areas. Second, young people are often underrepresented among entrepreneurs in spite of their high potential. In countries in transition there is a third crucial reason to deal with youth entrepreneurship: the young have been fast to adapt their attitudes, behaviour, aspirations, capabilities and skills to the requirement of a market economy and consequently became crucial actors of systemic transformation. Due to these reasons youth entrepreneurship is rapidly gaining ground among policy priorities in transition countries. However, policy and market failures are particularly high in this case, and beyond the general difficulties typical of mature market economies.

The proposed book foresees an important gap in the literature, in particular as youth unemployment is rampant in Central and Eastern Europe, brain drain of young skilled people is threatening, and youth entrepreneurship is often endorsed as a solution perhaps through returning migrants. Here, the book fills another gap in the literature in that it importantly provides for a number of case-studies.

The volume originates in an international seminar organized in Milan, Italy, in early 2006, by the Unidea/Unicredit Foundation together with the Joint European Master in Comparative Local Development (CoDe) of the University of Trento, and the OECD/LEED programme. The seminar, in which most contributors of the book participated, dealt with crucial issues that the post-communist economies face in the process of transformation, including high levels of youth unemployment, threatening out-migration of young people, and the absence of social cohesion.

The volume comprises the revised versions of most contributions to the Milan seminar as well as two additional chapters (the chapters by Sergio Arzeni and Jay Mitra, and of Miroslav Glas and Blaž Zupan), and is organized in two sections. The first section provides, on the one hand, a definition of the most significant issues with regard to youth entrepreneurship in Central and Eastern Europe, including youth unemployment, the potential of youth entrepreneurship for job creation and economic innovation, and the possibilities for and forms of policy-making to contribute to its development, while, on the other hand, it gives a comparative regional overview of these issues. The first chapter of Sergio Arzeni and Jay Mitra deals with a number of theoretically informed approaches to the potential of (youth) entrepreneurship and comparatively outlines its framework conditions in the Central and Eastern European context, and is complemented by the second chapter of Klaus Haftendorn, which provides a comparative-quantitative overview of the issue of youth unemployment and entrepreneurship in the region, and the possibilities for policy-making to counter this problem, also on the international and European levels. These two regional-comparative chapters are then complemented by two more qualitative and in-depth studies of the phenomenon. Ken Roberts' contribution in the third chapter provides region-wide qualitative research on the actual motivations for young people to engage in self-employment and entrepreneurial activities. And in the fourth and final chapter of this section, Péter Szirmai provides insights from the side of policy-making in an in-depth study of the experiences of a Hungarian NGO concerned with supporting youth entrepreneurship in various Hungarian regions.

In the second section of the volume, the major issues and problématiques outlined in the first part are given substance through a number of detailed country-studies, comprising a number of new member states that joined the EU in May 2004, i.e., Hungary (Mihály Laki in Chapter 5), Poland (Aleksander Surdej in Chapter 6), and Slovenia (Miroslav Glas and Blaž Zupan in Chapter 7), a new member state that recently joined the EU, Bulgaria (Rossitsa Rangelova in Chapter 8), and a prospective member state, Croatia (Ivo Bićanić and Marina Lang-Perica in Chapter 9).

Paul Blokker and Bruno Dallago, Liverpool and Trento, February 2007

Acknowledgements

The development of this volume would not have been possible without the continuous support and involvement of the Unidea/Unicredit Foundation, Milan, Italy.

Introduction

Economic Transformation and the Challenge of Youth Entrepreneurship in Central and Eastern Europe

Paul Blokker and Bruno Dallago

1. Introduction

The structural changes in advanced capitalist economies – in terms of a transformation to post-Fordism and a decline in the belief of the governmental capacity to govern the economy – and globalization have led to a new paradigm of socio-economic development. Within this paradigm and together with other critical components such as the production, transmission and use of knowledge and information, an increased focus is placed on and greater appreciation is made of (individual and collective) entrepreneurial activities, their role in economic growth and innovation, and the consequent need for promoting entrepreneurship and entrepreneurial activities. Such a renewed attention for the entrepreneur and his/her impact on the economy is not only relevant for advanced capitalist economies, but also for those societies that are new market economies or transforming their economies into capitalist systems.

At the same time and with particular reference to transformation countries, the social group that is often said to be more open to entrepreneurship, young people, is suffering from high unemployment rates and lower-than-average rates of entrepreneurial careers. This state of affairs is apparently puzzling. In fact and particularly in transformation economies, young people should suffer less from pre-established patterns of (passive) behaviour and (bureaucratic) social networks, be better qualified and skilled, more flexible, ready to change their lifestyles, adapt to new institutions and start new careers. These features should make this social group the ideal candidate for nurturing the entrepreneurship function in the new economic system. Reality turns out to be different and young people even show serious problems in finding their place in the labour market.

Here, we will focus on those societies that since the early 1990s have embarked on a systemic transformation from centrally planned to market economic systems. The prevailing attempts to create capitalism 'by design', in particular through the adoption of Western blue-prints, implies that the transformation countries have converged or are bound to converge towards, and consequently encounter similar problems as Western European economies in terms of difficulties of job creation, economic growth, and social stability. Yet the unprecedented nature of the transformation from communism to capitalism means that the transformation countries may not only face difficulties which are similar to those of the 'post-industrial economies'. Indeed, they also need to deal with additional problems related to systemic transformation as well as structural problems inherited from the past, such as the deep change in technology, related incentives, the surviving consequences of the emphasis on extensive rather than intensive growth, the distorted industrial structure and information flows, the weakness of innovative capacity – in some cases worsened by the suppression or delocalization of research and development activities by the transnational companies which have invested in those countries.

Young people in modern capitalist societies face an increasingly difficult situation in terms of satisfactory professional participation. The young have less access to employment in general, and to high quality and productive jobs in particular (see ILO 2004, 12). They also have less than proportional rates of participation in entrepreneurial activities (see Chapter 1 by Arzeni and Mitra in this book). The deteriorated situation of young people is not simply the result of a downward but cyclical economic trend, but should be understood in the wider context of profound changes in advanced capitalist economies. In transformation economies the situation of young people is not better, in spite of the hopes that systemic change opened particularly for this group of people.

This fact discloses a host of questions concerning the reasons for this situation. Is it because young people in former communist countries are not entrepreneurial, perhaps because of the effect of old habits of passivity? Is it because, due to the social and psychological effects of the enfolding transformation, they are interested in conspicuous life styles and uninterested in the hard work of the entrepreneur? Is it because policies during transformation, in particular macroeconomic stabilization and privatization policies, were wrong and disadvantaged particularly this age and social group? Is it because of the surviving power of the 'old boys' networks that disadvantages by definition young people? Or is it because, like in mature market economies, young people are simply less fit, less endowed in a competitive environment for whatever reason?

This introduction aims at defining the general framework of the above questions, which will be discussed in more detail in the following chapters. Since the issue of youth entrepreneurship is intimately linked to the more general issue of the young people's place in the labour market, we shall also discuss the latter issue in general terms together with that of the employment and unemployment of young people. This is necessary for different reasons, and in particular because the situation of young people in the labour market determines the social perception of the role of young people in the economy, reveals their skills and abilities, pulls them to play an active role in the economy (either as an employee or as an entrepreneur) or alternatively pushes them to look for alternatives to unemployment in the form of self-employment, further education, or emigration.

In the next section we will briefly review the most important features of the two fundamental components of the issue in advanced capitalist societies, youth employment and entrepreneurship, in order to clarify what is largely the standard reference for countries in transformation. As explained in the next section, by entrepreneurs we mean both innovators and businessmen, including the self-employed.

The following section deals with youth entrepreneurship in Central and Eastern Europe. It therefore contains references not only to the relevant literature, but also to the individual chapters in this book. In fact, the goal of this section is to critically connect the different chapters and highlight the messages that the book conveys. It sketches the critical features of the starting conditions by highlighting the specificities of transformation and goes on by discussing the relation between the disruption of the old system (destruction), economic transformation, and entrepreneurship (construction). The next sub-sections overview the features of youth unemployment and the labour market in Central and Eastern Europe, compare them to the situation typical in mature market economies, and stresses the importance of youth entrepreneurship and small business in Central and Eastern Europe. This section concludes with an overview of the major obstacles and difficulties that youth entrepreneurship meets during the process of transformation and subsequently looks at the support to small business creation that different entities (from local governments to entrepreneurial associations and private/public organizations, from national governments to international agencies) have set up to overcome those obstacles and difficulties.

The final section concludes by introducing a comparison of diversity and commonality of new and prospective EU members, and associated states. This group of countries includes respectively mature market economies, successful transformation countries and late-comers in transformation. The comparison considers three critical issues: legacies of the past, governance capacities, and policy-making. This section summarizes the overall conclusions of the book: lights and shades, achievements and disappointment are pervasive, albeit in a different mix in different countries, and a singular conclusion is impossible. Yet one aspect is clear: the issue of youth entrepreneurship, its promotion and success is critical to the success of transformation and the future of these countries. This conveys a clear criticism to policies implemented so far, and addresses a powerful, yet realistic and sober message to policy makers on the priorities upon which effort should be concentrated.

2. Youth employment and entrepreneurship in advanced capitalist societies

The nature of market economies has changed fundamentally compared to the situation existing in the 1960s. This transformation has involved profound restructuring in systems of production, economic governance, and relations between various actors. In general, a shift has taken place from nationally governed economies embedded in stable international arrangements (the Bretton Woods system) to decentralized economies governed on multiple levels (local, national as well as supranational) and through single-level networks and multi-level partnership, which are increasingly subject to the constraints and stimuli of the international and integrated global economy. The welfare state, which was based on a persistently growing economy of mass production (Fordism), mass consumption, and full or nearly full employment, has given way to an economy increasingly based on autonomous capitalist actors including powerful transnational corporations and influenced by international financial markets, making use of flexible production methods, and deregulated labour markets (cf. Amin 1994; Crouch and Streeck 1997).

This transformation to a 'post-industrial society' has, however, been accompanied by slow economic growth and high unemployment rates (OECD 2001). At the same time, the capacity for the macroeconomic steering of the economy (including the stimulation of full employment) by national governments has considerably diminished, while the emergence of multiple and multi-level forms of governance has shifted nodes of decision-making and collaboration to the sub-national as well as supranational and network levels (Crouch et al. 2001). From the 1970s onwards, nationally based macro-economic policy has shown to be insufficient to stimulate economic growth, employment, and general welfare in advanced economies (Crouch and Streeck 1997; Smith and Swain 1998).

One of the implications of the shift to 'flexible specialization' and 'lean production' and the perceived limits of the effectiveness of macro-economic steering is the requalification of small and medium-sized enterprises (Amin 1994), the endorsement of increased coordination and governance on the local level, and the stimulation of economic growth from the 'bottom up' by means of microeconomic policies. In a number of cases, local development has indeed shown to be important for the creation of market opportunities and strengthening development sustainability, the internationalization of local economies, higher productivity levels, and the reduction of unemployment levels (two important examples in the literature are North-East Italy and Germany, see, e.g., Crouch et al. 2001, 2004; Garofoli 2002; Piore and Sabel 1984). Also with regard to job creation and employment stimulation, in particular concerning young people, solutions are increasingly sought at the local level and by emphasizing the role of local governments and non-governmental actors such as enterprises, business associations, and a range of other non-state actors in the provision and stimulation of employment.

The transformation of state-governed and large-firms-led economic orders into multi-layer-governed and internationalized ones affects all those participating in the labour market. For both young people and adults it has become more difficult to keep employment or to acquire a new job when their roles and skills are not in demand. The transformation of the labour market has, however, disproportionally affected the employment position of the young. Young people not only need to confront the general difficulties on the labour market – less and less stable and protected forms of employment – which they indeed tend to experience in a more intense way (see ILO 2004, 5), as expressed in youth unemployment rates, which generally are between two to four times the rates of adult unemployment.

Young people also face particular problems that further affect their position in a negative way. First, employment regulation tends to protect those already employed, while newcomers are the first to be dismissed in periods of economic slump ('last in first out'). Second, young people are relatively unattractive for employers, as they lack working experience, and thus knowledge and skills, in particular of a tacit nature. The latter is also partially related to outdated or incomplete curricula and a weak relation or 'fit' between education and the economy. Third, in general, young people are paid lower wages than adults. Fourth, young people tend to have less 'voice' in matters pertaining to the economy (see ILO 2004, 13-14).

In all, young people tend to be affected more by growing unemployment in moments of recession and less by increasing employment in moments of recovery (OECD 2001, 15). In addition, the employment that young people take up has been mostly characterized by its unstable nature (part-time arrangements, short term and project contracts) and employment is less and less perceived as a lifetime engagement with a specific employer. The post-industrial economy, in which flexibility, specialized production, and globalization of production and finance are key elements together with deeply unbalanced public budgets, seizes to offer the stable employment positions and social benefits that the postwar 'marriage' of the Fordist production model and the welfare state could provide.

Although this general climate of flexibility, rapid change, and uncertainty leads to increased precariousness and occupational instability, it also seems to favour such entrepreneurial qualities as creativity, risk-taking, and innovation, thus giving an advantageous position to those inclined to self-employment and entrepreneurship (see OECD 2001). Instead of searching for ever scarcer opportunities of employment on the labour market, (young) people might set-up their own enterprises, so the argument goes.

The entrepreneur and its capabilities, which are usually defined as entrepreneurship, are considered in many different ways, of which two different although compatible ways are perhaps the most important. According to the one, in a Schumpeterian vein, the entrepreneur is the critical agent of innovation and entrepreneurship is the ability and the possibility to devise, plan and implement that innovation independently from the sector and branch of activity. The latter can be conceived, in a neoclassical perspective, as a novel allocation of resources or – in a more dynamic view – as a set of social and economic transformations that the entrepreneur promotes and that push the economy along an evolutionary path.

According to another view the entrepreneur is an employer or a self-employed economic agent, i.e. any businessman who chooses to start or manage an autonomous activity in the private sector. According to this latter view, the entrepreneur starts or manages a private economic activity and thus doing creates his own and others' jobs. In this perspective entrepreneurship coincides with job and enterprise creation, independently from the latter's innovativeness.

In the perspective of the present book, both conceptions are relevant. Indeed, the transformation going on in Central and Eastern Europe is primarily a complex set of innovative actions which require numerous and brave entrepreneurs and diffused entrepreneurship. However, the sustainability of transformation also requires that jobs are created and that new firms are founded. If these acts are innovative, they contribute to the very core of transformation. If they are merely survival-oriented actions, they nevertheless contribute to the sustainability of the process. They may even contribute to innovation if they imitate and diffuse previously developed innovative actions, which is likely to be the case with most activities in a time of transformation.

Finally, in a Baumolian perspective (Baumol 1993), the book shall also consider entrepreneurship as a resource that is allocated to different alternative uses. Indeed, one of the most important challenges for countries in transformation is not only to foster entrepreneurial abilities and create a proper playing ground for entrepreneurs:

it is also to create an incentive framework that directs the existing innovative abilities and energies in a productive direction. This depends much upon the set-up and working of institutions, including the development of markets, a new configuration and role for governments, the social perception of entrepreneurs and policies.

To summarise, it is generally held that youth entrepreneurship might have a number of significant positive consequences. First, youth entrepreneurship might contribute to the creation of employment for young people, both through self-employment and the creation of new enterprises, although, admittedly, most job creation takes place in well established and growing firms. In this way the high unemployment rates among young people could be somewhat reduced. Second, young people might be particularly innovative and develop new economic opportunities and trends. Third, the establishment of new small enterprises might contribute to the overall competitiveness of local economies, in particular if such small firms are situated in promising 'niches'. Fourth, self-employment might lead to increased job-satisfaction among young people, in material as well as in terms of increased autonomy (Blanchflower and Oswald 1998, 2).

Nevertheless, with regard to youth entrepreneurship as a solution for widespread youth unemployment, one should bear in mind that forms of youth entrepreneurship would even in the best of scenarios only be able to provide for a relatively small number of job places. In some instances, in particular in developing and transformation countries, self-employment is merely a response to the dire situations on the job market rather than the result of a positive choice for entrepreneurship (Scase 2003, but see Smallbone and Welter 2001, 2005; see also the chapter by Roberts in this book). Youth entrepreneurship can, however, still be of importance for a relatively small number of young people. And in more general terms, the argument usually made is that the promotion of youth entrepreneurship can have a positive impact on the wider economy, not only through (modest) job creation and economic growth, but also by contributing to the development of a wider entrepreneurial culture, stimulating the innovative and dynamic nature of (local) economies (Blanchflower and Oswald 1998; Smallbone and Welter 2001, 2003). In addition, in perhaps an optimistic vein, it is sometimes argued that the entrepreneurial activities of previously socially marginalized people might lead to increased social cohesion (see OECD 2001, 3).

3. Youth entrepreneurship in Central and Eastern Europe[1]

3.1 The specificities of transformation

Both the 'normal' problems of the 'post-industrial economy' and the distinct difficulties of economies in transformation are reflected in the youth unemployment rates in Central and Eastern Europe. While these rates reflect the overall structural problem that youth employment meets in market societies, at the same time they display the particularly complex economic difficulties of the transformation process.

---

1 We addressed this argument earlier in Blokker and Dallago (2006), on which this section is partially based.

As a consequence, unemployment rates of the young age cohorts in transformation countries are consistently higher than the levels of most Western European countries, and are sometimes on the increase since the start of the transformation in the early 1990s (for comparative data, see Sergio Arzeni and Jay Mitra's, as well as Klaus Haftendorn's chapters in this book). Such high figures show that the destruction of jobs and productive capacity in the transformation process have outrun the ability to create a substantial number of new employment opportunities.

Over time, this distinctness of transformation economies might, however, also turn into a pattern rather more familiar from the experience of late-comer or developing countries, as already suggested on the eve of transformation (Dallago et al. 1992) and as Tholen holds in an interesting comparison in the late 1990s (Tholen 1998). He concludes that the Central and Eastern European countries might be heading towards a 'Mediterraneanization' of their economies visible, for instance, in prolonged youth school-labour market transitions, a large and enduring second economy, and unstable jobs and a still pervasive role of the state. Such a trend – which would involve the 'normalization of [the Eastern European countries'] current levels and patterns of youth unemployment' (Tholen 1998, 166) – seems not to have been gainsaid by the developments of the early 2000s, thereby indicating the possibility of a structural peripheralization of part of the former communist countries in the European context, rather than their convergence with Western European standards.

One possible move away from the above-sketched scenario of 'Mediterraneanization' might be found in fostering entrepreneurial careers for young people and the establishment of small businesses that involve employment opportunities for the young unemployed. Entrepreneurship in economies in transformation can in this sense facilitate the emergence of a market economy (cf. Smallbone and Welter 2001; 2003, 95). This outcome may be seen as both resulting from purely spontaneous developments and from proper, both contextual and active policies. The former alternative, in which the emphasis is on the spontaneous emergence of private entrepreneurship, is in agreement with a more general liberistic approach to the issue of transformation (the 'Washington consensus'). During the 1990s, socio-economic policy-making was dominated by liberistic ('neo-liberal') recipes for state withdrawal, market creation, the redefinition and reallocation of property rights, the liberalization of the economy both domestically and internationally (Bönker et al. 2002, 7). The contingent rationale for these policies was the need to make change irreversible and capture a 'window of opportunity' for reforms that may not last for long (Gaidar and Pöhl 1995); rapidly establish a private property regime through privatization and liberalization that would support the unfolding of market institutions (Frydman and Rapaczynski 1994; Pejovich 1994; Rapaczynski 1996; for criticism see Nivet 2004); and avoid production disruption deriving from institutional and organizational change (Blanchard and Kremer 1997). However, the persistently high unemployment rates and the modest level of successful small business creation (although marked differences exist between countries in the region) indicate that this approach of 'market making' and state withdrawal is not conducive to create the basis for a sustained widespread entrepreneurial success on the longer term.

The latter alternative places the stress upon organic processes and is indeed of Austrian origin, albeit the neo-Keynesian contribution is also important. The core of organic processes is the foundation and development of new firms, be they totally new initiatives or spin-offs from existing firms and be they domestic or the result of foreign investment (Kornai 1990; Stiglitz 1998). New firms are less constrained by old habits and social relations, embody the new market institutions since the beginning, and force other firms to adapt through their competitive pressure. However, organic processes necessitate mechanisms of inter-firm relations to function, like reputation, trust and authority mechanisms, which may be lacking or are excessively weak during the first stages of the transformation process, perhaps until at least one full generation of business people has been changed. Moreover, entrepreneurship can take a variety of forms and entrepreneurs follow different motives in establishing a business, both of these not always conducive to wider social benefits or positive effects for (local) economic development and inclusive growth. Finally, the fact that young people are structurally disadvantaged in pursuing an entrepreneurial career indicates that the creation of market regulation, market institutions, and the diminishing of state interference are not sufficient to stimulate young people to take up an entrepreneurial career; quite to the contrary, it seems to point to the need for particular forms of public and private support and intervention. In the case of Poland, for instance, and as shown in Aleksander Surdej's chapter (Chapter 6), active policy-making seems to have had a positive impact on youth awareness of entrepreneurship and self-employment as alternatives to unemployment and migration,[2] and on employment opportunities in general, in a moment when the Polish labour market was overwhelmed by newly entering young people in the early 2000s. There is consequently a critical need for both contextual and active policies to foster entrepreneurial abilities and support the foundation and development of enterprises.[3] This book is in this line of analysis.

3.2 Post-communism, economic transformation, and entrepreneurship

Although the wide-scale changes of the former communist countries have been underway for nearly two decades, the transformation cannot said to be over, particularly among those transformation countries which have not entered the European Union. Distinct problems, directly or indirectly related to the communist past, remain important today and influence the possibilities of young people to

---

2 Arzeni and Mitra argue interestingly in their chapter that migration does not necessarily need to obstruct the development of local entrepreneurship in the home country, pointing to the role of returnees and global networks in the economies of countries such as Taiwan, Israel, China and India.

3 Many analyses are obviously intermediate. One important variant of the former approach, for instance, considered that there is a preliminary and transitory need for a strong role of politics in order to establish and enforce few critical institutions, such as prohibitions, private enforcement of public rules, voluntary compliance, self-protection and self-discipline. These institutions are intended to support direct action by private actors in cases when specialized public organizations such as courts are not available or are ineffective. Market processes can start enfolding based upon these urgency institutions (Black et al. 1996; Hay and Shleifer 1998).

play a productive role and support transformation. On the surface, the communist economies consisted of centralized economies that were virtually entirely regulated by the state. The 'command economy' (Grossman 1977) was steered from above by means of central planning of 'vertically integrated industrial networks comprising a relatively small number of large enterprises which sought to mass-produce standardized products' (Smith and Swain 1998, 34). The model of economic growth was one of extensive growth, that is, focused on the continued expansion of the means of production, low innovation rates, and full employment (Grilo and Thurik 2006, 75; Smith and Swain 1998, 33).

Nevertheless, in particular in later stages of the Soviet economic system, the budget constraint of economic actors became increasingly soft and local social forces and informal networks increasingly started playing an important role in the communist economies. On the one hand, the centralized planning system was increasingly evaded, which further increased shortage (Kornai 1980, 1992) while on the other hand, at least in some countries, 'private' activities in the 'second economy' were increasingly allowed. While in general very little room for private initiative existed, in some cases, such as Poland and Hungary, small, but persistent 'second economies' emerged from the late 1960s onwards (Dallago 1990) (see for the case of Poland, the chapter of Surdej). In Slovenia, as Glas and Zupan show in their chapter, a 'kind of Yugoslav "window" towards Western Europe' emerged, in that some forms of joint-ventures and cooperation with foreign companies were allowed. Varieties in centralization, the allowance of quasi-market regulation, and the semi-opening up of communist economies to the West form then one of the bases of emerging diversity in the post-communist world.

The eventual collapse of the Soviet system and the exhaustion of the centrally planned economy based on a rigid and non-adaptive model of extensive growth necessitated, together with the – mostly implicit – demand by the population for systemic change, the transformation of the communist countries to a radically different form of economic system. Such a systemic transformation consists – along with macroeconomic stabilization – of the comprehensive task of radically changing the fundamental economic, political and social institutions, the structure and functioning of the economy (among others, the development of markets, the introduction of new actors such as banks and other financial intermediaries, the restructuring of the boundaries, size and governance of firms, the moving away from older trade relations and patterns, and the integration into the capitalist world economy), and introducing private forms of ownership and independent economic activities.

The multilevel process of transformation (both political, social – including unemployment and social stratification – and economic) makes that the overall context for the setting up of businesses has been in a constant flux in the last decade and a half, much more so than in mature capitalist economies. If the external environment seems more risky for entrepreneurial activities, potential entrepreneurs themselves often lack long-term experience with entrepreneurial activities and related tacit knowledge. Some societies had a relatively pronounced experience with entrepreneurship before the advent of communism (such as the Czech Republic, Poland, and Hungary), so that one might presume that entrepreneurs can draw on such traditions in the transformation period (Grilo and Thurik 2006; Roberts and Tholen 1999). In some of these societies forms of private entrepreneurship re-emerged in the 1970s and 80s in the form of a – mostly shortage-led – second economy. But other countries do not share in such a tradition, and rather have the accumulated experience of 'capitalism from above' in the inter-war period and highly centralized and repressive 'state socialism' until the early 1990s.

The diverse trajectories of societies during communism created different legacies in the transformation period, influencing the construction of the market economy, including forms of entrepreneurship. Some societies, in particular those in which toleration for forms of private entrepreneurship was minimal in communist times, have seen a strong nomenklatura presence (members of the communist ruling elite) in the process of privatization. In these societies (such as Romania, Slovakia, and many of the former Soviet republics) former communist elites could use their political capital to acquire private capital, i.e. the private ownership of former state-owned property (see Eyal et al. 1998; Staniszkis 1999). Many private enterprises that were 'created' through privatization took the form of nomenklatura businesses, which were often characterized by persistent links with the state, and the securing of monopolistic markets and state subsidies. Such enterprises are often qualified as unproductive and hindering the development of a market economy (King and Szelenyi 2005; Smallbone and Welter 2001, 252). However, also in such reformed economies as those of Hungary and Poland various forms of 'spontaneous' privatization offered the old nomenklatura excellent opportunities to convert their old political capital into economic assets. The main difference was perhaps that in the latter countries the nomenklatura involved in the "spontaneous" privatization included more managers and technicians than in the less reformed countries. The technical ability of their "new" managers and the more competitive market context pushed these firms to obtain often a positive performance (Uvalic and Vaughan-Whitehead 1997).

A second form of entrepreneurship that emerged in economies in transformation is self-employment. Although sometimes this form of entrepreneurship derives from the opportunities created by the transformation, it is often a reaction to the loss of jobs in state-owned industries and the lack of alternative employment. A part of self-employment, even if not all of it (see Hanley 2000; Scase 2003), is a form of self-defence or survival in a rapidly changing economic environment, including the massive destruction of jobs following economic restructuring and a rapid de-industrialization (up to close to half of the previous employment level in countries such as Bulgaria and Romania). Indeed, overall employment is presently between two thirds and three fourths of pre-transformation level. In some countries this even led to a 'return' to the agricultural sector (particularly in Romania and Poland, but to a lesser extent also in other countries). In its latter manifestation, this form of entrepreneurship does hardly or not at all have a positive influence on local economic development as the self-employed are mostly engaged in personal survival and often at least partially operate in the informal economy, without investing in business expansion and creating additional employment.

A third form of entrepreneurship, small business development, is likely to be the most promising form as it involves small businesses owners who seek to accumulate capital and invest profit into the expansion of the enterprise. Such small businesses are the ones most likely engaged in innovative forms of businesses, potentially creating wider positive effects for local society (McIntyre and Dallago 2003).

As mentioned earlier, the dominant theory behind the overall economic transformations has for the greater part been the 'Washington consensus' (cf. Williamson 1990, Bönker et al. 2002; for a criticism see Stiglitz 1998). This implies that the emphasis in macro-economic policy-making, liberalization, and privatization in the 1990s has been foremost on 'rolling back' the state, in particular by means of the privatization of state-owned enterprises. In this way, enterprises have been created from the 'top down' by means of privatization, spin-offs from large state-owned enterprises and liquidation of state-owned assets. Each of these privatization approaches have gone to the advantage of insiders or foreign investors, much less so to new, including young, potential entrepreneurs. In this, the third form of entrepreneurship mentioned, small business development, has been largely neglected throughout the process of transformation.

The importance of the establishment of enterprises ex novo, that is, by singular individuals or families from the 'bottom up' has only recently gained more attention. While in many countries in the region such – often small-scale – private initiatives, although often at the survival level, have become increasingly important in creating economic growth, dynamism, and employment, attention and support from the part of the state has been relatively absent. In Romania, for instance, large-state firms have been able to survive with the help of 'soft budget constraints', while the development of the SME sector has been mostly ignored (Ahrend and Martins 2003). It is the latter, however, that in recent years has contributed most to employment creation. In many countries, including Poland and Hungary, governments in the region started paying more attention to local development and support to small business creation only at the end of the 1990s (see, e.g., Gorzelak 1999; McIntyre and Dallago 2003).

3.3 Youth unemployment and the labour market in Central and Eastern Europe

The transformation process has resulted in a moving away of the labour markets in these countries from centralized, state enterprise-based systems, oriented to full-employment and the state allocation of jobs to decentralized systems of labour force allocation based on market rationality and subject to the variegations of the world economy (Cazes and Nesporova 2003; Kovacheva 1999, 13). During communism young people were trained and educated mostly by state enterprises, provided with jobs by the state and guaranteed employment, even while still enrolled in education. In various cases social mobility was sooner the result of bypassing this state allocation system through social networking (social capital), than by climbing upwards by means of formal qualifications (Kovacheva 1999, 14). In contrast and in spite of continuously important social networks and illicit employment practices, in the economies in transformation young people have to count more and more on their own capacities to obtain suitable education and decent jobs, even if the state has set up national employment services and introduced specific policies.

In the 1990s, the socio-economic transformation of the post-communist societies was characterized by a serious decline in output and employment (the extent differed between countries in the region, but was significant everywhere), especially in the years up to the mid-1990s (see Chapter 2 by Klaus Haftendorn for comparative data). The loss of employment was concentrated in the public sector and the industrial and agricultural sectors.

Despite successful economic stabilization and restructuring and sustained growth rates since the mid-1990s, unemployment has shown to be a persistent phenomenon. This is especially true for unemployment amongst the young and in particular in rural regions. As confirmed by Haftendorn in this book, the levels of unemployment in Central and Eastern European countries remain significantly higher than in the old member states (see Table 2.4 in Haftendorn's chapter). And according to an ILO report cited by Haftendorn, the GDPs of economies in transformation would gain by at least six percentage points if the youth unemployment rate would be halved.

For instance, in Poland the highest unemployment rate at the end of 2002 was in the northern region of Warmia-Mazury, at almost 30%, while the lowest was in the central region of Mazowsze, at 13.9% (European Industrial Relations Observatory, EIRO). At the end of 2004, the overall unemployment rate in the Zachodniopomorski voivodship – a predominantly rural area with one of the highest unemployment rates in Poland – was 27.4% compared to a national rate of 19.1% (Foundation for the Development of Polish Agriculture, FDPA). In terms of access to the labour market young people face a serious disadvantage and their level of unemployment remains very high (often more than two times the – already exceptionally high – adult rate), even if their participation in the labour market is low and the number of those looking for a job is relatively modest. Indeed young people remain for longer periods in secondary and higher education, while the transition from education to work is increasingly difficult, and formal education often incompatible with the demands of the labour market (Cazes and Nesporova 2003, 11). In addition, many young people go into the informal economy, simply abstain from looking for a job, or choose for out-migration, as is, for instance, shown in Surdej's chapter on Poland.

Not only the quantity of available employment, its division by sector and branch of activity and by enterprise size changed. Also the qualitative nature of employment changed through a tendency towards flexibilization and an increasing lack of stable, long-term career paths. There is presently demand for higher and sophisticated technical content of labour skills and the necessity to learn continuously and adapt one's knowledge to the endlessly changing requirements of production. Apparently, these are developments that should favour the demand for young labour and skills (Haftendorn and Salzano 2003). However, it is significant that economic growth of recent years has not led to an equivalent rise in overall employment, thanks to the remarkable upsurge of labour productivity. It may be surprising that economic growth led even less so to jobs for young people. Indeed and in spite of their advantages in terms of flexibility and formal skills, young people may lack those forms of tacit knowledge and capabilities, social relations and political power that may be particularly important when restructuring and rebuilding the production system.

Even with economic growth, then, young people have more difficulty finding employment, and when they do find a job, it is likely to be of a precarious nature and low-quality (as a result of the creation of 'junk jobs' in the service sector and the shadow economy) (La Cava et al. 2005). In addition, official figures do not reflect unregistered unemployment, which means that real youth unemployment is likely to be even higher than reflected in national statistics. At the same time, perhaps a substantial number of young people work in the underground economy and are consequently unregistered as employees or self-employed (Kovacheva 1999).

3.4 Importance of youth entrepreneurship and small business in Central and Eastern Europe

An increasingly popular solution to overcoming this structural problem in economies in transformation – high levels of youth unemployment and threatening out-migration in particular of more highly educated and skilled young persons – is proposed in the form of youth self-employment and youth entrepreneurship (Blanchflower and Oswald 1998; Curtain 2000; OECD 2001; UN/ECE 2003). It is seen to be a significant, alternative way to integrate young people into the labour market in economies in transformation and to contribute to the overall dynamism of these economies. From the early 1990s until today, and as attested by the chapter of Haftendorn in this book, the labour market does not offer sufficient and decently paid jobs for a large part of the young people who are looking for employment, particularly for those who are without the skills sought after in the labour market, and those belonging to minorities. And as Arzeni and Mitra argue in this book, it is especially the malfunctioning of and discrimination on the labour market and the concomitant joblessness of young people that pushes youth into 'necessity entrepreneurship'. Gender discrimination (Kovacheva 1999; Wallace and Kovacheva 1998, 20-1) is also important among the young looking for employment.

In economies in transformation, the starting up of a business can be an alternative to unemployment or seeking a job abroad, even if its impact on the overall economy is likely to be rather limited and even if doubts remain as to whether the people who do not find a job are apt to set up an independent business. An alternative, perhaps more convincing interpretation of the issue is that, by activating entry mechanisms into business and self-employment, those who start an independent career may liberate jobs for others. As the restructured state sector and large companies substantially reduced employment, the small and medium size enterprise sector and self-employment could be an important source for job creation for young people. In Central and Eastern Europe in general, it seems that potential entrepreneurial capacities are relatively underutilized (see Grilo and Thurik 2006), and Arzeni and Mitra argue in Chapter 1 that there is a 'huge potential for improving the rates of entrepreneurship in the region by providing opportunities for youth to participate actively in entrepreneurial activities'.

To be sure, in particular in economies in transformation, young people lack experience and other important features, and consequently may have difficulties in managing successfully the intricacies of entrepreneurship and innovation. However, they may be less conditioned by past experiences and more open to novelty. As a result, they might prepare future innovation based on their novel ideas. They may be more prone to support discrete innovation than elder entrepreneurs, who are instead better equipped to implement incremental innovation. In the particular context of countries in transformation, an additional advantage of young entrepreneurs is that they were economically and socially born in the new system and consequently they are more likely to embody the new market and innovation-friendly institutions. Related innovative ideas and behaviour, particularly in the small and medium size enterprise sector, can lead to diversification, flexibility and adaptability, and can foster the positive process of 'creative destruction' that Joseph Schumpeter identified as so significant for economic development. However, for this to happen in a socially productive manner, proper institutions are necessary (Baumol 1993) and the relevant economic actors (the young entrepreneurs) should have such an advantage in their strengths (in terms of formal knowledge, abilities, flexibility, and adaptability) that compensates for their likely disadvantage in other spheres (particularly tacit knowledge and capabilities, social networks and political relations).

3.5. Obstacles and difficulties of youth entrepreneurship

Confronted with widespread youth unemployment policy-makers can choose to rely on spontaneous development, i.e. leaving the young to find their own way[4] or pursue two strategies: stimulate job creation and promote enterprise foundation (entrepreneurship). We will concentrate on active policy-making below. With regard to the former, spontaneous developments are hardly a solution in Central and Eastern Europe. As indicated above, young people have a particular importance in societies in transformation, since they embody in the fullest way the new institutions and consequently are most pro-reform and most willing to support significant change in their economies and societies. However, young people simultaneously face a relatively disproportional part of the difficulties and strains of transformation: in a sense, they are among the victims of transformation due to a lack of labour demand, the fiscal crisis of the state (in particular, social security) and disruption of the welfare state amidst surviving privileges, principally for the elderly.

The start-up of new businesses in economies in transformation faces a number of difficulties, particularly when young people are involved. These regard overall cultural environment, the institutional setting, and access to financial resources. In transformation settings, the wider cultural and social context often does not provide incentives for entrepreneurship. Also, a certain continuity in behaviour and attitudes from the communist past – the 'habits of the heart' – might be expected (see, for instance, Sztompka 1995). These might have been reinforced by the problematic experiences with transformation in general and privatization in particular, even if many countries have undergone drastic transformations, not least in youth culture. In Central and Eastern Europe, social and cultural acceptance of entrepreneurial behaviour – pro-active, individualist – sits uneasy with the dependent, conformist,

---

4 This alternative to active public policy presupposes that young people will spontaneously engage in independent enterprise foundation or self-employment to avoid unemployment and the low wage standards of the average employee. In reality, however, this alternative proves to be a difficult option for young people in Central and Eastern Europe. The undeveloped institutional, financial and real infrastructure and other negative contextual features apart (e.g. spreading criminality), young people often lack the necessary personal features (including skills, tacit knowledge, and business reputation). These negative conditions may render the start up of a business difficult for young people and may even more so render prohibitive the expansion and modernization of activities.

and collectivistic forms of behaviour of the past ('Homo Sovieticus') (Pejovich 1998). One cannot, of course, generalize here, as there are significant differences between different countries in the region, rural and urban areas, jobs in the branches of old industrial sectors and new branches, as well as between older and younger generations.

As direct experience with forms of entrepreneurial activities and familiarity with business practices and related tacit knowledge are seldom at hand, the transmission of codified and re-contextualized knowledge and entrepreneurial skills through formal and informal education becomes important if entrepreneurial behaviour among young people is to emerge. Furthermore, the connection between formal educational curricula and local economies and business communities are in many of the new member states far from optimal, leading to a mismatch between the skills young people learn and those demanded by the labour market. Also, the administrative and regulatory framework is often burdensome, outdated and not conducive to entrepreneurship.

Targeted policies of small business promotion and financial, operational, logistical, and post start-up support are often lacking. Entrepreneurs perceive the instability of macroeconomic policies and frequent changes of regulation as conducive to business uncertainty, regulations as unresponsive to business needs, taxes as too high, and bureaucratic structures as non-transparent and uncooperative (for instance, in the form of complex and lengthy licenses) (GEM; OECD-EBRD 2003). In addition, as mentioned earlier, the state and the financial sector can be non-cooperative with SMEs by being disproportionately favouring large enterprises, also due to the different forms of capture (Fries et al. 2003; Hellman et al. 2000; Yakovlev 2006). In countries in transformation, SMEs are typically weak in lobbying for more favourable conditions and young entrepreneurs are nearly irrelevant in doing so.

The lack of access to finance through regular credit channels and the conditions attached to it, although serious, are usually not a particularly important obstacle for setting-up small firms. However, they are an important obstacle to their growth and modernization (Dallago 2006). Young entrepreneurs may have a particularly hard time even finding the start-up and working capital to found a business, since the typical financial sources of small businessmen – own savings and relatives' and acquaintances' support – are also modest in the case of young entrepreneurs, due to the weakness of their social and business networks. Banks are averse to provide small loans to young entrepreneurs, in particular because young aspiring entrepreneurs have no business reputation, can hardly provide collateral to underpin loans, and lack in soundly elaborated business plans.

3.6 Support to small business creation

In various transformation countries, with apparently important exceptions in Central Europe, much of the policy-making towards development and economic growth since the early 1990s has had more of a regressive character – combating unemployment and industrial decline – than a progressive one, stimulating innovation and competitiveness. For small business creation and entrepreneurship, it is exactly this element that is often missing: a supportive institutional, infrastructural and governmental environment. Also the support by business associations, chambers of commerce and similar private or mixed organizations is typically weak or inexistent in the case of young entrepreneurs, since those organizations support primarily their long-lasting members and are usually oriented towards large size. In reality then, and as attested in Szirmai's case-study of a Hungarian non-governmental organization promoting youth entrepreneurship (Chapter 4), it have often been foreign Non-Governmental Organizations (NGOs), in particular through their support to local civil projects, that have had a substantial impact on local capacities. But such foreign support cannot remain without national and local efforts of the state, local governments, and semi-public as well as private actors.

There are at least three areas where, in particular, (local) governments but also the other actors mentioned, could intervene much more effectively and with wider social benefits. The first area is that of information, awareness-building and education. For young people to make a conscious choice for entrepreneurship they need to be aware of its potentialities as well as risks. But there is also the need to disseminate entrepreneurial attitudes to young people that can be useful in a variety of jobs in an innovative and competitive context. In the case of a person deciding in favour of pursuing an entrepreneurial career, there emerges the need for much more specific training in business and entrepreneurial skills. Promotion programmes of youth entrepreneurship need to deal with the translation of a business idea into a convincing business plan, knowledge of how to run a business on a daily basis, including management and technical skills, administrative and legal knowledge, and financial/accounting skills.

The second area that is relevant for policy-making is the provision of actual start-up and development assistance. Although in general access to capital does not constitute a prohibitive obstacle for starting a business, for young people the situation may be less favourable. Here, local governments as well as other institutions such as business organizations, business angels and mentors from among established entrepreneurs can support young people by providing micro-credit, mutual credit guarantee schemes, and venture capital funds. These solutions would provide a more balanced access to regular capital channels, as those young people who do not have access to informal resources often have to face the discrimination and risk-aversion of banks against young entrepreneurs.

Next to financial support, and as a third element, young entrepreneurs are in need of logistic support in terms of the actual premises, equipment and materials, as well as support with legal matters for their business to operate normally. Here, local governments and other organizations can support young people by offering premises and the usage of equipment at favourable conditions through different channels (OECD 2001). Finally, it is essential to underline the need for post start-up support. It seems not enough to help young people merely to start up new businesses; continued support, mentoring, and legal and financial advice are crucial in contributing to the development of new small enterprises into competitive flourishing and expanding businesses, rather than to create unstable forms of precarious self-employment.

4. Conclusions: commonality and diversity

The post-communism transformation makes up an arduous challenge for the entire Central and Eastern European region. All countries in the region, including those of formerly non-conformist states such as Yugoslavia, had economies in which a number of key aspects of communist economic governance – to a more or lesser extent – prevailed, although economic reforms from the 1960s on attenuated these features in some of the countries. As mentioned above, key aspects included extensive and centrally steered economic planning, industrial structures dominated by large state-run enterprises, and an economic culture hardly conducive to entrepreneurial activities. As a consequence, the framework of opportunities and problematics of post-communist restructuring and transformation sketched above, including the issues related to youth employment and entrepreneurship, are relevant for the whole region.

In other words, it can be argued that all the former communist societies are facing similar challenges, but, at the same time, intraregional differences and variations clearly exist. While the region as a whole is often counterposed to Western Europe, it is also divided in various subregions or groups with regard to the speed and depth of political and economic transformation, the reform approaches followed, and prevalent conditions and circumstances. A common distinction is that between the new European Union (EU) member states (the eight countries that joined the EU in May, 2004, and which are normally regarded as the 'front-runners' in transformation), the new members that joined later on (Bulgaria and Romania in 2007), the prospective member states that are involved in the pre-accession process of restructuring (Croatia), and the remaining former communist – Western Balkan and post-Soviet – societies, often considered 'laggards' in transformation.[5]

In the book, several similar classifications are made. In Haftendorn's chapter, a distinction is made between the new member states, South-Eastern Europe, and the Commonwealth of Independent States, mostly on the basis of different levels of economic development and growth (but Haftendorn also strongly emphasizes the similar challenge that these countries face, in particular in terms of high youth unemployment). Arzeni and Mitra note significant differences with regard to employment trends and forms of entrepreneurship between Central and Eastern European countries, on the one hand, and the countries making up the Commonwealth of Independent States, on the other. At the same time, Arzeni and Mitra, and somehow contrary to Haftendorn's and our own interpretation, argue for the treatment of Eastern Europe as largely similar to Western Europe in terms of

---

5 The dominant interpretation of such different transformation trajectories in transition studies – all countries moving at different speeds along the same time scale – is better avoided, see Blokker (2005). In addition, general indicators should be used with caution. For instance, general differences in Gross Domestic Product levels can be observed between the new and the prospective member states, but these differences do not necessarily indicate significant difference between East and West, as, for instance, the GDP level of Croatia as a prospective member is higher than that of Latvia, while new member Slovenia's GDP level in 2004 (72.02% of the EU-15 mean) was higher than that of old member Portugal (67.49%) (Eurostat 2005).

youth unemployment rates. Ken Roberts identifies a difference mainly between the former Soviet countries, Russia included, and what he calls East-Central Europe. According to Roberts, '[b]usiness had become a basically legitimate, respectable way of earning a living' throughout East-Central Europe in the late 1990s, whereas in the former Soviet countries business seemed to be more related to continuing (local) state involvement, and informal and illegal practices.

Overall, it seems sensible to speak, on the one hand, of a set of similar (structural) legacies and challenges that need to be confronted by all transformation societies, therefore warranting the label 'post-communist', and significant diversity in the trajectories and outcomes of transformation, on the other. Even if this book is not driven by a systematic intra-regional comparison, the chapters touch on aspects of transformation that indicate a variety of responses to the creation of capitalism, rather than a singular transformation pathway. Diversity can be more convincingly approached if a number of aspects are taken into consideration. A first aspect consists of legacies of the past, in terms of diverse experiences with communism and pre-communism. Such legacies do not necessarily play a decisive role in economic transformation, but do pose significant constraints as well as provide resources. A second aspect consists of the institutional and governing capacities available in the various transformation economies. Such capacities are clearly related to distinct legacies from the past, but also to institution-building in the transformation period. A third aspects entails the specific choices made and policies pursued by key transformation actors (political and economic elites) (cf. Ekiert and Hanson 2003, 2; King and Szelenyi 2005; Stark and Bruszt 1998).

4.1 Legacies of the past

Many authors have pointed to the importance of legacies of the past for the present trajectories of the transformation countries, a phenomenon often referred to as 'path dependency' (see Eyal et al. 1998; King and Szelenyi 2005; Pickles and Smith 1998; Stark and Bruszt 1998). In general terms, legacies of the past have been understood in two ways. First of all, legacies of the (communist) past have often been interpreted as mostly negative and as a burden for the present. The 'Leninist legacy' (Jowitt 1992) consisting of, among others, authoritarianism, centralized states and bureaucracies, and clientelistic behaviour, negatively conditions the emergence of democracy and capitalist market economies. But, secondly, others have pointed to the potential resources that past legacies can provide in the post-communist context, above all indicating the importance of education and innovative institutional forms, as in the case of 'recombinant property' in the creation of post-communist capitalism (Stark 1990). The emphasis is on innovative resolutions based on the original combination of available resources.

The positive and negative aspects seem, however, unevenly divided among Central European countries and those situated further to the East and South-East (cf. Ekiert and Hanson 2003, 3; King and Szelenyi 2005, 213). Thus, where many of the constraints of the communist legacies seem to have subsided in Central European countries and made place for more innovative forms of development, the Leninist legacy seems more burdensome in especially South-Eastern Europe and the post-

Soviet societies. In this book, no conclusive evidence for such suppositions can be given, but the diverse impact of legacies of the past is attested by many of the chapters.

As, for instance, shown in Mihály Laki's chapter (Chapter 5), in the Hungarian case the socialist state tolerated a 'second economy' with a number of small private businesses in the industrial and service sectors, which involved a 'remarkable minority of the Hungarian population' and served as a 'pre-school for thousands of entrepreneurs in the post-communist era'. However, Laki quickly points out a related, in many ways negative legacy, in that former nomenklatura members were far more likely to acquire privatized state-owned property than non-party members in the 1990s, while those that were active in the private sector before 1989 could not profit in the same way and often needed to set up entirely new businesses.

Surdej's chapter on Poland highlights the peculiar trajectory of the Polish transformation both before and after 1989, which was relatively similar to the Hungarian one. The most remarkable and well-known aspect is that the Polish socialist state allowed for some private economic activities, in particular from the mid-1980s onwards, in sectors such as trade, construction and agriculture, preparing Poland in a certain way for the economic transformation after 1989. But Surdej also points to another legacy, i.e., the much better preparation of those with higher education levels, skills, and social capital, often found among the former nomenklatura, to confront the challenges of economic transformation.

Miroslav Glas and Blaž Zupan indicate in their chapter on Slovenia (Chapter 7) that the socialist economy was relatively less dependent on large industrial conglomerates than the other Yugoslav republics and primarily rooted in an economy with a strong tradition of small industry and crafts. In addition, the Slovenian economy was relatively open towards Western Europe during socialism and could therefore avoid a drastic reorientation of trade relations and the loss of the Yugoslav market after the collapse of the socialist state.

Turning away from the group of 'front-runners', Rossitsa Rangelova's chapter (Chapter 8) points out that the socialist regime in Bulgaria, in partial contrast to the above-mentioned experiences of Hungary, Poland, and Slovenia, did not tolerate private economic activity, eliminated a perception of entrepreneurship for at least two generations, and profoundly changed the value-system of the population. Rangelova relates this lack of entrepreneurial spirit not only to the socialist period, but also to pre-socialist legacies of statist paternalism and economic protectionism.

Finally, in their chapter on Croatia, Ivo Bićanić and Marina Lang-Perica (Chapter 9) argue that the post-socialist Croatian economy is best characterized as a form of 'crony capitalism' (Bićanić first developed this notion in Bićanić and Franicevic 2000), in which the state has been captured by particularist groups who seek to promote their own private interests (Weber's classical definition for this phenomenon was 'political capitalism', a definition also picked up in the debate on transformation, see Staniszkis 1999; Eyal et al. 1998). This development can be partially explained by reference to social capital, accumulated in the past by specific groups, which takes the form of paternalistic inclinations and social networks. At the same time, and in partial contrast to paternalistic and statist tendencies, Bićanić and Lang-Perica point out that during socialism a 'dynamic and entrepreneurially-oriented tradition of second jobs in the unofficial economy', which contributed to 30% of the Croatian GDP in the late 1980s, was tolerated. While this unofficial economy persisted and even increased during the transformation in the 1990s, Bićanić and Lang-Perica argue that it can be regarded as a 'as a training and testing ground' for self-employment and youth entrepreneurship that might eventually bring forth businesses operating in the official economy.

4.2 Forms of governance

Significant differences in state capacities, governance competencies, and market-making between countries in Central and Eastern Europe are confirmed by research on distinct trajectories of transformation. While the liberistic view of transformation invariably endorses the market as the sole producer of economic growth, innovation, and socio-economic well-being, a more nuanced position holds that a variety of 'modes of governance' can in reality sustain a market economy (see the literature on governance, e.g., Boyer and Hollingsworth 1997; Crouch et al. 2001; Crouch 2005; Williamson 1996). Governance of the economy can thus be based on various modes of governance, ranging from the market, state, hierarchy, and community, to forms of association.

Often, the assessment of governance capacities is reduced to a distinction between a prioritization of the state, on the one hand, and of the market, on the other. King and Szelenyi, for instance, argue that two different trajectories can be identified in Central and Eastern Europe: 'capitalism from without' or liberal, market-based capitalism in the case of the Visegrad countries and 'capitalism from above' or 'patrimonial capitalism', in which the state plays a dominant role, in the case of Eastern and South-Eastern Europe.[6] While the former have sought to create Western-style capitalism by opening up the economy, attracting foreign investment, and rapidly privatizing state property, the latter have, at least in the early years of transformation, opted for a more protective and statist path of transformation. In the latter, state-owned enterprises have often been protected from market competition by means of 'soft budget constraints', while the economy has only been slowly liberalized and privatization has been allowed to proceed notably slower than in the Visegrad countries.

Such a macro-distinction in favour of market governance as a producer of growth and development seems to hold in general. Roberts, for instance, sustains in his chapter on youth self-employment in the region that the actual impact of the state on starting entrepreneurs seems rather modest. But such an observation should not be taken to mean that the state and other forms of public or semi-public governance are not important. In particular, according to Roberts, the state can use its 'unique capacities to broker', mediating between various relevant actors (such as foreign NGOs or firms with important know-how). But in order to perform such a role successfully, the state needs to have distinct capacities, be relatively free from interference by particularist groups, and needs to be aware of its potentially important role.

---

6 They further identify 'hybrid capitalism' which applies to China's experience, see King and Szelenyi (2005).

In general, the various country studies in the book indicate that the market alone can hardly be a solution for the successful development of forms of entrepreneurship, business development, and economic innovation. In the specific case of Hungary, the immediate post-1989 context proved to be favourable to the creation of private businesses, in particular due to the conditions shaped by government policy in terms of deregulation and the protection of SMEs. These developments seem to largely support an argument in favour of market spontaneity in the development of entrepreneurship. Laki, however, shows that the market mechanism was deemed as insufficient, and that, even before the state acknowledged the importance of specific educational and promotional policies to sustain emerging entrepreneurship, it were organizations operating in the civil sphere, such as NGOs and non-profit organizations that recognized the need for focussed educational programmes. It was only at a later stage, notably in a moment when SME-creation was slowing down, that the state stepped in.

In his chapter on Poland, Surdej shows that the economic transformation started off with the so-called Balcerowicz-plan, a largely neo-liberal recipe for transformation. However, this neo-liberal approach, which as a core premise endorsed a shift of responsibility for social well-being from the state to the individual him/-herself, could not prevent a process of social differentiation in the Polish society between those who were able to take up opportunities and others who could hardly do so. Such a social situation, particularly experienced in terms of extremely high unemployment rates, could not remain without answers from policy-makers and active state intervention, through, among others, the promotion of SME-creation and labour market policies.

The Slovenian economic transformation can overall be considered a success story in terms of the creation of a liberal market economy, according to Glas and Zupan. At the same time, new SMEs faced significant obstacles in the early 1990s, in particular with regard to bureaucratic hurdles, lack of finance, and difficulty in finding premises. Despite such obstacles, the number of new enterprises grew enormously initially, to slow down dramatically again in 1994, not least because of strong foreign competition and detrimental legislation. As the early wave of SME-creation was dominated by adults, after its exhaustion there is more and more public attention for the potential of forms of youth entrepreneurship. Glas and Zupan indicate, however, that youth entrepreneurship is only slowly coming off the ground, in particular also because of the lack of sustained support and policy-making by the government. They point to the crucial nature of complementary forms of public intervention to a in many ways relatively successful market.

Also in the case of Bulgaria, the conditions for SME creation and youth entrepreneurship have hardly been optimal, as shown in Rangelova's chapter. Youth entrepreneurship emerged primarily in a spontaneous and 'trial-and-error' kind of way. The economic transformation was characterized by a very slow implementation of reforms and high level of political instability, resulting according to Rangelova in inconsistent economic policy-making. It is only from the end of the 1990s onwards that general conditions for economic growth, and therefore, entrepreneurship seem to be ameliorating. Similarly, the role of the state has only rather recently been turned into an actively intervening one, for instance, by means of employment policy and the promotion of enterprise start-ups.

Finally, Bićanić and Lang-Perica argue that a state that is highly present in the economy, through, for instance, the provision of subsidies and extensive state ownership in the economy, is not necessarily an effective state. They refer indeed to a 'large but weak state' in the case of Croatia. But rather than supporting a neo-liberal argument of far-reaching retreat of the state and market governance, in their argument on barriers for entrepreneurship on the local level, Bićanić and Lang-Perica endorse a reformed *local* state that is capable of supporting targeted projects for youth entrepreneurship and self-employment.

4.3 Policy-making

One would expect that regional/national differences in state capacities and governance competencies have their repercussions for the development and promotion of SMEs and, in particular, for young persons attempting to set up a private enterprise. It seems warranted to argue that, based on the various country studies in this book, that the section of the youth that is willing to engage in entrepreneurship and self-employment, is in need of educational, financial, as well as administrative and operational resources. As argued above, a supportive institutional context for youth entrepreneurship needs to address three issues: education, start-up and development assistance, and logistic support. Although no general conclusions can be drawn on the basis of the country studies presented here, in general most governments, often in concomitance with NGOs, non-profit as well as business organizations, are (or recently got) involved into some kind of support for youth employment and youth entrepreneurship.

In the case of Hungary, Laki argues that in a later stage of the transformation, the need for the education of business skills in secondary schools was first picked up by NGOs and later also by the state, which made such education a compulsory part of the curriculum. But Laki also shows that, even if pro-active state policy regarding entrepreneurship and young entrepreneurs has been developed, it fails to address the variegated nature of young people trying to start up a business (in terms of social background and status, education, accumulated skills). Policies should, according to Laki, distinguish between business success and social equality. From a general, comparative perspective, Roberts points to the same problem: if the policy objective is to target those groups in society that are most likely to have success in creating and developing new businesses, and therefore to enhance economic success, policies should target those (males) that are well-educated and have already had contact with financial institutions for the development of businesses. If, alternatively, an important policy aim is employment promotion, social inclusion, and equality, then governments and other relevant institutions should devise targeted and tailor-made policies, for instance for young women and people belonging to minorities.

In Poland, policies aiming at SME-promotion were started in the mid-1990s, and included the simplification of procedures, access to finance, and business support (in centres that combine the functions of information provision, incubation, support for innovation and technology, and training as well as financial services). Surdej also notes, however, that substantial governmental support for such promotional policies and supportive institutions only came available in the immediate run-up to the EU accession. Regarding youth entrepreneurship, this argument is even more true, and support was particularly the result of the increased awareness of the problem of youth unemployment. The promotional policies, implemented from the early 2000s onwards, were firstly part of wider labour market policies, while in 2005 entrepreneurial policies became more autonomous. These policies include awareness promotion and the amelioration of the social image of entrepreneurs, financial support, and the teaching of entrepreneurial skills,

Even in the – in a comparative sense – less problematic transformation in Slovenia, policies towards the support of young people with regard to the labour market as well as entrepreneurship might be said to be insufficiently developed. Glas and Zupan refer to a number of expert studies that indicate the lack of financial support, the absence of developed relations between academics and business, the lack of professional infrastructure, and an overall lack of focused government policies. Nevertheless, a few initiatives have taken off since 2002, in particular the set-up of business incubators. Glas and Zupan argue, however, that more sustained and long-term measures are necessary.

In the case of Bulgaria, Rangelova relates that during the 1990s employment policies were mostly passive; only at the end of the decade more active policy-making was implemented, accompanied the promotion and expansion of state employment services. Youth employment was generally not regarded as a distinct phenomenon, but as part of the general problem of unemployment. This lack of targeting hampers more comprehensive and profound forms of policy-making, according to Rangelova. But the recently created active policies – in the form of job creation and the promotion of business development – seem to contribute to a more favourable situation.

Bićanić and Lang-Perica argue that Croatia can be seen as a 'laggard' in economic transformation (as is the case with the other Western Balkan states) and that it has only been since 2000 that specific policies promoting employment and entrepreneurship targeting the youth have gotten off the ground (even if general policies regarding entrepreneurship started in 1997). The authors are, however, relatively doubtful about the future. The general framework for entrepreneurship – regulations, policies, and their applications – is, according to them, not endorsing entrepreneurship, making that 'starting a business in Croatia is not easy'. Despite pro-active policy-making, high formal costs, additional administrative costs (including corruption), high start-up costs, and a general 'bias to bigness' of the state bureaucracy create a rather unfavourable environment for entrepreneurship.

The chapters that follow cannot exhaust the argument on youth entrepreneurship and its implications for societies in transformation. But they do give an elaborated, introductory account of the major potentialities and impediments involved in the development of entrepreneurial activities by young people, and the wider institutional and societal context of such activities. And while the country chapters cannot possibly cover the whole region, they do provide rich and comparative material with clear significance beyond their immediate context.

References

Ahrend, R. and J.O. Martins (2003), 'Creative Destruction or Destructive Perpetuation: The Role of Large State-owned Enterprises and SMEs in Romania During Transition', *Post-Communist Economies* 15:3, 331-356.

Amin, A. (ed.) (1994), *Post-Fordism: A Reader* (Oxford, UK/Cambridge, Mass. : Blackwell).

Baumol, William J. (1993), *Entrepreneurship, Management, and the Structure of Payoffs* (Cambridge, Mass. and London: The MIT Press).

Bićanić, I. and V. Franicevic (2000), 'Dismantling Crony Capitalism: The Croatian Case', CERGE-EI Research Seminar Series, Prague, http://www.cergeei.cz.

Black, B., R. Kraakman and J. Hay (1996), 'Corporate Law from Scratch', in R. Frydman, C.W. Gray and A. Rapaczynski (eds.), *Corporate Governance in Central Europe and Russia*, Vol. 2: *Insiders and the State* (Budapest: Central European University Press).

Blanchard, O. and M. Kremer (1997), 'Disorganization', *The Quarterly Journal of Economics*, 112:4, 1091-1126.

Blanchflower, D.G. and A.J. Oswald (1998), 'Entrepreneurship and the Youth Labour Market Problem: A Report for the OECD', http://www.dartmouth.edu/~blnchflr/papers/OECD.pdf.

Blokker, P. (2005), 'Post-Communist Modernization, Transition Studies, and Diversity in Europe', *European Journal of Social Theory* 8:4, 503-525.

Blokker, P. and B. Dallago (2006), 'Doing Business in the East? Difficult for the Young'/'Intraprendere a Est? Difficile se si è giovani', *EAST: Europe and Asia Strategies* 9, 34-41, http://www.eastonline.it/.

Bönker, F., Müller, K. and Pickel, A. (2002), 'Cross-Disciplinary Approaches to Post-Communist Transformation: Context and Agenda', in Frank Bönker, Klaus Müller and Andreas Pickel (eds), *Postcommunist Transformation and the Social Sciences: Cross-Disciplinary Approaches* (Lanham, MD: Rowman & Littlefield), 1-38.

Boyer, R. and J.R. Hollingsworth (1997), *Contemporary Capitalism: The Embeddedness of Institutions* (Cambridge/New York: Cambridge University Press).

Cazes, S. and A. Nesporova (2003), *Labour Markets in Transition. Balancing Flexibility and Security in Central and Eastern Europe* (Geneva: ILO).

Crouch, C. and W. Streeck (1997), *Political Economy of Modern Capitalism: Mapping Convergence and Diversity* (London/Thousand Oaks, Calif: Sage).

Crouch, C. et al. (2001), *Local Production Systems in Europe: Rise or Demise?* (Oxford/New York: Oxford University Press).

Crouch, C. et al. (2004), *Changing Governance of Local Economies: Responses of European Local Production Systems* (Oxford/New York: Oxford University Press).

Crouch, C. (2005), *Capitalist Diversity and Change: Recombinant Governance and Institutional Entrepreneurs* (Oxford/New York: Oxford University Press).

Curtain, R. (2000), 'Concept Paper: Identifying the Basis for a Youth Employment Strategy Aimed at Transition and Developing Economies', at http://www-ilo-mirror.cornell.edu/public/english/bureau/exrel/partners/youth/yen/1-curtain.pdf.

Dallago, B. (1990), *The Irregular Economy. The 'Underground' Economy and the 'Black' Labour Market* (Dartmouth: Aldershot).

Dallago, B. (ed.) (2006), *Transformation and European Integration. The Local Dimension of Transformation* (Houndmills, Basingstoke: Palgrave Macmillan).

Dallago, B., Ajani, G. and Grancelli, B. (eds.) (1992) *Privatization and Entrepreneurship in Post-Socialist Countries: Economy, Law and Society* (Basingstoke - New York: Macmillan - St. Martin's Press).

Ekiert, G. and S.E. Hanson (eds.) (2003), *Capitalism and Democracy in Central and Eastern Europe. Assessing the Legacy of Communist Rule* (Cambridge: Cambridge University Press).

Eurostat (2005), *Europe in Figures. Eurostat Yearbook 2005* (Luxembourg: Office for the Official Publications of the European Communities).

Eyal, G., I. Szelényi, and E. Townsley (1998), *Making Capitalism Without Capitalists. Class Formation and Élite Struggles in Post-communist Central Europe* (London/ New York: Verso).

Fries, S., T. Lysenko and S. Polanec (2003), 'The 2002 Business Environment and Enterprise Performance Survey: Results from a Survey of 6,100 Firms', London: European Bank for Reconstruction and Development, *Working Paper N° 84*, November.

Frydman, R. and A. Rapaczynski (1994), *Privatization in Eastern Europe: Is the State Withering Away?* (Budapest: Central European University Press).

Gaidar, Y. and K. Otto Pöhl (1995), *Russian Reform, International Money* (Cambridge, Mass.: The MIT Press).

Garofoli, G. (2002), 'Local Development in Europe. Theoretical Models and International Comparisons', *European Urban and Regional Studies*, 9:3, 225-239.

GEM (various years) *The Global Entrepreneurship Monitor* (London: London Business School/Babson College and the Kaufmann Foundation).

Gorzelak, G. (1999), 'Regional Policies and Regional Capacity-Building in Poland', in Martin Brusis (ed.), *Regional Policy-Making in Bulgaria, the Czech Republic, Estonia, Hungary, Poland and Slovakia*, CAP Working Paper, Munich, December, http://www.cap.uni-muenchen.de/download/RPPoland.PDF.

Grilo, I. and A.R. Thurik (2006), 'Entrepreneurship in the Old and New Europe', in Enrico Santarelli (ed.), *Entrepreneurship, Growth, and Innovation: the Dynamics of Firms and Industries: International Studies in Entrepreneurship* (Berlin: Springer Science), 75-103.

Grossman, G. (1977), 'The "second economy" of the USSR', *Problems of Communism*, 26, Sept.-Oct., 25-40.

Haftendorn, K. and C. Salzano (2003), 'Facilitating Youth Entrepreneurship. Part I. An Analysis of Awareness and Promotion Programmes in Formal and Non-formal Education', Series on Youth and Entrepreneurship, SEED Working Paper No. 59, (Geneva: International Labour Organization).

Hanley, E. (2000), 'Self-employment in Post-communist Eastern Europe: A Refuge From Poverty or Road to Riches?', *Communist and Post-Communist Studies* 33, 379-402.

Hay, J.R. and A. Shleifer (1998), 'Private Enforcement of Public Laws: A Theory of Legal Reform', *American Economic Review*, 88, 398-403.

Hellman, J.S., Jones, G., Kaufman, D. and Schankerman, M. (2000) 'Measuring Governance, Corruption, and State Capture. How Firms and Bureaucrats Shape the Business Environment in Transition Economies', World Bank Policy Research Paper 2312 (Washington, DC, World Bank), April.

ILO (2004), *Improving Prospects for Young Women and Men in the World of Work. A Guide to Youth Employment* (Geneva: International Labour Organisation).

Jowitt, K. (1992), *New World Disorder: The Leninist Extinction* (Berkeley: University of California Press).

King, L. and I. Szelenyi (2005), 'Post-Communist Economic Systems', in N. Smelser and R. Swedberg (eds), *The Handbook of Economic Sociology*, Second Edition (Princeton University Press), 205-32.

Kornai, J. (1980), *Economics of Shortage* (Amsterdam: North-Holland).

Kornai, J. (1990), *The Road to a Free Economy. Shifting from a Socialist System. The Example of Hungary* (New York: W.W. Norton).

Kornai, J. (1992), *The Socialist System. The Political Economy of Communism* (Princeton: Princeton University Press and Oxford: Oxford University Press).

Kovacheva, S. (1999), 'Flexibilisation of Youth Transitions in Central and Eastern Europe', working paper, www.hwf.at.

La Cava, G., P. Lytle, and A. Kolev (2005), 'Young People in South Eastern Europe: From Risk to Empowerment', Social Development Team, Washington D.C.: World Bank, http://lnweb18.worldbank.org/ECA/ECSSD.nsf/ECADocByUnid/DD691E9C6CEAED2785256F0F0079B81E?Opendocument.

McIntyre, R.J. and B. Dallago (eds.) (2003), *Small and Medium Enterprises in Transformational Economies* (Basingstoke and New York: Palgrave Macmillan).

Nivet, J.-F. (2004), 'Corporate and Public Governances in Transition: The Limits of Property Rights and the Significance of Legal Institutions', *The European Journal of Comparative Economics*, Vol. 1, N° 2, pp. 3-21 (http://eaces.liuc.it).

OECD (2001), *Putting the Young in Business. Policy Challenges for Youth Entrepreneurship*, LEED Notebook No. 29.

OECD-EBRD (2003), *South East Europe Region. Enterprise Policy Performance: A Regional Assessment*, Paris and London, October.

Pejovich, S. (1994), 'The Market for Institutions vs. Capitalism by Fiat: The Case of Eastern Europe', *Kyklos*, 47, 519-529.

Pejovich, S. (1998), *Economic Analysis of Institutions and Systems*, Revised Second Edition (Dordrecht: Kluwer Academic Publishers).

Pickles, J. and A. Smith (1998), *Theorising transition. The political economy of post-communist transformations* (London: Routledge).

Piore, M.J. and C.F. Sabel (1984), *The Second Industrial Divide: Possibilities for Prosperity* (New York: Basic Books).

Rapaczynski, A. (1996), 'The Roles of The State and The Market in Establishing Property Rights', *Journal of Economic Perspectives*, 10, 87-103.

Roberts, K. and J. Tholen (1999), 'Young Entrepreneurs in the New Market Economies', in *South-East Europe Review*, 1, 157-78.

Scase, Richard (2003), 'Entrepreneurship and Proprietorship in Transformation: Policy Implications for the SME Sector, in Robert J. McIntyre and Bruno Dallago (eds.), *Small and Medium Enterprises in Transformational Economies* (Houndmills, Basingstoke and New York: Palgrave Macmillan), 64-77.

Smallbone, D. and F. Welter (2001), 'The Distinctiveness of Entrepreneurship in Transition Economies', *Small Business Economics*, 16, 249-262.

Smallbone, D. and F. Welter (2003), 'Entrepreneurship and Enterprise Strategies in Transition Economies: An Institutional Perspective', in D. Kirby and A. Watson (eds), *Small Firms and Economic Development in Developed and Transition Economies* (Aldershot: Ashgate), 95-114.

Smallbone, D. and F. Welter (2005), 'Entrepreneurship in Transition Economies: Necessity or Opportunity Driven?', paper presented at the VII ICCEES World Congress, Berlin, July 25th-30th.

Smith, A. and A. Swain (1998), 'Restructuring and Institutionalising Capitalisms: The Micro-foundations of Transformation in Eastern and Central Europe', in Pickles, J. and A. Smith (eds.), *Theorising Transition. The Political Economy of Post-communist Transformations* (London: Routledge), 25-53.

Staniszkis, Jadwiga (1999), *Post-communism: The Emerging Enigma* (Warsaw: Polish Academy of Sciences).

Stark, D. (1990), 'Privatisation in Hungary. From Plan to Market or from Plan to Clan', *East European Politics and Societies*, 4:3, 351-392.

Stark, D. and Laszlo, B. (1998), *Postsocialist Pathways: Transforming Politics and Property in East Central Europe* (Cambridge: Cambridge University Press).

Stiglitz, Joseph E. (1998), 'More Instruments and Broader Goals: Moving toward the Post-Washington Consensus', WIDER Annual Lectures 2, Helsinki: UNU/WIDER, January.

Sztompká, P. (1995), 'Cultural and Civilizational Change: The Core of Post-communist Transition', in B. Grancelli (ed.) (1995), *Social Change and Modernization. Lessons from Eastern Europe* (Berlin/New York: Walter de Gruyter), 233-248.

Tholen, J. (1998), 'The Young Unemployed, Self-Employment and the Mediterraneanisation of Youth Transitions in East-Central Europe', *South-East Europe Review*, 4/98, 151-67.

UN/ECE (2003), 'SME policy and youth entrepreneurship in countries in transition', ECE/OPA/CONF.3/2003/22, Geneva: UN/ECE.

Uvalic, M. and D. Vaughan-Whitehead (eds) (1997), *Privatization Surprises in Transition Economies – Employee Ownership in Central and Eastern Europe* (Cheltenham: Edward Elgar).

Wallace, C. and S. Kovacheva (1998), *Youth in Society: The Construction and Deconstruction of Youth in East and West Europe* (Basingstoke: Macmillan).

Williamson, J. (1990), 'What Washington Means by Policy Reform', in J. Williamson (ed.), *Latin American Adjustment: How Much has Happened?* (Washington, D.C.: Institute for International Economics).

Williamson, Oliver E. (1996), *The Mechanisms of Governance* (New York and Oxford: Oxford University Press).

Yakovlev, A. (2006), 'The Evolution of Business – State Interaction in Russia: From State Capture to Business Capture?', *Europe-Asia Studies*, 58:7, 1033-1056.

PART 1
Youth Entrepreneurship and Self-Employment in Transition Economies

Chapter 1

From Unemployment to Entrepreneurship: Creating Conditions for Change for Young People in Central and Eastern European Countries

Sergio Arzeni and Jay Mitra

We must develop strategies that give young people everywhere a real chance to find decent and productive work that will allow them to become independent and responsible global citizens.
– Kofi Annan, UN Secretary-General, International Youth Day, August 2003

1. Introduction

The shift in the political structure of countries in Central and Eastern Europe (CEE) marked the beginning of a long period of transition from a socialist to a capitalist system of a free market economy, following the collapse of the command economies between the end of the 1980s and the beginning if the 1990s. However, almost all the expert economic projections of productive change, based on the adoption of policies supported by the International Monetary Fund and the World Bank, turned out to be unrealistic as the outcomes of the transition were manifest in the sharp rise in unemployment problems, the reality of which blew away the dreams of many. The group or class of people most overwhelmed by this predicament were the 'youth', as their unemployment rates soared in some cases almost twice the national average.

Joblessness often results in certain push factors which could propel people to become 'necessity entrepreneurs' (GEM 2005). Entrepreneurship can, therefore, be considered to be an alternative to the wage economy especially when the latter fails to meet the aspiration of the young. The purpose of this chapter is to examine the role of entrepreneurship as a viable tool for the systematic reduction of youth unemployment in CEE countries. Framework conditions affecting entrepreneurship development in the CEE are investigated in order to obtain an understanding of the local factors affecting entrepreneurship in the region. More specifically, the chapter sets out to explore the literature for:

- the nature and causes of youth unemployment in the region and the prospect of entrepreneurship (new business creation and self-employment) as an alternative to employment in the wage economy; and

- policies affecting entrepreneurship and small business development and whether positive outcomes can be observed in terms of new venture creation.

Based on the findings from the exploration, the authors conclude with an overview of the strengths, weaknesses, opportunities and threats (SWOT) affecting youth entrepreneurship in the CEE countries.

A Rationale

The rationale for this chapter stems from the recognition of the difficulties policy makers face in many countries, and specifically in the transition economies, in tackling the problem of youth unemployment. A large segment of the world population falls under the classification of 'youth', thereby making unemployment issues take an important place on the agenda of policy makers. It is estimated that there are more than one billion people between the ages 15 to 24, and that 85 percent of them live in developing countries. According to recent estimations by the ILO (World Youth Report 2003), 40 percent of the 160 million people unemployed today in the world are youth. In the case of the CEE countries, youth unemployment is above that of their adult counterparts. The resulting negative impact on the productive potential and future economic prospects of young people, and the regions in which they live, raises serious concerns among policy makers and the wider society. These concerns are exacerbated when illegal means of livelihood offer tangible alternatives to legitimate opportunities of livelihood.

A report by the OECD (2001) explains that continual youth unemployment wastes human resources that could contribute to economic progress in the short-run; influences widespread unhappiness (amongst which rising suicide rates are a symptom), and social discontent among the youth, and may leave long-term scars on the working adults of the next generation. In the absence of jobs in the wage economy, supporting youth entrepreneurship can be an important policy consideration for many economies, regardless of their stage of development, and a valuable complement to policies supporting wage employment. This is especially the case as recent trends in the United States and a number of OECD countries show a high interest of youth in participating entrepreneurship (OECD 2001). For example, about 40 of young people finishing secondary school in the USA expresses a high interest in forming their own businesses; while in the United Kingdom, more than a third of the nation's young people express a desire to start their own businesses, and each year about 50,000 of them actually do so (OECD 2001). Likewise in France, a survey on pupils beginning and finishing secondary school and those in the first year study for a BTS (*Brevet de Technicien Superieur*) professional qualification, carried out in 1999, showed that 32 percent of the respondents were seriously foreseeing the creation of an enterprise as their first professional work (OECD 2001). Thus, promoting youth entrepreneurship carries with it potentials for reducing unemployment, as there may be a direct effect on employment if new young entrepreneurs hire fellow young persons from the 'dole' queues (Curtain 2000). Can similar models or approaches be adopted in CEE countries?

To achieve the objectives stated above, this chapter relies on secondary data sources and key policy documents, including data relating to entrepreneurship framework conditions, such as the existing state of education and availability of venture capital. The work of different researchers on CEE country economies, such as Saveska (n.d.), Blanchflower and Oswald (1998a) and others, also inform this chapter.

In the absence of comprehensive data across all CEE countries it can be tempting to extrapolate the state of the youth entrepreneurship from general sources of information. But rather than following that hazardous route, this chapter sets out to examine the overall framework conditions for entrepreneurship in a transition environment. Certain assumptions underpin this examination and they include the following:

a. the basic framework conditions of attitudes to and capabilities for entrepreneurship, levels of education, appropriateness of support and supply systems, have a direct impact on entrepreneurship among all groups of people;
b. the peculiar conditions of the state of specific economies together with their framework conditions allow for either the prevalence of positive externalities emanating from good business practice or 'rent-seeking' entrepreneurship which cashes in on corrupt form of opportunism (Baumol 2002; Dallago 2005);
c. the specific conditions of youth in particular countries, as in a mix of higher levels of unemployment combined with higher educational attainment levels in CEE countries, can result in a dangerous and volatile mix of social unrest and economic decline;
d. successful youth entrepreneurship in any economy is path dependent in that it is more likely to flourish in places where there is a tradition of entrepreneurial activity, supportive infrastructure, and cultural acceptance; and,
e. transition itself provides for the kind of tensions generated by economic and social disequilibria, which offer opportunities for entrepreneurs to seek and realize, either for genuine wealth creation or socially dysfunctional individual gain.

This chapter does not aim to address specific problems of youth entrepreneurship in the CEE countries. The lack of reliable, empirical data (Aidis 2003) prevents us from undertaking such an enterprise. Instead, by interpreting existing material and, partly through extrapolation of material from related policy areas (education, employment, etc.), an attempt is made to provide an overview of 'what is' and 'what is possible' in the area of youth entrepreneurship in the transition economies of the CEE. This is not sufficient to also cover the specificities of both the different transition economies or indeed the peculiarity of youth entrepreneurship. Also, while in policy terms, the primary equation between policy-making and job creation has been taken for granted, other aspects of entrepreneurship, namely creativity, networking, and innovation have inevitably been ignored. This deficit is unfortunate and will need to be addressed by all concerned with the subject.

2. State of the Economy in Central and Eastern Europe

During the early years of the transition to the market economy there was a decline in economic performance of the countries marked by a recession. The recession intensified in 1991 with recorded falls in GDP ranging from 9 to over 15 percent. The transition did not occur in all the countries at the same time in terms of implementing market reforms. The recession suffered by the region particularly affected industry. Almost all the countries, with the exception of Poland, had a fall in output of a fifth or more in 1991.

The privatization of shops led to the creation of a small, private business sector. The first countries to launch plans for privatization were Czechoslovakia, Hungary and Poland, with Hungary having started to test market-oriented reforms since the 1980s. But the *creation of new businesses* did not form part of the agenda of regional policy makers. Perhaps the dramatic growth in newly created private enterprises in the early 1990s, driven by high levels of consumer demand for products and services previously unavailable in the command economy (Aidis 2005), generated an environment of myopic complacency.

By the mid to late 1990s, most of the transition economies witnessed a fall in new business development (Glas et al. 2000; Kontrovich 1999; UNDP 1998), with the problems being attributed to an increase in regulations, new competition both at the local and international levels, poor financing, and a reduction in consumer demand.

In recent years however, there has been some improvement in terms of economic growth, averaging steadily over 5 percent in the region (see Figure 1.1 below). In 2005, economic growth was favourable at 5.4 percent, although in comparison to the previous year it had slowed down slightly. Nevertheless, growth remained strong, in excess of 5 percent, more than three times higher than in the EU 15. Projections made over the next few years show the rate of growth will continue at the rapid pace of more than 5 percent, and is expected to remain higher than the EU 15. Thus, in general, the region is gradually recovering from the recession it suffered during the earlier days of transition.

The opening up to the world markets by the CEE economies, through the introduction of economic measures that allowed rapid price liberalization, combined with a strict macroeconomic stabilization policy, had an effect on employment. Many believed that the transition from a communist to a capitalist system of free market economy offered hope of individual freedom, protection of individual human rights and an assurance of rising living standards. Yet, it did not 'take long for the optimism and enthusiasm to vanish' (Saveska, n.d., 1). The result was an immediate decline in the demand for labour, followed shortly by a decline in employment. The employment fall was striking in the early years of the economic transition.

According to Nesporova (2002), even at this early stage, a notable difference in employment trends had emerged between the transition countries of CEE and those of the Commonwealth Independent States (CIS), with the three Baltic countries moving gradually from the second to the first group. In terms of unemployment, young people, in particular school leavers without work experience, were the group hardest hit by unemployment (Nesporova 2002). Unemployment rates of young people (those younger than of 25 years of age) are significantly higher than those of the population 25 years and above in all CEE countries, as is the case in the EU Member States. This implies that young people face more difficulties in finding employment than their peers. Generally, in these transition economies, unemployment rates of youth below 25 are twice as high as or even higher than the national average.

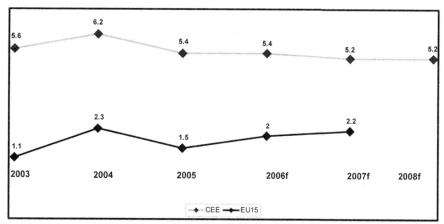

Figure 1.1 Real GDP Growth of the Central Eastern European Region and the EU 15, 2003 to 2008

f-forecast

Note: Forecast of EU 15 countries based on European Commission data Forecasts on CEE represent the projections of PMR publications; Average GDP growth in the region was based on proportionate weight of individual economies in the region's GDP.

Central and Eastern Europe (CEE) – Czech Republic, Hungary, Poland, Russia and Slovakia
Source: PMR Press release, 26 April 2006.

However, the CEE countries do not constitute a special case. Blanchflower and Oswald (1998a) investigated the relationship between youth and adult unemployment by plotting a correlation between the levels of youth unemployment and adult unemployment for a sample of advanced OECD countries. The slope gradient recorded line is approximately two, which suggests that for every 1 percent rise in adult unemployment there is on average a 2 percent point increase in young people's joblessness (see Figure 1.2 below). Blanchflower and Oswald (1998a) also identified a relationship between youth and adult unemployment by plotting a correlation between the levels of youth unemployment and adult unemployment derived from micro data on nations of Eastern Europe (see Figure 1.3 below). This time, although a comparable relationship was observed for Eastern Europe, the gradient of the slope as depicted in Figure 1.3 is slightly smaller than that of the Western European countries (see Figure 1.2 below), at 1.5 rather than 1.8. The comparative scatter of correlates is also a little less well-defined.

It could, therefore, be argued that youth unemployment is correlated with adult unemployment rates not just in CEE nations but also in other Western European economies. Understanding the features of youth unemployment necessitates a wider appreciation of the causes of unemployment among adults (Blanchflower and Oswald 1998a). Researchers have observed that the rate of unemployment tends to decline with age, reaching the lowest levels for the pre-retirement population (Nesporova 2002). Nesporova (2002) explained that this is related to the perpetuation of seniority rules and insiders' power, especially in large enterprises, and the frequent willingness of older workers to accept 'lower-level' jobs. Given the correlations stated above and the stranglehold of old institutional practice on employment, it would appear that the youth of CEE countries face a major problem emanating from these constraints and that the opportunity to break out is provided through either entrepreneurial activity or by remaining longer in education.

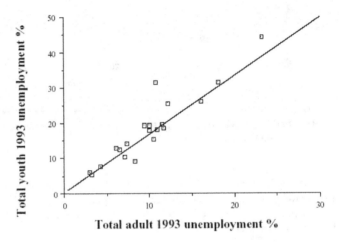

Figure 1.2 The cross-country relationship between adult unemployment and youth unemployment in the OECD economies in the 1990s
(y = - 3.6289e-2 + 1.8231x R^2 = 0.861)

Note: The countries covered here are Canada, Switzerland, Japan, Sweden, Norway, France, Australia, USA, Netherlands, UK, West Germany, Belgium, Denmark, Finland, Luxembourg, New Zealand, Ireland, Italy, Spain, and Portugal. Youth unemployment covers those 15-24. Both kinds of unemployment rates are standardized OECD figures for 1993.
Source: Blanchflower and Oswald (1998a).

Nesporova (2002) compared the participation rates in economic activity of youth in the 15-24 year age bracket with two other age groups in selected transition economies. The comparative groups were 'prime-age' (25-49) and older (50-64) workers. The comparison shows that between the years 1990 to 1999, the steepest decline in labour supply was amongst the youth, that is, within the 15-24 years age group. They explained that there are several factors that influenced the rate of unemployment particularly amongst the young, including:

a. increase in the rates of participation in higher education;
b. difficulties in the transition from education to work;
c. lack of demand for newly gained professional qualification;
d. employers complain about the lower quality of education;
e. demographic changes.

The first factor is that higher education has become considerably more attractive to young people in the course of transition, with many of them extending the time period of their studies. Irrespective of the benefits derived from such a choice, it has led to delays in direct youth participation in the economy. A second factor is the increasingly difficult transition from education to work. Employers in the region are not willing to put up with the additional costs of on-the-job training of inexperienced young workers. Also, a considerable number of young people are faced with a lack of demand for their newly gained professional education in consequence of unsatisfactory reforms to national education systems, which lag considerably behind labour market needs and lead to skill mismatches coupled with employers' complaints of the lower quality of education (Nesporova 2002).

Demographic changes have also had considerable influence on youth unemployment in the CEE countries. Although there was a strong entry of youth aged between 15-25 years into the labour market particularly in the early 1990s, substantial changes taking place during the economic restructuring process of the transition economies, resulted in the erosion of demand for 'old' skills, which favoured the youth. Soon after the first wave of restructuring, however, [sentence seems to contradict what is stated above not really because it (this sentence refers to the priod that follows the first period of economic restructuring)] the preference of employers changed to prime-age workers with work experience. Furthermore, with the notable exception of Poland, there was also a sharp decline in fertility rates in the transition economies. Falling incomes of young families and housing problems faced by young people accounted for this particular decline. On the other hand, in Poland, the proportion of persons aged between 15 and 24 in the total population increased constantly over the whole decade. This is often cited as one explanation for the accelerating unemployment in Poland after 1997 and exceptionally high youth unemployment rates at more than double the national average.

Youth flight or migration to developed countries has been the source of many debates in European circles. Its potential impact on CEE economies can be devastating, especially in terms of a 'brain drain'. It would appear that there is no clear appreciation of the ways in which migration policy can be developed to incorporate innovative ways in which to make use of migrating and settled talent abroad to create new business opportunities, along the lines of developments in countries which have undergone similar problems but which have converted the crippling effects of 'brain drain' (Taiwan, Israel, China and India) into the flourishing prospects of 'brain circulation' (Saxeninan 2005). CEE countries have a long history of migration to countries such as the USA and in Western Europe, and for this reason alone, some steps could be taken to reduce the problems of talent loss and economic stagnation or decline. Issues of migration are outside the scope of the chapter, so reference is made to the subject only in passing, as one way of exploring possibilities for future economic gain for the youth of CEE countries.

Transition also brings fresh challenges for youth, and to some extent their effort in overcoming difficulties is a measure of their ability to use the advantage of 'less baggage' against the entrenched mind sets of those in established authority positions, simply capitalizing on the benefits of capitalism.

In this context, do entrepreneurship or small and medium sized enterprises make a difference? Do they simply offer escape routes or can they genuinely contribute to wealth creation and spillover effects that have an impact on both the economies and society? Aidis and Sauka (2005) argue that SMEs are able to provide economic benefits beyond the boundary of the individual enterprise in that they open up additional opportunities for experimentation, learning and adaptation. Moreover, even when new SMEs do not generate new jobs, they help to mitigate the negative effects of underutilized human capital by allowing for alternatives to traditional forms of employment and opportunities for self-employment or new business creation for relatively skilled yet unemployed workers (EBRD 1995) For the youth of CEE countries, seeking entrepreneurial alternatives acquires a special significance when there is considerable economic, structural, demographic and political pressure to fit into the global economy.

The Alternative of Entrepreneurship

In the early post-war era, which was characterized by relatively well-defined technological trajectories, stable demand, and seemingly clear advantages of diversification, small businesses were considered to be a vanishing breed with preserving them having more to do with democratic and political values than with economic efficiency (Verheul et al. 2002). Giant corporations were seen as the sole and most powerful engines of economic and technological progress (Audretsch, Carree and Stel 2001, 4), with Schumpeter's work in the 1950s creating an image of the large corporations gaining competitive advantage over small and new ones, and of giant corporations ultimately dominating the entire economic landscape (Audretsch, Carree and Stel 2001). The dominant image of the large firm reigned up until the 1970s, when David Birch arguably became one of the first scholars to discover the important contribution small firms make to the economy. Birch's (1979) work showed that 81.5 percent of net new jobs created during the period 1969 to 1976 were created by small firms. Careful, systematic empirical evidence documented in the 1980s also showed the shift in the burden of economic activity from large firms to small, predominantly young enterprises (Verheul et al. 2002, 2).

Many policy makers around the world have embraced entrepreneurship policy as a viable means of generating employment and economic growth. Lundstrom and Stevenson (2002, 5) define entrepreneurship policy by the following measures:

- aimed at the pre-start, the start-up and post-start-up phases of the entrepreneurial process,
- designed and delivered to address the areas of motivation,
- opportunity and skill,

- with the primary objective of encouraging more people in the population to consider entrepreneurship as an option, to move into the nascent stage of taking the steps to get started and then to proceed into the infancy and early stages of a business.

In CEE, all of the transition economies have formulated strategies aimed at overcoming employment difficulties, and many of them embrace a variety of aspects of entrepreneurship policy. Although variations in these policies exist between the countries, most of them have tried to establish institutional frameworks that are to serve as a basis for promoting not just labour market policies, but also entrepreneurship and small business development as means of encouraging self-employment.

3. Entrepreneurship and Youth Unemployment

The high levels of unemployment in many countries of the world have led policy makers to seek solutions, with entrepreneurship promotion emerging as one of the popular policy tools for job creation, the reduction of unemployment and even poverty eradication. Job creation has been central to such policy measures mainly because of the need to address both economic and social inequalities and also for the need to have relatively straightforward evaluation measures (Storey 1994, 2003).

Entrepreneurship scholars have advanced a number of theories aimed at explaining the relationship between entrepreneurship and unemployment. These arguments sometimes offer contradictory points of view on the relationship between entrepreneurship and unemployment. Income choice has been the starting point for numerous studies focusing on the decision confronted by an individual to start a firm and become an entrepreneur (Blau 1987; Evans and Leighton 1990; Evans and Jovanovic 1989; and Blanchflower and Meyer 1994). The suggestion is that increased unemployment will lead to an increase in new venture creation on the grounds that the opportunity cost of not starting a firm has decreased. Yet, Lucas (1978), and Jovanovic (1982), have argued that the unemployed tend to possess lower endowments of the human capital and entrepreneurial talent required to start and build a new firm, suggesting that high unemployment is associated with a low degree of entrepreneurial activities. A low rate of entrepreneurship may also be a consequence of low economic growth levels, which also reflect higher levels of unemployment (Audretsch 1995).

Oxenfeldt (1943) is acknowledged as one of the first researchers who investigated the link with unemployment with entrepreneurship. His work is more of an extension of Knight's view that individuals make a decision among three states – unemployment, self-employment and employment. The actual decision is shaped by the relative prices of these three activities (Audretsch, Carree and Thurik, 2001). Thus, he argues that people faced with unemployment and low prospects for wage employment turn to self-employment as a viable alternative. Therefore, entrepreneurship is viewed here as positively related to unemployment.

Empirical evidence compounds the problem of contradictions ands ambiguities Storey (1991). While some studies find support for Oxenfeldt's (1943) claim that greater unemployment serves as a catalyst for startup activity (Evans and Leighton 1989; Reynolds, Storey and Westhead 1994; Reynolds, Miller and Makai 1995), other scholars found that unemployment reduces the amount of entrepreneurial activity (Audretsch and Fritsch 1994; Audretsch 1995).

The theoretical and policy formulation logic referred to above is also applied to the question of youth entrepreneurship and its role in reducing unemployment among young people. Regarding youth entrepreneurship, reference is being made to the 'practical application of enterprising qualities, such as initiative, innovation, creativity, and risk-taking into the work environment (either in self-employment or employment in small start-up firms), using the appropriate skills necessary for success in that environment and culture' (Schnurr and Newing 1997; cited in Chigunta 2002). However, the focal point of this study is self-employment, defined here as anyone who works for himself or herself but not for anyone else, except under arm's-length contracts (OECD 2001). Specifically with regard to the issue of unemployment amongst young people and the role of entrepreneurship, Blanchflower and Oswald (1998b, 2) stated that many commentators seem to agree on the following benefits of youth entrepreneurship promotion:

1. There may be a direct effect on employment if new young entrepreneurs hire fellow youths from the dole queues.
2. New small firms may raise the degree of competition in the product market, bringing gains to consumers.
3. Young entrepreneurs may be particularly responsive to new economic opportunities and trends.
4. Entrepreneurship may promote innovation and thus create new jobs.
5. Greater self-employment among young people may go along with increased self-reliance and well-being.

It is worth noting that economists have little evidence on whether these hypothetical benefits exist in practice (Blanchflower and Oswald 1998b). However, an important survey of OECD countries was conducted by Blanchflower and Oswald (1998b), which investigated young people's employment, attitudes and entrepreneurial behaviour. One of the key findings emerging from the study is that *although many people would like to run their own businesses across all age groups, this preference is particularly marked for youth*. The researchers also found that young self-employed people have higher life-satisfaction (holding other things constant) than other young people with similar characteristics. The survey by Blanchflower and Oswald (1998b) also found that although *young people are more likely to have a positive attitude towards self-employment, older people are more likely to be self employed.* One possible explanation to this, at least in part, is that youth lack collateral and business experience, and are, therefore, considered a very high risk proposition by lenders, making it difficult for them to gain access to credit (World Youth Report 2003). These empirical findings seem to suggest that tapping into the positive attitudes of youth towards entrepreneurship could have a significant influence on reducing or solving many aspects of youth unemployment.

In terms of policy support, although the different aspects of entrepreneurship policy are of relevance to youth entrepreneurs, scholars argue that young people as a group are distinct in terms of policy support as they require more time and attention than older people and this may exceed what general development agencies wish to provide to one client (Chigunta 2002). Chigunta (2002) argues that this requires staff trained and experienced in dealing with young people. Dealing with young people requires skills and sensitivity quite different from those required when dealing with adults (White and Kenyon, 2000, 23). Thus, scholars are united on the view that supporting youth entrepreneurship requires special programmes designed to support the youth (White and Kenyon 2000; Chigunta 2002).

4. Entrepreneurship Framework Conditions

The efforts of many countries in creating more dynamic and competitive entrepreneurial economies is often impeded, at least in part by the lack of proper institutional context. Regarding institutions, reference is made to 'the rules of the game in a society' (North 1990), which may reduce the risk and uncertainty that individuals face during the entrepreneurial process of starting or developing a business, and they include 'formal' institutions, such as political and economy-related rules and organizations, but also 'informal institutions', which refer to codes of conduct, values and norms that 'come from socially transmitted information and are part of the heritage that we call culture' (North 1990). Examples of relevant institutional frameworks for entrepreneurship and small business development include the availability of finance (e.g. venture capital), higher education institutions (especially relevant for high-tech entrepreneurship), but also the legal and tax systems that may enable or constrain entrepreneurship. The existence or lack of these institutions in the CEE countries is likely to affect the development of entrepreneurship.

Policies Affecting Enterprise Creation and Development

Policy makers in many countries around the world come up with specific policies designed for the promotion of entrepreneurship and small business, in recognition of the argument that new enterprises contribute to economic growth, employment and wealth generation (Wennekers and Thurik 1999; Audretsch and Thurik 2001). Over the years, there has been an increased pressure on policy makers, academics, and business practitioners to identify and implement effective public policy for the creation of conditions under which entrepreneurial organizations can flourish, thereby providing local employment opportunities that help to alleviate poverty and contribute to wealth generation.

Framework Conditions and Entrepreneurship in the CEE countries

One of the reasons for the variations in policies and instruments used to develop entrepreneurship in the transition economies is the nature of the transition process itself. Loose definitions that explain the transition process simply in terms of a move from a communist environment to an 'advanced market economy' do not help to account for the variations. Similarly, the fact that eight Eastern European countries have now joined the European Union and are, therefore, regarded as post-transition economies, does not indicate that the structures and processes of an 'advanced market economy' have suddenly become embedded in these countries. Clearly new, empirical work has to take into account the economic, social and individual processes by which people in the CEE countries influence 'transition'. In the absence of any clear definition (or indeed reliable data), both the observation of the characteristics of entrepreneurs and the different stages of enterprise development the reality provide for some understanding of the development of entrepreneurship in these environments.

In general terms, the entrepreneurial characteristics of transition economies resemble those of their counterparts in many developed economies. However, the vary fact of 'transition' distinguishes the economic environment of these CEE countries. Contending with issues such as the 'reorganization of work' (Johnson and Loveman 1998, cited in: Aidis 2005), including the acceptance of the practice of private enterprise, and the creation of a climate of support for free enterprise, has not been easy. As stated earlier, the transition process has been characterized by an inclement economic environment exacerbated by a recession that followed early promises of positive change. Aidis (2005) also refers to the lack of a private enterprise tradition, the absence of relevant finance, low purchasing power levels, poorly qualified workers, a debt spiral resulting from the absence of a credit system, and the concentration of firms in the industrial and manufacturing sectors, as some of the key characteristics (World Bank 1995; Bartlett and Bukvic 2001; Puissarides 2004). When these issues are complemented by larger ones, such as property rights and unfair competition from an informal economy (Glas et al. 2000), then the barriers to enterprise development appear to be significantly high.

The governments' response to the kind of environment stated above to some extent compounded the problem. Policies concerned with business legislation, the introduction of a business tax system, and over-regulation, in general coupled with interference in small business affairs, have been the norm. The unfortunate outcome of these responses has been an increase of corruption ands rent-seeking enterprise development activities (Dallago 1997; Bartlett and Bukvic 2001; Baumol 2002). It is perhaps understandable that the destabilizing factors referred to above are products of a negative attitude to private enterprise inherited from the past (Marot 1997 cited in: Aidis 2005).

The typical public sector approaches adopted in the CEE countries have not necessarily captured the imagination of typical entrepreneurs or small business owners. But their's has been a passive attitude of acceptance to these developments, along the lines of what was expected of people in general in command economies (Kobeissi 2001). If there is no previous experience then, inevitably, the typical private business person has difficulties coping with the legislation and institutional systems necessary for the proper operation of a market economy.

There is something to learn from the phenomenon of legitimization of illegal entrepreneurship, which occurred while private enterprise was still a restricted activity. Earle and Sakova (2000), found that those who ran such illegal businesses in the pre-transition period had a greater chance of employing people than others, and that they were motivated positively to run legal outfits.

Aidis, however, differentiates between Central and Eastern European countries, including the Baltic States (CEEB), and the entrepreneurs in the Commonwealth of Independent States (CIS). As the following table shows, CEEB countries have smore affinity with European countries, thanks to the existence and retention of a small private sector during the socialist period. However, in the CIS countries, the dominance of Russian language networks has generated a 'Mafia- style capitalism' linking Russia with the newly independent countries. Unlike the CEEB countries where the old political elites were replaced by new regimes, the former remained in power with their alter egos (Aidis 2005).

The size of the countries also has a bearing on the differences between CIS and CEEB countries. Thus smaller countries such as the Kyrgyz Republic do not appear to have the problems with financial support that countries such as Albania, Belarus and the Ukraine have faced.

How the characteristics and conditions will influence the youth of these countries remains to be seen. It is difficult to predict whether an affinity with Western European institutional norms and operations in the formal economy will necessarily result in entrepreneurial success at a level higher than where both the formal and informal economies are prevalent. Europe does not offer an enviable model for entrepreneurship and it is possible that growing CEEB and CIS countries might need to look further for examples of dynamic enterprise.

Within the transition economies, promoting entrepreneurship and developing small businesses have become important elements in facilitating growth in the private sector. During the transition period, changes arising from macro-economic and structural reforms provided opportunities for many people to start their own businesses. This proved to be a major source of new jobs, entailing at the same time major modifications in economic structures throughout the region (UN *Report on the World Social Situation* 1997, 122). Several measures have been adopted by the respective countries. Hungary, the Czech Republic, Bulgaria and Poland have all introduced measures to encourage more people to consider self-employment.

According to Smallbone and Welter (2003), Estonia has made considerable progress in terms of institutional development. Until recently, policy support measures designed directly to aid small business development in Estonia were not in place, with the role of government viewed as one of limited intervention (Phare Report 1999). As a candidate country for the European Union (EU), Estonia introduced a new Commercial Code in 1995, in order to harmonize regulations and the business environment with EU requirements. This resulted in the introduction of legal forms of entrepreneurship similar to mature market economies; an increase in the minimum capital requirements for public and limited liability companies; and the creation of a new, central Business Register (Smallbone and Welter 2003). Smallbone and Welter (2003) also stated that the basis of small business policy in Estonia is embedded in the National Program for the Adoption of the 'Aqcuis Communitaire' 2002-2003 (NPAA). This includes the use of pre-structural funds and other foreign assistance instruments to assist in the implementation of the Action Plan; developing an infrastructure for entrepreneurship, supported through Phare projects; offering state support services to start-up businesses, and strengthening the capacity of relevant institutions in preparation for receiving assistance through EU Structural Funds (Smallbone and Welter 2003).

Table 1.1 Differences between entrepreneurship in CEEB and CIS countries

Factor	CEEB countries	CIS countries
Environment	Affinity with Europe and EU countries	Dominance of old soviet language networks
	Western-oriented development	Mafia-style capitalist development
	Memory of private business	No memory of private business
	During socialist period, small and limited private business culture sustained	During socialist period, private business culture non-existent
	Communism collapsed and resulted in a rotation of political elites	Communism collapsed with only a partial rotation of political elites
	Lack of financing	Lack of financing
	Lower levels of corruption	Higher levels of corruption
The role of the state	Invisible hand model	Grabbing hand model
		Inspection culture
		Lack of rule of law – social networks
Business owner characteristics	Specialization of business activities	Business development focused on the 'big strike' or getting rich quickly; coping with unstable market conditions
	Full time private business	Generic business activities
	Diversified business sectors	Business activities primarily engaged in trade
	Business development seen as a gradual step-by-step process	Part-time businesses in combination with employment in the state sector
	Individual businesses are the dominant form	Part-time business protection and survival predominate
	Businesses function in official economy	Businesses function in both official and informal economy

Slovenia followed two basic stages for the promotion of self-employment (Saveska, n.d.). First, the responsibility for the provision of basic information for people who have an interest in starting new ventures is handled by employment offices. These individuals have to present a viable project to the agencies. Secondly, costs associated with services rendered by the employment agencies are reimbursed after the unemployed person has become self-employed. According to 1992 data, 833 people out of the 3,840 that participated in the program became self-employed (Drobnic 1997, 172).

The Czech Republic has a rather robust approach to enterprise promotion. The program for enterprise promotion is divided into two activities. A part of the program is aimed at regulating the development of SMEs in general, while the other part promotes specific fields of activity or the development of a depressed region. The government tries to facilitate not only the provision of basic information, but also tax concessions, capital, advice on accounting and business planning to new entrepreneurs. New business owners also benefit from training. These programs are available to both the employed and the unemployed, thereby making it possible for some youth to benefit from the programs.

Table 1.2 Self-employment as a share of total employment, selected transition economies, 1993 and 2000 (percentage)

Country	1993			2000		
	Men	Women	Total	Men	Women	Total
Bulgaria	12.9	9.2	11.2	18.3	10.6	14.7
Croatia	25.1[1]	15.4[1]	20.7[1]	23.3[7]	14.4[7]	19.2[7]
Czech Republic	15.8	9.4	12.8	18.8	9.0	14.5
Estonia	10.4	6.2	8.4	9.7	6.4	8.1
Hungary	17.4	11.3	14.6	18.7	9.6	14.6
Kazakhstan	0.1[3]	0.2[3]	0.1[3]	–	–	–
Latvia	12.4[2]	6.9[2]	9.8[2]	12.5	8.4	10.5
Lithuania	21.5[4]	14.6[4]	18.3[4]	19.2	12.7	15.9
Macedonia	74.0[5]	68.5[5]	71.8[5]	–	–	–
Poland	32.2	29.9	31.2	25.9	18.4	22.5
Romania	24.4	19.4	22.1	32.6	17.4	25.4
Russian Federation	10.1[6]	5.6[6]	8.0[6]	8.4	6.2	7.4
Slovakia	9.0	3.5	6.6	10.9	4.1	7.8
Slovenia	16.0	7.6	12.2	15.3	6.5	11.2
Ukraine	–	–	–	8.3[7]	9.0[7]	8.6[7]

Notes: [1]1996 [2]1995 [3]1989 [4]1997 [5]1991 [6]1994 [7]1999
Sources: Labour force surveys; author's calculations.

The program for enterprise promotion in Bulgaria was introduced in 1991. This policy received a rather slow response from the citizens of the country, with only 27 people applying in 1991. Later on, this figure rose after some legislative changes had taken place. The program is designed such that funds are allocated to individuals who submit projects equivalent to their benefit payment for the entitlement period. Although the program had a very slow start, the number rose dramatically in 1992 with up to 4000 people starting their own businesses and around 6000 in 1993. A decline in response was however observed in 1994, with numbers dropping down to 911 people (Bobeva 1997, 41-42).

Poland's heavy reliance on start-up loans generated serious difficulties. Labour offices were overwhelmed by administrative expenses in running the program. Thus, expenditures devoted to this program in 1994 were much lower than the initial funds allocated to the program in 1990 (Gora 1997, 131). Neither were the banks in the country strong enough to provide sufficient support to labour offices.

The success of the programs introduced by the transition countries varies to a considerable extent in relation to the overall business environment. In general, there is a strong correlation between the share of self-employed workers, a country's economic performance and its labour market situation (Nesporova 2002). However, several problems that deserve considerable attention remain (Saveska n.d.). First, the legal and regulatory environment make it difficult for private businesses to prosper. Entrepreneurs across the region are often faced with rapid and unforeseen changes in regulations or budget allocations. Often, they tend to be frustrated by red tape, paperwork and fees. High taxes, bribery and corruption are all important issues that provoke businesses to avoid paying their taxes in full.

Educational Qualifications of Youth

In common with most European countries, the educational attainment levels of younger people in the CEE countries are superior to those of older people (Mansuy and Couppié 2001). The population of young people entering the labour market with low or no qualification is decreasing. Estonia, Slovakia and the Czech Republic are the key countries with the lowest rates of early school leavers.

On the other hand, the countries that display the highest rates school leavers are Hungary and Bulgaria, while those with lowest rates of school leavers are the Czech Republic, Estonia and Slovakia. The issue of education and youth entrepreneurship has some importance depending on the policies pursued by the different CEE countries. For example, those countries wishing to support technology entrepreneurship amongst the youth have to pay particular attention to the education of the youth especially in sciences courses. This will give them the scientific background and competence to engage in the development and exploitation of technologies. Silicon Valley and the Cambridge cluster serve as living examples of the combination of scientific education and entrepreneurship, as many of their high-tech start-ups were founded by engineers and scientists. On the other hand, countries not pursuing high-tech entrepreneurship are less likely to consider education as important to youth entrepreneurship. This is because the link between education and nonhigh-tech entrepreneurship is not well established. In fact, many, if not all of the worlds leading entrepreneurs are not necessarily highly educated people.

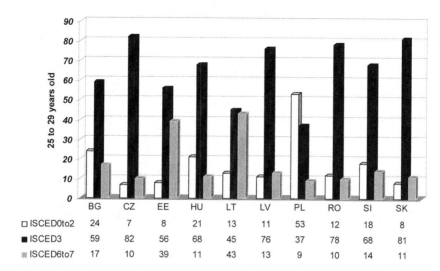

	BG	CZ	EE	HU	LT	LV	PL	RO	SI	SK
☐ ISCED0to2	24	7	8	21	13	11	53	12	18	8
■ ISCED3	59	82	56	68	45	76	37	78	68	81
▨ ISCED6to7	17	10	39	11	43	13	9	10	14	11

Figure 1.3 Educational attainment levels of the population, 1997

Methodological note: Estonia and Lithuania display a relatively high percentage of people having acquired a qualification at International Standard Classification of Education (ISCED) levels 5 to 7. This is due to the specificity of the education and training system in these two countries. Both countries have vocational education and training courses classified at ISCED level 5. The majority of people in the ISCED 5 to 7 category have actually acquired a vocational qualification at this level.

Source: Mansuy, and Couppié (2001).

Private Equity Finance

In terms of venture capital finance in the region, recent data shows that there has been a significant increase in investment in the region. There was an overall increase of 22 percent in 2004 in comparison with 2003, with a total of 547 million euros invested across the Central and Eastern European region (EVCA 2005). Amongst the countries in the region, Bulgaria had the highest increase by amount, with others, such as Hungary and Latvia also showing a marked increase in investment. However, the private equity investments in Poland, Romania and the Czech Republic decreased in 2004, in comparison to 2003.

In terms of venture capital investment in the region as a percentage of gross domestic product in 2004, Bulgaria again has the highest score (higher than the European average). All other transition economies scored lower than the European average.

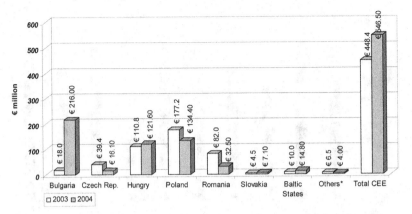

Figure 1.4 Private equity – annual investment volume central and eastern European region, 2003-2004

Source: EVCA (2005).

Table 1.3 Type of investment by country – 2004

€'000	Bulgaria	Czech Republic	Hungary	Poland	Romania	Slovakia	Baltic States	Others
Seed	–	–	–	–	–	–	–	–
Start-up	–	2,245	501	–	–	947	706	1,759
Expansion	3,421	13,829	120,561	44,100	7,339	6,112	14,102	2,262
Replacement Capital	20,684	–	–	59,494	25,204	–	–	–
Buyout	191,871	–	500	30,843	–	–	–	–
Total 2004	215,976	16,074	121,562	134,437	32,543	–7,059	14,808	4,021
Total 2003	18,043	39,422	110,775	177,213	82,020	4,479	10,000	6,513

Source: EVCA (2005).

All of the countries had equity investments made for the expansion of businesses in the region. Hungary clearly had the highest for expansion investment with 120 million euros, followed by Poland with 44 million euros. In terms of start-up investment, the Czech Republic and Slovakia were ahead of the other CEE economies. In general, investments made at the start-up stage are considerably lower than those made at the expansion stage. In the case of Bulgaria, despite having the highest equity investments in the region, it had no start-up stage investment in 2004. Others without start-up stage investment in 2004 are Poland and Romania.

Whether venture finance is directed to young people starting their own ventures is a moot question. The absence of verifiable data across the different countries makes it difficult to check out the prospects of youth endeavour in this respect, especially young people's ability to raise new venture capital for high growth and sustainable businesses in the knowledge economy. Suffice it to state that essential framework conditions are being generated for different levels of participation among varying groups of entrepreneurs. To exten to which these conditions also suffer from constraints in the wider economy will determine whether young entrepreneurs will take up opportunities.

5. New Business Start-ups and Growth in the Transition Economies

Prior to the transition period, the size of the officially recognized private sector in the CEE countries was considered to be small, accounting for less than 5 percent of total employment in Czechoslovakia and Bulgaria, 10 percent in Hungary and just about 30 percent in Poland. Despite the rise in both youth and adult unemployment, especially in the early 1990s, this small size of the private sector has been nevertheless been boosted by the outburst of new business start-ups. New enterprise development in the transition economies is now considered to be among four factors making a significant contribution to the reduction of unemployment in the first decade of transition from a socialist to a free market economy. The other three factors are the privatization of state-owned enterprises; foreign direct investment; and legal and institutional reforms (Nesporova 2002). Many new firms were started due to the newly available market opportunities, creating jobs not only for their owners but also for wage-workers. Although it is not entirely possible to determine the contribution of new businesses to employment growth in the private sector as opposed to the transfer of jobs to the private sector, Table 1.4 gives an idea of the growth in number of private firms.

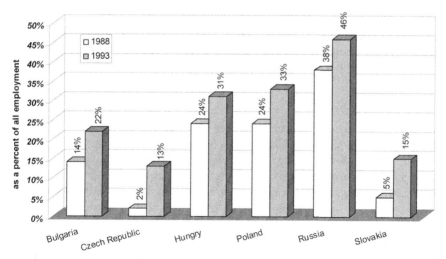

**Figure 1.5 Self-employment dynamics in transitional economies:
all self-employment**
Source: Earle and Sakova (1998).

Table 1.4 Indicators of the growth in the number of private firms

Bulgaria	Dec 1989	Dec 1990	Dec 1991
Joint ventures and foreign subsidies	51	204	-
Private firms	9583	18300	-
Czechoslovakia	**Dec 1989**	**Dec 1990**	**Dec 1991**
Foreign companies	-	0	3225
Joint ventures	-	229	4984
Registered entrepreneurs (1000s)	87	488	1338
Romania	**Dec 1989**	**Dec 1990**	**Dec 1991**
Private businesses (1000s)		97.5	154.5
Independent persons (private businesses)		50.4	101.5
Small enterprises & family associations (private businesses)		47.0	53.0
Poland	**Dec 1989**	**Dec 1990**	**Dec 1991**
Joint ventures*	429	1645	4796
Private firms*	11693	29650	45077
Individual business establishments**	813.5	1135.5	1420.0
Number of employed persons (000s)	1475.5	1915.5	2591.1
Hungary	**Dec 1989**	**Dec 1990**	**Dec 1991**
Limited liability and joint stock companies (Incorporated [a])	4792	18963	42278

*   Commercial law partnerships – number of firms
** Number of firms
a) Enterprises with "legal entity" (including state enterprises)
Sources: Bulgaria, *Statistical Reference Book of Republic of Bulgaria*, Central Statistical Office, 1991; Czechoslovakia, *Bulletin*, FSU, Number 1, 1992; Poland, *Monthly Statistical Bulletin*, GUS (various issues); Romania, *Buletin de Informare Publica*, CNS (various issues); Hungary, *Statisztikai Havi Kozlemenyek*, KSH (various issues).

As Table 1.4 above suggests, there has been an increase in the number of registered entrepreneurs in Czechoslovakia by over one million just from the end of 1989 to the end of 1991. The majority of the rise was in activities related to industry, mostly repair and maintenance, construction and trade. One of the countries with the most significant increase in entrepreneurship in terms of new venture creation is Hungary, which recorded a start-up figure of about 37,000 limited liability and joint stock companies. A similar rise in number of new enterprises occurred in Poland, with a four-times increase in the two years that ended in 1991. In Romania, despite the existence of legislation covering both the formation of private firms and privatization of state enterprises, there has been little progress made in its implementation. From about 97,000 single owner/employee firms in 1990, the figure for 1991 was just 155,000.

Another important study on self employment, conducted by Earle and Sakova (1998), suggests that all of the countries in the analysis have recorded a rise in self employment (Figure 1.5). As the figures show, nearly half of the Russians in employment engage in some significant self-employment activity, followed by Hungary and Poland at around 30 percent, Bulgaria about 20 percent, and the Czech Republic and Slovakia at about 10 percent.

New jobs created by the new enterprises include both the highly skilled and professional jobs, but also jobs that do not require much education such as farming and other forms of services. Also, most of the businesses created in the beginning were family-owned sole proprietorships with key activities in retailing, services such as automobile repairs. However, there has been a shift in direction towards wholesaling, manufacturing and transportation, and the number of newly created limited liability companies has increased (Crane 1995, 37).

Table 1.5 Changes in size of industrial enterprises (percentage shares)

Employment							Enterprises		
Number of employees		0-49		50-99	100-499	500+	0-99	100-499	500+
Czechoslovakia	1989	–	0.0	–	3.4	96.5	44.3	28.6	27.2
	1990	–	0.5	–	8.0	91.6	58.2	23.6	18.2
Hungary	1989	2.0		2.5	16.3	79.3	56.9	26.8	16.4
	1990	4.4		4.1	19.5	72.0	76.5	15.3	8.2
Poland	1989	0.3		1.1	18.2	80.4	9.6	48.9	31.0
	1990	0.5		1.6	19.9	78.0	12.6	48.4	27.6
Romania	1989	–	0.5	–	3.6	96.0	7.2	20.2	72.6
	1990	–	0.7	–	4.4	95.0	7.5	20.3	72.1
France	1989	13.7		9.6	24.1	52.1	79.5	16.8	3.7
Sweden	1991	20.0		8.0	22.8	49.3	99.4	0.4	0.2

a) The employment sizes are 0-200, 201-500 and 501+
b) The breakdown of enterprises by employment size refers to 1990
Source: National Statistical yearbooks.

Changes in sizes of enterprises have also been observed over the years. For example, as Table 1.5 (above) shows, there has been a decline in the importance of large enterprises with up to 500 employees, while smaller enterprises have increased in magnitude. Nevertheless, large enterprises still remain the biggest employers although the structural changes taking place seem to demonstrate a shift in focus from large to small enterprises. The small enterprise sector has therefore been identified as the main new job generator for the transition economies (Nesporova 2002), and the promotion of small and medium-sized enterprises (SMEs) has become one of the more popular active programs in transition economies (Saveska n.d.). Many governments of the transition economies have designed several policies aimed at promoting entrepreneurship and small business development.

6. Attitudes to and Motivations for Entrepreneurship and Growth

The growth in private firms, and especially the visible shift in the positive presence of smaller businesses, suggest that the overall attitude to entrepreneurship in CEE countries is healthy. While the general economic and institutional constraints can have an adverse effect on their growth, their continuing presence marks their resilience to problems. A focus on niche markets, flexibility of operations derived from smallness, and related factors, are all likely to account for their survival and growth. Mitra and Matlay (2004) found that as new firms were embedded in the economy, owner-managers also became more appreciative to the training needs of their employees. This positive attitude did not always translate into reality as training was seen as more of a good prospect in the abstract. Few employees actually received regular formal training. Such contradictions make up a typical small-firm owner-manager, whether in the West, the CEE countries, or other parts of the world.

The apparent move away from traditional family businesses to other areas of business activity also indicates growing signs of maturity. The extent to which entrepreneurs rely on their immediate family or personal sources for starting a business is also indicative of a growing cultural belief in the value of entrepreneurship for society (see Figure 1.6 below). There is nothing necessarily unusual in this trend. But the relatively low levels of involvement of either other sources or the state have to be monitored over time. Families appear to be accommodating both the pains of unemployment and the difficulties of establishing new start-ups, and unless the availability of different forms of support structures are firmly established it could be difficult to sustain entrepreneurship, especially among the young.

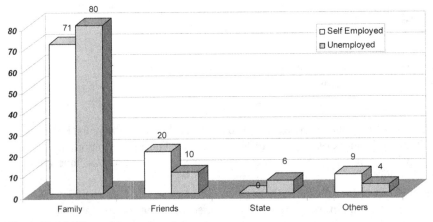

Figure 1.6 Main sources of assistance
Source: Kovacheva (1999).

Coupled with the establishment of appropriate framework conditions in the wider economy, the changing nature of the market place for new, high growth businesses, the fragility of transition can potentially be overcome in the future. This can only bode well for younger entrepreneurs who can find possible role models in the previous generation and rely on a growing infrastructure to support their endeavour. In this connection the high levels of migration among young people to the West appears to present different problems. These young people tend to take both their skills and their 'enforced' self-employment status away from their home countries. If, however, successful economic growth re-attract such people to their countries then the period of economic exile would have provided them with a better sense of entrepreneurial capabilities with which to overcome odds in different environments. Together with an enhanced set of skills and experience, the young migrants could be harnessed for the future.

Concluding Observations

In this chapter, we have explored the efforts in the Central and Eastern European region in creating more dynamic and competitive entrepreneurial economies. Findings from the review seem to indicate that considerable progress has been made, as manifested in the rise of entrepreneurial activities in the region. However, very little attention has been given specifically to the design of measures to address youth entrepreneurship. This is despite the fact that youth unemployment rates are clearly higher than those of adults. This suggests that there is a huge potential for improving the rates of entrepreneurship in the region by providing opportunities for youth to participate actively in entrepreneurial activities. Table 1.6 summarises the main strengths (plus opportunities) and weaknesses (and threats) in the economies of CEE countries as far as youth entrepreneurship is concerned.

The potential for young CEE entrepreneurs to succeed is high, especially since recent research in OECD countries has shown that youth tends to have more positive attitudes towards self-employment than adults (Blanchflower and Oswald 1998b).

The rising levels of new venture creation and the rapid growth of the economy at 5 percent and higher in the region are positive developments towards improving an entrepreneurial culture in the region. Rising levels of education amongst the youth, which have surpassed their adult counter parts, also carry hopes of a brighter future in generating high value businesses in the region. The growth of venture capital investment is also a welcome development, although more work needs to be done in attracting venture finance for the start-up stage as most of the investment goes into expanding firms and buyouts.

One of the key themes emerging from the analysis of secondary data is the diversity in the use of policy instruments to support entrepreneurship in the region. Different countries have adopted various approaches to promoting enterprise. Although many firms were started up as a consequence of these policies, it seems that high levels of unemployment have equally forced people into necessity entrepreneurship, while others have benefited from the opportunities that the free market system has generated.

Table 1.6 Strengths, weaknesses, opportunities and threats for entrepreneurial youth in the CEE countries

Strengths and Opportunities	Weaknesses and Threats
• Positive attitudes of governments of transition economies towards entrepreneurship and small business development • Youth tend to have higher educational qualifications than adults • Rising interest in postgraduate education amongst youth • Rising rates of new venture creation in the transition economies • A shift from starting small family businesses to new ventures in wholesale, manufacturing and transportation • Change taking place from large to small enterprises • Increase in venture capital investment in the region (2003-2004)	• Very high rates of youth unemployment • Not many policies directly aimed at supporting youth enterprise • Young are considered very risky lenders • Self-employment is higher in countries with more developed economies in the region • Recent economic transition that affected the economies of the region • Bribery and corruption • Start-up stage investment in venture capital is very low (2004) • Legal and the regulatory environment (too much paper work)

Developing and operating in a free market economy means participating in and working out the trials, tribulations and benefits of the global economy. CEE countries have a long experience of emigration, and this has taken on a new meaning ever since the decision of most countries to join the European Union. The particular attractions of frustrated youth and their families to the richer parts of Europe have resulted in large scale migration leaving a problematic deficit back in their countries of origin. It is believed that 60,000 Latvians have left their country since accession to the EU, 120,000 Lithuanians work in Ireland, 37,000 Slovaks have taken up jobs in the UK, and 15 percent of the Moldovian (not an EU member) work force labour abroad. The staggering statistics fuel anxiety with regard to the loss of skilled people and the brain drain that results from mass emigration. Whether foreign remittances shore up local economies is a moot question and the absence of these people at a time when foreign inward investment is being attracted can be a serious problem. It is likely that in the short-run these problems will not go away, especially if the youth do not return home. But medium to long-term strategic thinking and planning can yield surprising results.

Countries such as Taiwan and Israel, and more recently, China and India, have faced similar problems of a youth brain drain, mainly to the USA. However, over the years, prospective economic growth coupled with clever policy making, including winning over the hearts and minds of the diaspora community abroad, has led to an influx of money and talent together with the return of emigrants to their home countries. These returnees have established strong networks with their counterparts in the USA, identified niche business prospects and established global networks of technologies, venture capital and entrepreneurship. The positive outcome of these developments has been as staggering as the negative implications of the brain drain referred to earlier. They have contributed to Taiwan's semi-conductor industry leadership, to China's manufacturing dominance and to India's software edge. It is possible that CEE countries can adopt similar strategies, forging innovative links with their diaspora abroad while cultivating new networks with the dynamic growth prospects in China and India. This subject requires serious, special attention.

In conclusion, despite the progress being made in the region, there is still work to be done in supporting youth entrepreneurship. In consideration of youth being highly risky lenders, other initiatives can be considered such as grants or venture capital finance to young people who are capable of producing feasible business plans. Also, in the current era of the knowledge based economy, which is associated with high skills, technological change and innovation, efforts need to be made to ensure that youth in the region is taking up science and technology courses, coupled with entrepreneurship studies, as a way of building their competencies and to ensure that they emerge as key players in the global economy. Recognizing the higher levels of positive attitudes to entrepreneurship among youth, government policies can perhaps focus less on the peculiarities of the young and more on removing the systemic barriers, such as aversion to the particular risk factors among young people, that thwart entrepreneurial endeavour. Understanding youth as partners and deriving value from their ability to constantly change between employment, and temporary work, as part of a process of 'self-actualization and exploration' (Du-Bois-Raymond 2001) requires a step change in the institutions working with young people in society. Finally, efforts could also be directed at different forms of social entrepreneurship (not part of the discussion in this chapter) where entrepreneurship extends into the community beyond the efforts of a select few starting up new businesses.

Note

Special thanks are due to Yazid Abubakar for his considerable support in bringing together some of the secondary data and for his insights during the discussion of the content of this chapter. Thanks also to Aneta Milczaryck for her efforts in sourcing some of the resources referred to in this chapter. Both Yazid and Aneta are Ph.D. students at the Centre for Entrepreneurship Research, School of Entrepreneurship and Business, University of Essex.

References

Aidis, R. (2003), 'Entrepreneurship and Economic Transition' (Amsterdam: Tinbergen Institute), Discussion paper (http://Tinbergen.nl).

Aidis, R. (2005), 'Entrepreneurship in Transition Countries: A Review', Working Paper no. 61, *Centre for the Study of Social Change in Europe* (UCL School of Slavonic and East European Studies), December (2005) London.

Audretsch, D.B. and Thurik, A.R. (2001), 'What is New About the New Economy: Sources of Growth in the Managed and Entrepreneurial Economies', *Industrial and Corporate Change* 10(1), 25-48.

Audretsch, D.B., Carree, M.A. and Thurik. A.R. (2001), *Does Entrepreneurship reduce Unemployment* [Online], Available:www.spea.indiana.edu/ids/pdfholder/ISSN%2002-1.doc[2006, Oct. 8].

Audretsch, D.B. and Thurik, A.R. (2001), 'What is New about the New Economy: Sources of Growth in the Managed and Entrepreneurial Economies', *Industrial and Corporate Change*, 19, 795-82.

Audretsch, D.B. and Fritsch, M. (1994), 'The Geography of Firm Births in Germany', *Regional Studies*, 28(4), July, 359-365.

Audretsch, D.B. (1995), *Innovation and Industry Evolution* (Cambridge, Mass.: MIT Press).

Audretsch D.B., Carree, M.A. and Stel, A.J.V. (2001), *Impeded Industrial Restructuring, The Growth Penalty*, ISSN 01-2.

Bartlett, W. and Bukvic, V. (2001) 'Barriers to SME Growth' in Slovenia' *MOST 11*, 177-195.

Baumol, W. (2002), *The Free-market Innovation Machine: Analyzing the Growth Miracle Of Capitalism* (Princeton: Princeton University Press).

Blanchflower, D. and Oswald, A. (1998a) *Unemployment, Well-Being and Wage Curves in Eastern Europe. [Online]*, Available: www2.warwick.ac.uk/fac/soc/economics/staff/faculty/oswald/europeeast.pdf [2006, Oct. 4].

Blanchflower, D. and Oswald, A. (1998), *Entrepreneurship and the Youth Labour Market Problem: A Report for the OECD. [Online]*, Available: www.dartmouth.edu/~blnchflr/papers/OECD.pdf [2006, Oct. 8].

Blanchflower, D. and Meyer, B. (1994), 'A Longitudinal Analysis of Young Entrepreneurs in Australia and the United States', *Small Business Economics*, 6(1), 1-20.

Blau, D.M. (1987), 'A Time Series Analysis of Self Employment in the United States', *Journal of Political Economy*, 95(3), 445-467.

Bobeva, D. (1997), 'Employment Policies and Programmes in Bulgaria', in M. Godfrey and P. Richards (eds.), *Employment Policies and Programmes in Central and Eastern Europe* (Geneva, Switzerland: ILO), 19-47.

Crane, K. (1995), 'The Costs and Benefits of Transition', in J.P. Hardt and R.F. Kaufman (eds.), *East-Central European Economies in Transition* (New York, NY, USA: M.E. Sharpe), 25-49.

Chigunta, F. (2002), 'Youth Entrepreneurship: Meeting the Key Policy Challenges, Produced for the *Youth Employment Summit* (YES2002)', *[Online]*, Available: www.yesweb.org/gkr/res/bg.entrep.ta.doc [2006, Nov. 8].

Curtain, R. (2000), 'Towards a Youth Employment Strategy', *Report to the United Nations on Youth Employment.*

Dallago, B. (2005), 'Institutions and Entrepreneurship: A Comparative Evaluation of South Eastern Europe' Working Paper 01/2005, University of Trento, School of International Studies, Trento, Italy.

David, S.E. and Jovanovic, B. (1989), 'Estimates of a Model of Entrepreneurial Choice under Liquidity Constraints', *Journal of Political Economy*, 97(3), 657-674.

Drobnic, S. (1997), 'Employment Policies and Programmes in Slovenia', in M. Godfrey and P. Richards (eds.), *Employment Policies and Programmes in Central and Eastern Europe* (Geneva, Switzerland: ILO), 157-183.

Earle, J.S and Sakova, Z. (1998) 'Self-Employment in Transitional Economies: Entrepreneurship or Disguised Unemployment', http://wwww/eerforum.org/ conferences.

Earle, J and Sakova, Z. (2000), 'Business Start-Ups or Disguised Unemployment? Evidence on the Character of Self-employment from Transition Economies', *Labour Economics*, 7, 575-601.

Earle, J. and Sakova, Z. (2001), 'Entrepreneurship from Scratch', *SSRN Working Paper.*

Evans, D.S., and Leighton, L.S. (1989), 'The Determinants of Changes in U.S. Self-Employment, 1968-1987', *Small Business Economics*, 1(2), 111-120.

Evans, D.S. and Leighton, L. (1990), 'Small Business Formation by Unemployed and Employed Workers', *Small Business Economics*, 2(4), 319-330.

EVCA (2005), 'Central and Eastern Europe Statistics 2004 - Special Paper', *European Venture Capital and Private Equity Association. [Online],* Available: www.evca.com/images/attachments/tmpl_13_art_86_att_925.pdf [2006, Oct. 8].

GEM (2005), *The Global Entrepreneurship Monitor* (London Business School, UK Babson College and the Kaufmann Foundation, USA).

Glas, M., Drnovvsek, M., and Mirtic, D. (2000), 'Problems Faced by New Entrepreneurs: Slovenia and Croatia', paper presented at the 30th *European Small Business Seminar*, Gent, Belgium.

Gora, M. (1997), 'Employment Policies and Programmes in Poland', in M. Godfrey and P. Richards (eds.), *Employment Policies and Programmes in Central and Eastern Europe* (Geneva, Switzerland: ILO), 115-135.

Johnson, S. and Loveman, G. (1995), *Starting Over in Eastern Europe: Entrepreneurship and Economic Renewal* (Cambridge: Harvard Business School Press).

Jovanovic, B. (1982), 'Selection and Evolution of Industry', *Econometrica*, 50, 649-670.

Kobeissi, N. (2001), 'Residual Communism and Entrepreneurship Development in Post-Communist Countries', Working Paper, Rutgers University, New Jersey.

Kontrovich, V. (1999), 'Has New Business Creation in Russia come to a halt?', *Journal of Business Venturing*, 14: 451-60.

Kovacheva, S. (1999), 'Flexibalisation of Youth Transitions in Central and Eastern European Countries', working paper, http//:www.hwf.at.

Lucas, R.E. (1978), 'On the Size Distribution of Business Firms', *Bell Journal of Economics*, 9, 508-523.

Lundström, A. and Steveson, L. (2002), 'On the Road to Entrepreneurship Policy Summary', *Entrepreneurship Policy for the Future Series*, Volume 1.

Mansuy, M. and Couppié, T. (2001), 'The Transition from Education to Working Life Key Data on Vocational Training in the European Union', *Cedefop Reference series. [Online]*, Available: http://www2.trainingvillage.gr/download/publication/ keydata/kdt3/2202/2202EN. htm[2006, Oct. 4].

Marot, B. (1997), 'Small Business Development Strategy in Slovenia', Chapter 3, in *Entrepreneurship and SMEs in Transition Economies*, The Visegrad Conference (Paris: OECD), 51-64.

Mitra, J. and Matlay, H. (2004) 'Enterprise and Vocational Education and Training in the Accession Countries', *Industry and Higher Education Journal*, 18(1), February, 2004.

Nesporova, A. (2002), 'Why Unemployment Remains so High in Central and Eastern Europe', International Labour Office, Employment Paper 2002/42. *[Online]*, Available: www.ilo.org/public/english/employment/strat/download/ ep43.pdf [2006, Oct. 4].

North D.C. (1990), *Institutions, Institutional Change and Economic Performance* (Cambridge: University Press).

OECD (2001), *Putting the Young in Business: Policy Challenges for Youth Entrepreneurship*, The LEED Programme, Territorial Development Division, Paris.

Oxenfeldt, A. (1943), *New Firms and Free Enterprise* (Washington, D.C.: American Council on Public Affairs).

Phare (1999), 'The State of Small Business in Estonia: *Report 1998*', *PHARE Support to Small Business Development in Estonia* (Tallinn, 1999).

Pissarides, F. (1999), 'Is Lack of Funds the Main Obstacle for Growth? EBRD Experience with Small and Medium-sized Businesses in Central and Eastern Europe', *Journal of Comparative Economics*, 31, 503-531.

PMR (2006), *Strong but Fading Economic Growth in Russia and Good Prospects for Slovakia and the Czech Republic, Press release: 26 April 2006*, PMR Publications. *[Online]*, Available: http://www.pmrpublications.com/index. php?pr_id=43 [2006, Oct. 12].

Reynolds, P., Storey, D.J. and Westhead, P. (1994), 'Cross-National Comparisons of the Variation in New Firm Formation Rates', *Regional Studies*, 28(4), July 443-456.

Reynolds, P., Miller, B. and Maki, W.R. (1995), 'Explaining Regional Variation in Business Births and Deaths: U.S. 1976-1988', *Small Business Economics*, 7(5), 389-707.

Reymond du-Bois, M. (2001), 'World Youth Report', *Journal of Youth Studies*, 4(1).

Saveska, S. (n.d.), 'Unemployment as a Social Cost of Transition in Central and Eastern Europe: Applicability for the Republic of Macedonia', [Online], Available: www.nispa.sk/news/saveska.rtf [2006, Oct. 12].

Saxenian, A. (2006), *The New Argonauts: Regional Advantage in a Global Economy,* (Cambridge: Harvard University Press).

Smallbone, D. and Welter, F. (2003), 'Institutional Development and Entrepreneurship in Transition Economies', Paper Presented at the ICSB 48th World Conference - Advancing, Entrepreneurship and Small Business, held on 15-18 June1 2003 in Belfast (Northern Ireland). [Online], Available: http://www.unece.org/indust/ sme/institutional%20development.html (2006, Oct. 13).

Storey, D.J. (1991), 'The Birth of New Firms – Does Unemployment Matter? A Review of the Evidence', *Small Business Economics*, 3(3), September, 167-178.

United Nations (1997), *Report on the World Social Situation* (New York, NY, USA).

Wennekers, A.R.M. and Thurik, A.R. (1999), 'Linking Entrepreneurship and Economic Growth', *Small Business Economics* 13(1), 27-55.

Verheul, I., Audretch, D., Thurik, R., Wennekers, S. (2002), 'Explaining Entrepreneurship and the Role of Policy: An Eclectic Theory', Research Report 0012, EIM.

White, S. and Kenyon, P. (2000), 'Enterprise-Based Youth Employment Policies, Strategies and Programmes', *Draft Report to ILO*, Geneva.

World Youth Report (2003), *World Youth report – 2003: Report of the Secretary-General, United Nations,* Official document: A/58/79 & E/CN.5/2003/4, *[Online],* Available: www.un.org/esa/socdev/unyin/wyr03.htm [2006, Oct. 12].

Chapter 2

Youth Entrepreneurship and Self-Employment as a Source of Employment in Eastern Europe, South-Eastern Europe, and Central Asia

Klaus Haftendorn

1. Introduction

Employment is the central subject in all transition economies.[1] High unemployment is one of the characteristics of these transition economies. Young people are particularly affected by unemployment in all these countries. The present chapter will give a short overview of the economic situation of the countries in Eastern Europe, South-Eastern Europe and Central Asia and look into the specific situation of unemployment of young women and men. Wage employment in the public and private sector is not sufficient to provide enough jobs for the active population and this in a situation where the population is ageing in a number of countries of Eastern Europe, while in countries of Central Asia the youth population is steadily increasing. Job seekers often do not have the right qualifications for the new requirements of enterprises competing in a global market. The education programmes for vocational training and higher education are outdated and the reform process is not fast enough to respond to changing requirements.

During recent years, the international community and national governments have taken a number of measures to improve the entrance conditions of young women and men in the labour market. The EU, with its European Employment Strategy, has made a strong case for the integration of youth employment in the policy agenda. A particular effort had been made by the Secretary General of the United Nations who created in 2001, as a first measure in line with the Millennium Development Goal 8 which also aims to reduce youth unemployment, a High Level Panel on Youth and the Youth Employment Network YEN. The Youth Employment Network, connecting together the UN Secretariat, the World Bank and the ILO, which also acts as Secretariat to the Network, promotes the application of the High Level Panel recommendations at national level through the commitment towards youth employment from the highest authorities of the member States.

---

1 Term usually employed for former central-planned economies in Eastern Europe, South-Eastern Europe and Central Asia.

Against this backcloth, the chapter will give an overview of youth unemployment and self-employment in the transition countries and some of the programmes designed to promote youth employment and entrepreneurship. In addition, recommendations will be made of how governments can promote enterprise creation in general and help young women and men to create their own income-generating activity.

2. Socio-economic environment in South-Eastern and Eastern Europe, and Central Asia

This region covers countries with large economic disparities. In order to better compare the data of the countries, they have been grouped together as follows:

- EU New Members with 8 countries belonging to Eastern Europe;
- SEE, South-Eastern Europe with 7 countries;
- CIS, covering 12 countries.

The first group of countries that belong to the EU since May 2004 shows the best economic figures. Already, during the years immediately before accession, these countries had well sustained economic growth. This development is expected to continue as a result of the accession. All countries have been able to improve the living conditions of their citizens between 1998 and 2002 (except Slovakia) as indicated by the ranking of the UNDP Human Development Index. However, the unemployment rate remains high; only Hungary, Latvia and Lithuania could significantly create jobs to reduce unemployment while in Poland unemployment increased strongly.

Table 2.1 Socio economic data from EU New Member States

Country	GDP/capita, PPP current US$ (2002)	Real GDP growth/year % (2003)	Unemployment rate 1995–2003	UNDP H D I ranking 1998–2002
Czech Republic	15 148	2.6	4.0 – 4.1	32 –
Estonia	11 712	4.4	9.7 – 10.0	46 – 36
Hungary	13 129	2.9	10.2 – 5.3	– 38
Latvia	8 965	6.0	18.9 – 10.7	63 – 50
Lithuania	10 015	6.6	17.1 – 12.4	5 – 41
Poland	10 187	3.3	13.3 – 19.6	44 – 37
Slovakia	12 426	3.8	13.1 – 17.5	40 – 42
Slovenia	17 748	2.1	7.4 – 6.6	29 – 27

The countries belonging to the Western Balkans have been able to perform an important and steady growth during the last four years (with the exception of Serbia and Montenegro due to the inter-ethnic conflict in 2001) and it is expected that growth will continue. However, the GDP per capita lags behind the EU New Member countries. The living conditions in these countries have certainly improved, but they rank well behind those of the EU New Member countries. Also, the unemployment figures show double digits and unemployment might be even higher, as in some of the countries the statistics take into consideration only the registered unemployed instead of those of Labour Force Survey (LFS) data.

Table 2.2 Socio economic data from SEE countries

Country	GDP/capita, PPP current US$ (2002)	Real GDP growth/year % (2003)	Unemployment rate 1995–2003	UNDP H D I ranking 1998–2002
Albania	3 973	6.0	12.9 – 15.2	94 – 65
Bosnia & Herzegovina	5 538	3.2	39.4 – nn	nn – 66
Bulgaria	6 909	4.8	15.7 – 13.7	60 – 56
Croatia	9 967	4.7	14.5 – 14.3	49 – 48
Romania	6 326	4.8	8.0 – nn	64 – 69
Serbia & Montenegro		1.0	13.4 – nn	
FRY Macedonia	6 262	3.1	35.6 – 36.7	nn – 60

The economic performances of the 12 CIS countries are extremely disparate. The economically strongest country, the Russian Federation, produced a GDP per capita that is near to those of SEE countries, while the weakest country, Tajikistan, is equal with some of the least developed countries. The growth rates are quite considerable, but they are based on a very low economic level. The unemployment rates are high, and in most of the countries, worse than in 1995. The living conditions, according to the UNDP HDI, rank lowest of all considered countries.

Table 2.3 Socio economic data from CIS

Country	GDP/capita, PPP current US$ (2002)	Real GDP growth/year % (2003)	Unemployment rate 1995–2003	UNDP H D I ranking 1998–2002
Armenia	2 957	13.0	6.7 – 10.1	93 – 82
Azerbaijan	3 115	11.2	0.8 – 1.4	90 – 91
Belarus	5 344	6.0	2.9 – 3.1	57 – 62
Georgia	2 190	8.6	10.8 – nn	70 – 97
Kazakhstan	5 769	9.1	2.1 – nn	73 – 78
Kyrgyzstan	1 572	4.1	50.4 – nn	98 – 110
Rep. of Moldova	1 431	6.3	1.0 – 7.9	102 – 113
Russian Federation	7 926	7.3	9.5 – nn	62 – 57
Tajikistan	916	10.2	2.0 – nn	110 – 116
Turkmenistan	4 622	17.0	31.0 – nn	100 – 86
Ukraine	4 714	8.5	5.6 – 9.1	78 – 70
Uzbekistan	1 336	5.0	0.3 – 0.4	106 – 107

The informal economy has taken a significant share in the national economies of the countries belonging to the EU New Members, to SEE and to the CIS. In some countries, it is the main source for creation of national wealth as shown in the following table. Employment conditions in the informal economy are highly exploitative; however, it often provides the first and only job opportunity for young people.

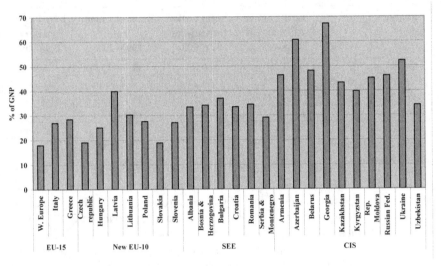

Figure 2.1 Informal economy as a percentage of GNP, 1999/2000
Source: Schneider (2002).

The labour market situation remains difficult in all countries under review. The EU New Member states' labour markets are characterized by regional disparities and a severe educational mismatch. Some developing regions face shortage of manpower while in other regions high unemployment is persistent with an informal economy that cannot provide decent jobs. As new EU members, these countries embark now on employment policies based on EU employment guidelines adopted in 2003 with the employment targets of full employment, promotion of quality and productivity at work, and fostering of social cohesion and inclusive labour markets.

In SEE, the unemployment rates will remain high for the next years, despite some economic improvements. Many of the job seekers are young women and men who are looking for wage employment for the first time. The best they can expect is short-term employment with precarious legal and working conditions.

The decline of employment in CIS countries was rather low after the desegregation of the Soviet Union. However, figures show only registered unemployment and do not take into account those unemployed who do not expect any support from public labour offices and therefore do not register. Some of the CIS countries dispose of considerable natural resources that led to steady growth in the past and will be the engine of economic development in the future. This growth, however, could not be transformed in growth of employment as it is based on capital-intensive production for export. There are few links or trickle-down effects to the other economic sectors that are often dominated by small and micro enterprises operating in the informal economy.

In general, the high pressure of job seekers on the labour market has led to a liberalization or non-respect of labour legislation that makes the employment situation more and more precarious. Many job seekers, who in most of the countries are only entitled to unemployment benefits for a short period, try to make their living through informal employment or self-employment like micro commercial activities or the creation of a micro enterprise.

3. Youth unemployment

In general, in transition countries but also in advanced economies, even if to a lesser extent, the youth[2] unemployment rate is high and the ratio to adult unemployment often more than double. The following table gives some ratios that characterize the situation of young people in the labour market and its changes between 1993 and 2003.

Table 2.4 Principal youth labour market indicators, 1993 and 2003

	Youth unemployment rate (%)		Youth labour force participation (%)		Youth employment-to-youth population ratio (%)		Ratio of youth-to-adult unemployment rate	
Region	1993	2003	1993	2003	1993	2003	1993	2003
EU-15	20	14.5	48.6	45.9	38.9	39.2	2.24	2.15
New EU Member States (EU-10)	22.5	30.7	47.3	36.8	36.6	25.5	2.54	2.43
EU-25	20.4	17.3	48.4	44.1	38.5	36.5	2.29	2.24
South-Eastern Europe (SEE-8)[1]	23	22.4	51.3	40.3	39.5	31.2	2.91	2.45
CIS (12)	9.4	14.6	47.4	40.8	42.9	34.8	3.58	2.46
Europe & Central Asia (49)[2]	17.2	17	48.6	42.3	40.3	35.1	2.63	2.36
World	11.7	14.4	58.8	54.9	51.9	47	3.1	3.5

Source: ILO.
[1]Including Turkey [2]Without San Marino

With the exception of the "old" EU Member States, the youth unemployment rates increased quite significantly in the accession countries, in SEE and in the

_____

2 Youth according to UN definition covers the age group between 15 and 24.

CIS. This is the same trend that is observed worldwide. However, there are large differences among the countries. Western European countries show an important decrease on average. Nevertheless, youth unemployment can be as high as 26 to 28% like in Greece or in Italy. Poland shows the highest peak with over 40% of youth unemployment but also countries from SEE approach the line of 38%.

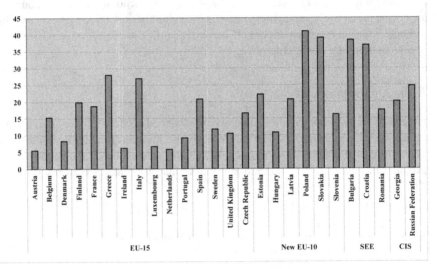

Figure 2.2 Youth unemployment rates in Europe, 2001
Source: ILO (2003b).

In the Central Asian countries of the CIS the situation is even worse. Labour Force Surveys in Kazakhstan (2002) and Georgia (1999), the Survey of Population on Problems of Employment in Azerbaijan (2001), calculations based on micro-samples and the Population Census in Kyrgyzstan (1999) have revealed unemployment figures of youth ranging between 50 and 60%. To these bleak figures another has to be added, i.e., the unemployment rates of young women which are in general worse than those of young men. In some countries the difference can attain 10 to 15%.

The increase of youth unemployment rates is even more alarming as during the same period the labour force participation of young women and men was decreasing as well. The main reason for this lower participation is mainly due to higher enrolment in secondary and higher education. In the EU New Member countries the changes in education enrolment count largely for the decrease in labour force participation, while in SEE and CIS countries, in most cases, the enrolment in secondary and higher education is not the main reason for the drop in labour force participation; they are the result of young workers leaving the labour market for other forms of activities and migration. While the youth population in most of the countries grows (except the Western European countries), the ratio to youth employment decreases; in other words, more and more young people are without employment.

Macro-economic measures should provide employment for the whole active labour force; unfortunately, over the last decades, unemployment increased or remained stable on a high level with particular adverse effects for young people whose unemployment rate is in general 2 to 3.5 times higher than the adult unemployment rate. There are only a few countries where this ratio is nearly 1, like Germany, Austria and Switzerland. The enterprise-based vocational training system (also called dual system) in these countries provides an entry point for young school leavers to the world of work and, due to this practical experience, makes them immediately operational for employment.

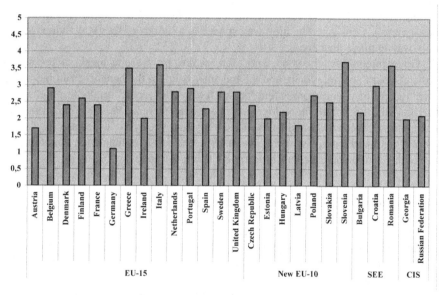

**Figure 2.3 The ratio of youth unemployment rates to adult unemployment
rates in Europe, 2001**
Source: ILO (2003a).

When looking behind these aggregate figures of the labour market, we will find a number of reasons for the high unemployment rates in general and for youth in particular:

- Loss of markets due to the breakdown of the centrally planned economy with down-sizing of large public companies;
- Release of redundant workers in public services;
- Emergence of capital-intensive extraction of national resources turned to export markets with little effect on local and regional economies;
- High competition from imported consumer goods from emerging countries like China, India, South Korea and others;

- Mistrust towards private companies from the administration which rather discourages than encourages the creation of private SMEs;
- Timid emergence of Small and Medium-Sized companies that were not supported and therefore not able to compensate the job losses in large companies and in administration;
- Mismatch of education and training with its labour requirements of SMEs; therefore young people who are leaving school or vocational training institutions seldom find a remunerated job whose requirements correspond to the aptitudes and skills they have acquired.

In this context, after completing their education, young adults very often find themselves directly in unemployment and with little hope that this situation will change soon. Consequently, they are exposed to all kinds of illegal activities as the only way to make their living.

Governments become more and more aware, on the one hand, of the social costs of youth unemployment and, on the other hand, of the benefits from increased employment of young women and men. A recent ILO report[3] on youth pointed out that halving the youth unemployment rate would increase the GDP of transition economies between 6.6% and 10.6%. Orienting these young adolescents towards self-employment and enterprise creation would be one of the policies that governments in South-Eastern and Eastern Europe and CIS should adopt.

4. Entrepreneurial potential of Youth

Today's youth generation is much better educated than in the past and ready to take its destiny in its own hands. Research on youth entrepreneurship reveals a considerable level of latent entrepreneurial potential. A research carried out in Great Britain by the Prince's Scottish Youth Business Trust in 1993 discovered that 20% of 18 to 30 year old persons had the potential to become entrepreneurs. Experiences from internationally operating youth entrepreneurship promotion programmes, like Youth Business International with its mentorship programmes, confirm that this indicative figure is quite realistic. Nowadays, young women and men are more inclined to take the risk to become entrepreneurs; they are better educated than the elder generation, are independent from family, and entrepreneurial activities become more socially acceptable.

In the age group of 18 to 30 years of age, more and more consider self-employment or becoming an entrepreneur as a possibility for income generation or as a career option. The DG Enterprise of the European Commission initiated a survey on entrepreneurship "The Flash Eurobarometer" which is conducted annually. The survey tried to find out if the active population of EU member states prefers being employed or being self-employed. The survey provides data from 2000 to 2004. The idea of self-employment has a high preference among the age group of 15 to 24. In

---

3 ILO, *Global Employment Trends for Youth*, 2004.

2000, 50% of this group preferred self-employment and in 2005, still 45% were of the opinion that they would rather be independent and self-employed.

Research from the Global Entrepreneurship Monitor shows that the most active age group of business starters are persons 25 to 34 years old, followed by the age group of 18 to 24 years old. In particular, low-income countries have the highest start-up rates for the entire active population, as well as for youth.

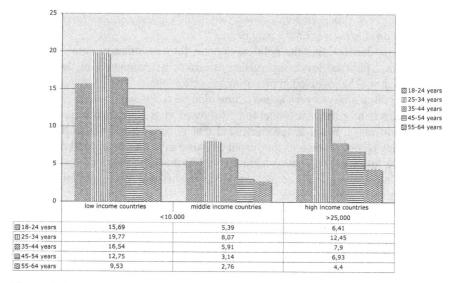

	low income countries <10.000	middle income countries	high income countries >25,000
18-24 years	15,69	5,39	6,41
25-34 years	19,77	8,07	12,45
35-44 years	16,54	5,91	7,9
45-54 years	12,75	3,14	6,93
55-64 years	9,53	2,76	4,4

Figure 2.4 Total Entrepreneurial Activity (TEA) (index) by age and by income group (2004)

Source: GEM (2004) – Figures kindly provided by GEM coordination team.

5. Youth employment policy

At the international level, a number of significant policy initiatives with regard to youth employment policy can be found. In November 2001, the European Commission published the White Paper on youth policy "A new impetus for European Youth".[4] This White Paper is the result of a large consultation involving young people, researchers, policy makers and public administration through 17 national conferences and hearings with the Economic and Social Committee. The suggestions made during this consultation process are laid down in the paper. For young people, a coherent youth policy should cover five major fields:

- Participation;
- Education;
- Employment, vocational training, social inclusion;

---

4 Commission of the European Communities; COM (2001) 681 final.

- Well-being, individual autonomy, culture;
- European values, mobility, relations with the rest of the world.

A further initiative is the UN Secretary General's Youth Employment Network (YEN), which recommends developing a national youth policy with all relevant cross-cutting elements. Therefore YEN invites countries to become Lead Countries for Youth Employment by taking the following policy engagements:[5]

1. *Confirm the government's commitment at the highest political level to decent and productive work for young people*
   It is understood that the political impetus for this initiative comes from the highest political level, supervising governmental ministries or departments which will be involved in preparing the action plan.
2. *Prepare a national review and action plan on youth employment*
   There is no particular model to be followed in preparing these reviews and action plans, but it is recommended that governments refer to the panel's policy recommendations for overall guidance as to the content and the process to be followed. The governments should furthermore invite civil society, the business community, employers, trade unions and youth organizations to contribute to this process.
3. *Contribute to international development cooperation in sharing national experience with other countries and with the international community*
   Lead countries will be expected to not only develop national reviews and action plans on youth employment, but to furthermore share their plans and experiences with others. Lead countries may wish to organize regional or international meetings or exchanges in order to build momentum for broader action at the regional and global levels in favour of youth employment.
4. *Contribute to a broader political process within the United Nations General Assembly in the overall framework of follow-up to the Millennium Declaration[6] and within the ILO for a coherent and integrated international strategy on employment*
   Lead countries are expected to support the Millennium Development Target on youth employment, not simply as an objective in its own right, but furthermore as a means to support the overall roadmap for implementation of all the Millennium Development Goals. Also, action on youth employment can be expected to contribute to broader employment policy within both the national and international dimensions.

For many governments education and employment are the key elements of their youth policy. The European Commission in the White Paper stipulates lifelong learning through formal education and higher recognition of non-formal learning. The

---

5 Up to March 2006, 19 countries had joined the group of lead countries.
6 General Assembly resolution 55/2 of 8 September 2000.

employment policy[7] is centred around four main "pillars": improving employability; developing an entrepreneurial spirit and creating jobs; encouraging firms and their employees to be adaptable; strengthening equal opportunities for men and women. The High Level Panel of the Secretary General's Youth Employment Network formulated a number of recommendations covering four aspects for the promotion of youth employment:

- Employment creation through macro economic measures;
- Equal opportunities to make sure that all measures are gender balanced and extended to vulnerable groups among young women and men;
- Employability to give all the means through education, training and personal development to young people to match the labour market requirements;
- Entrepreneurship as a valuable career option for youth.

A number of countries in Europe, like Austria, Denmark and Germany, have a strong tradition in enterprise-based vocational training and apprenticeship schemes which increases employability and contributes largely to the fact that the youth unemployment rate in these countries is not much higher than the general unemployment rate.

The German Ministry for Economic Cooperation and Development issued, in 2006, a strategy paper entitled "Cornerstone of Youth Employment Promotion in Development Cooperation". The centerpiece of the strategy is a three-dimensional integrated approach which combines employability through a mediation and matching mechanism with employment opportunities. In order to increase employability (labour supply), interventions are proposed in basic education, in labour market-oriented technical vocational training and education, including entrepreneurship education and promotion of non-formal education and training.

The matching and mediation mechanism is based on an Active Labour Market policy (ALMP) composed of a sound labour market information system, youth-oriented services and instruments like career guidance, occupational orientation, consultancy and placement services. Further, better labour market regulations should reduce entry barriers for young people and more participation of youth in policy making should be promoted. On the employment opportunity (labour demand) side, creation of more jobs for young people is stipulated through the setting of incentive schemes for employers; the promotion of apprenticeship schemes; and the implementation of labour intensive infrastructure programmes. A strong case is made for the promotion of young entrepreneurs and self-employment through business start-up programmes, micro finance schemes and consultancy services and mentor programmes.

---

7 European employment strategy, based on the new "employment" chapter in the Treaty of Amsterdam.

6. Recommendations for a coherent youth entrepreneurship policy

A coherent youth entrepreneurship policy should be embedded in an overall youth employment policy which should always be taken into consideration when governments take decisions in social and economic matters. The formulation of this policy should be based on a large consultation of young people. Governments are very conscious about the fact that high youth unemployment has high social costs and bears the risk of social unrest.

On the other hand, high social benefits can be gained if governments are able to unlock the strong potential of young people for self-employment and entrepreneurship and employability. Young entrepreneurs, in turn, create national wealth and create employment not only for themselves but also for others. The UN Secretary-General Kofi Annan[8] made the following recommendations for a coherent Youth entrepreneurship policy:

> Governments at national and local level need to encourage a broad and dynamic concept of entrepreneurship to stimulate both personal initiative and initiative in a broad variety of organizations which include but reach beyond the private sector: small and large enterprises, social entrepreneurs, cooperatives, the public sector, the trade union movement and youth organizations.

Based on these recommendations, the High Level Panel Group on Youth Entrepreneurship[9] developed a road map for policy makers which shows the impediments for young entrepreneurs and what would stimulate youth entrepreneurship. For a coherent youth entrepreneurship policy, governments should take policy measures that are centred on the key-factors of the road map[10] with the aim:

- to create a positive entrepreneurship culture;
- to encourage more young women and men to start an entrepreneurial undertaking;
- to have a conducive legal and regulatory framework for enterprise creation; and
- to support youth during the pre-start-up phase, the start-up phase and the post start-up phase of the entrepreneurial process.

Creating a positive enterprise culture

Cultural standards are determinant for a national culture. They are understood as all kinds of recognition, thinking, values and activities that the majority of members belonging to the same culture consider for themselves personally or for others as normal, natural, typical and binding. Behaviour is controlled on the basis of recognized cultural standards. Central cultural standards in one culture can be

---

8 Report to the General Assembly of the UN, A/RES/55/2, September 2000, New York.
9 Working Group on Entrepreneurship.
10 www.ilo.org/yen.

completely missing or only have peripheral meanings or fundamental different functions in another culture.

Entrepreneurship is understood in a wide social, cultural and economic context, as well as being innovative at home, school, leisure and at work. Entrepreneurship involves life attitudes including the readiness and the courage to act in a social, cultural and economic context. Entrepreneurial qualities or behaviour include:

- creativity and curiosity;
- motivation by success;
- willingness to take risks;
- ability to cooperate;
- identification of opportunities; and
- being innovative and tolerate uncertainty.

A positive enterprise culture values and rewards such behaviour whereas cultures that reinforce conformity, group interests, and control over the future are not likely to show risk-taking and entrepreneurial behaviour. In order to create a positive enterprise culture, governments should take the following initiatives:

- assess awareness of youth about entrepreneurship as a career option;
- increase interest in business and entrepreneurship within the society;
- promote the social role of entrepreneurs; and
- organize PR campaigns, media coverage on entrepreneurship, competitions and awards and youth business events.

Promoting youth entrepreneurship and enterprise creation through entrepreneurship education

The importance of education and training for an entrepreneurial society has been underlined on several occasions through United Nations Declarations and Conventions. A key event in the international development of enterprise education was the Intergovernmental Conference on Education and the Economy in a Changing Society held under the auspices of the Organization for Economic Co-operation and Development (OECD) in Paris in 1988. The OECD educational monograph, *Towards an Enterprising Culture*, issued soon after that conference, said: "Changes in educational methods are needed to foster competence in 'being enterprising' as a vitally important qualification needed by the young as they enter society. This competence means having the ability to be creative and flexible, to be flexible to take and exercise initiative and to be able to solve problems".

The importance given by the European Community to entrepreneurship education was underlined in the European Charter for Small Enterprises (adopted by the General Affairs Council, 13 June 2000, and welcomed by the Feira European Council, 19/20 June 2000) which stated:

Europe will nurture entrepreneurial spirit and new skills from an earlier age. General knowledge about business and entrepreneurship needs to be taught at all school levels.

Specific business-related modules should be made an essential ingredient of education schemes at secondary level and at colleges and universities. We will encourage and promote youngsters' entrepreneurial endeavours, and develop appropriate training schemes for managers in small enterprises.

More recently,[11] the EU Vice-President Günter Verheugen, responsible for industry and enterprise policies said: "We need a more favourable societal climate for entrepreneurship, in particular to encourage young Europeans to become the entrepreneurs of tomorrow. We need a systematic approach to entrepreneurship education at all levels, from primary school to university".

Increasingly, the concern of governments at a national level is generally to foster a spirit of enterprise and a number of countries, especially in the European Union, promote self-employment as an important part of their efforts to reduce youth unemployment. Promoting entrepreneurship and enterprise creation is therefore high on the policy agenda of almost all countries in the world as successfully created enterprises generate additional employment. However, few, if any, countries have created clear and comprehensive education policies to promote youth entrepreneurship and self-employment. Instead, what we find are elements of education and training policy at different levels as they relate to the world of work and the world of business. Entrepreneurship education involves getting young people to think about entrepreneurship and the role of business entrepreneurs in economic and social development. They also get an opportunity to analyse the changes taking place in their country and are encouraged to consider self-employment as a career option.

Some recommendations for the introduction of entrepreneurship education in the national education system

The responsibility for appropriate education and training programmes to this end is located within the Ministry of Education and sometimes in collaboration with the Ministry of Labour or with Ministries of Trade and Industry or other ministries. In some cases, special inter-ministerial committees have been convened. Concrete actions should focus on programme interventions at secondary and tertiary levels, awareness-raising campaigns or providing technical and financial support and training through specifically-designed government interventions.

Awareness raising programmes at primary and secondary school levels with the aim of familiarizing pupils with the philosophy of entrepreneurship by developing beliefs, behaviours and motivation will have a long-term effect and have a positive influence on enterprise culture. Such programmes integrated in vocational training curricula and lectured at universities will prepare the ground for a career option as entrepreneur. Programmes that aim at immediate enterprise creation for young people can be run at vocational training schools and universities but should also include the upper age-group of youth outside the education system as this will have

---

11 February 2006, EU commission IP/06/148 http://europe.eu.int/comm/education/ policies.

the greatest effect. The University of Durham (United Kingdom) suggests (Enterprise Education: A briefing paper by Dr. N. Iredale, 2002) that there are a number of different objectives and outcomes which can be achieved:

- Firstly, and most universally, enterprise education can be a path towards developing enterprising skills, behaviours and attitudes *through* any curriculum subject at every phase of education to provide a wider preparation for autonomy in life. That relates to work, family or leisure.
- Secondly, it can provide insight into and help young people understand *about* the entrepreneurial and business development processes through business education in secondary schools and in further and higher education allowing young people to work more effectively in a flexible labour market economy or working in a small business.
- Finally, it can develop awareness of, and capability *for*, setting up a business now or sometime in the future. This approach can be used in vocational and professional education.

The learning effectiveness of such programmes should be measured not in terms of knowledge but the acquisition of practical life skills and the ability of students to anticipate and respond to societal changes more easily. Programmes at vocational training schools are supposed to have medium-term effects while at universities the programmes can produce results in term of business creation in the medium and short term. Within schools and non-formal education programmes, the agents of change are teachers who have to become facilitators of a process.

Studies by the European Commission have highlighted the need for the professional development of teachers in order to provide them with the confidence to develop enterprise education and to make them more aware of how they can assist pupils or students in the development of their entrepreneurial attitudes and skills. The need for support for teachers has also been reflected in a number of projects and initiatives undertaken in Central and Eastern Europe. An example is the national programme to develop enterprise and business understanding within secondary schools undertaken in Slovenia between September 1996 and March 1998. The overall aim was to provide a solid base for the national development of enterprise and business understanding within the core curriculum of all general secondary schools in Slovenia. Under this programme a core group of teachers attended a *train the trainers* type of workshop, in order to be able to disseminate their knowledge and skills to other schools across the country.

Resource materials and training packages

The emergence of entrepreneurship education over the last decade has increased the need for curriculum and training packages and resource materials. The latter vary in the scope of the information and methods presented based on the intended socio-economic and educational audience. At lower levels of education, many educational materials are intended to impart a basic-to-intermediate understanding of business and market systems, and will inculcate in students a desire to learn more about entrepreneurship and business in the future. At higher levels, texts are designed to provide a balance between theory and practice.

The ILO has developed and successfully implemented an entrepreneurship education programme called Know About Business (KAB).[12] Know about business means to understand the role of business in society, its contribution to the wealth of nations and its social responsibility, entrepreneurial attitudes and behaviour and to be informed about how an enterprise is functioning. KAB is a programme for vocational education, secondary education and higher education designed for an 80 to 120 hours course in formal education. The general objective of KAB is to contribute towards the creation of an enterprise culture in a country or society by promoting awareness among young women and men of the opportunities and challenges of entrepreneurship and self-employment, and of their role in shaping their future and that of their countries' economic and social development. The specific objectives of KAB are to:

- develop positive attitudes towards enterprises and self-employment among the population by targeting youth but also stakeholders for enterprise development;
- create awareness of enterprise creation and self-employment as a career option for young people as part of education;
- provide knowledge and practice about entrepreneurial competencies and challenges in starting and operating a successful enterprise;
- facilitate school-to-work transition as a result of better understanding of functions and operations of enterprises.

The KAB package has been developed for instructors of TVET institutions, teachers of secondary schools and lecturers/professors of higher education to enable them to teach entrepreneurship to trainees, pupils and students.

The KAB package comprises a Facilitator's Handbook, a business game, nine modules and a Learner's Handbook. Each module represents a key area of entrepreneurship and is divided into several topics. KAB has been translated into 10 languages. The implementation of KAB starts always with a local adaptation of the modules, the training of teachers followed by the one-year school test in selected vocational and/or secondary schools and/or polytechnics or universities. After the school test, governments can make informed decisions on a general integration of the programme in the national curriculum. Till now KAB had become part of the national education programme in 7 countries, among them Kazakhstan and Kyrgyzstan, and is in the test phase in 15 countries in Central Asia, South-East Asia, Africa and Latin America.

Set-up a conducive legal and regulatory environment

The legal and regulatory environment of a country should facilitate enterprise creation and decent work conditions for their employees in order to create economic

---

12 www.ilo.org/seed, Youth Entrepreneurship.

growth. A coherent youth employment policy should take into consideration the specific needs of young business starters, particularly in the following fields:

- Business registration;
- Legal form of business;
- Tax regimes;
- Access to credits;
- Investment incentives for start-ups of small enterprises;
- Property rights, copy rights, trademarks; and
- Bankruptcy laws.

Promotion of self-employment and youth entrepreneur start-ups

To assist young business starters to turn a business idea into a business opportunity and to increase the survival rate of these nascent small enterprises, governments should put in place organizations that provide assistance during this critical phase. These are usually enterprise promotion agencies, local Chambers of Commerce, the business community, public education and training institutions, community-based organizations and regional governments working often with international development assistance partners, local and international NGOs and the private sector.

A programme which is used in more than 80 countries is the training programme Start Your Business (SYB) of the ILO. It provides training to develop those skills necessary to start a small business. SYB uses participatory training methods and brings together basic theory, relevant information and practical activities. The course is a cost-effective means to help potential entrepreneurs think through the most important issues related to starting a business. One practical result of the training is the self-developed business plan for the potential business that can be presented to a credit institution. The training materials consist of a handbook and a workbook for the trainees, a business game that is a dynamic tool for creating a simulated business environment where trainees can experience the consequences of their business decisions, and a guide for trainers.

The SYB programme was not specifically designed for young starters. However, more than 50% of the participants of the course are young women and men. Youth Business Centres are specialized enterprise promotion agencies which provide tailor-made services to potential business starters, among young women and men, and to young entrepreneurs already in business, e.g.:

- advisory services;
- mentorship programmes;
- linkages to micro finance organizations and banks;
- linkages to innovation centres and specific public funding programmes; and
- organization of young entrepreneur associations and business linkages.

Business incubators, either as stand-alone organizations or linked to business centres or universities, are powerful (but also costly) instruments to help young starters to overcome the start-up phase and the first year of the business. Governments should also include in their youth policy the actions of national and international foundations (both civil society and corporate) which could form partnerships with national governments and NGOs to promote enterprise growth among young entrepreneurs nationally and internationally. NGOs, throughout the world, tend to have a focus on the education and training opportunities for youth at risk.

Specialized NGOs have evolved dealing with different dimensions of self-employment and micro-enterprise. Some NGOs are concerned with the promotion of free market values. Others focus entirely on the small-scale credit side, product development, women entrepreneurs, or the vocational training of the young people in rural and urban situations. Here, NGOs are probably a more significant source of support than central or local government schemes.

However, a very large number of NGOs is interested in training for its social benefits above all else. Such NGOs have developed frameworks for dealing with issues such as HIV/AIDS awareness, health, environment and support for women by focusing on the holistic development of the individual and through activities to create sustainable livelihoods.[13] Micro finance programmes in this context are relatively new and such programmes tend to develop much more specific linkages between different social problems affecting youth or community development strategies.

To sum up, youth entrepreneurship and self-employment can significantly contribute to a substantial reduction of youth unemployment. As research shows, 20% of the active youth population could engage in entrepreneurial activities and thus create their own employment and employment for others. Governments could freely use this potential by developing a coherent entrepreneurship promotion policy that also takes into consideration the specific needs of young women and men.

Bibliography

Axmann, M. (2004), 'Facilitating labour market entry for youth through enterprise-based schemes in vocational education and training and skills development', SEED working paper No 48 (Geneva: ILO).

Bahri, S., Haftendorn, K. (eds) (2006), 'Towards an entrepreneurial culture for the twenty-first century, stimulating entrepreneurial spirit through entrepreneurship education in secondary schools' (Paris: UNESCO; Geneva: ILO).

Commission of the European Communities (2001), *European Commission White Paper. A New Impetus for European Youth*, COM(2001) 681.

---

13 A livelihood is everything people know, have, and do to make a living. Applied to youth, the livelihoods approach comprises a broad and interrelated set of programmes and policies that include: giving youth opportunities to generate and earn income; providing credit, savings and other financial services and related training in job and business skills; developing institutions, alliances and networks for youth to advance their economic interests; and promoting policy and social changes that improve young people's livelihood prospects. In many cases, training is provided in diverse skills and specialities in order to diversify the economy and reduce reliance on one product.

Commission of the European Communities (2004), *Aktionsplan: Europäische Agenda für unternehmerische Initiative*, KON(2004) 70.

European Union (1997), *The Treaty of Amsterdam.*

Flash Eurobarometer (2004), 'Entrepreneurship', realised by EOS Gallup Europe upon request of the European Commission, No. 160.

GEM (2005), *Global Entrepreneurship Monitor 2005 Executive report* Babson College, London Business School, (MA USA; London UK).

Haftendorn, K. and Salzano, C. (2003), 'Facilitating Youth Entrepreneurship, Part I. An analysis of awareness and promotion programmes in formal and non-formal education, Part II, A directory of awareness and promotion programmes in formal and non-formal education, SEED working paper No. 59, (Geneva: ILO).

ILO (2005), 'Cooperation in a changing development, Report of the Director General, volume I'.

___ (2005), 'Managing transitions: governance for decent work; report of the Director General, volume II', (Budapest).

___ (2005), 'Pathways to decent work: background report of the International Labour Conference', 93rd session.

— (2004), 'Global employment trends for youth'.

___ (2004), 'Starting right: Decent work for young people, background report of the ILO tripartite meeting on youth employment: The way forward'.

___ (1998), 'Guide to ILO recommendation No. 189', adopted by the ILC June 1008.

Johannsen, A., Kausch, I. and Tibitanzl, F. (2006), 'Cornerstone of youth employment promotion in development cooperation', BMZ Discourse series No. 007 (Berlin, BMZ).

O'Higgins, N. (2001), 'Youth unemployment and employment policy: A global perspective' (Geneva: ILO).

Schoof, U. (2006), 'Stimulating youth entrepreneurship, barriers and incentives to enterprise start-ups by young people', SEED working paper No. 76 (Geneva: ILO).

Sievers, M., Haftendorn, K. and Bessler, A. (2003), 'Business centres for small enterprise development, experiences and lessons from Eastern Europe', SEED working paper No. 57 (Geneva: ILO).

YEN (Youth Employment Network) (2003), 'Consolidated outcome of the high-level panel's working groups on employability, equal opportunities, employment creation and entrepreneurship' (Geneva: ILO).

Chapter 3

The Young Self-Employed in East-Central Europe[1]

Ken Roberts

1. Introduction

As soon as communism collapsed it was realised that, complementing the privatisation of state enterprises, successful transitions into market economies required the rapid creation of swathes of small and medium-sized enterprises (SMEs). All competitive market economies need small and growing businesses as well as large established companies. And there were further reasons, aside from the strictly economic, for seeking to stimulate a rapid growth of SMEs. This was believed to be a way of ensuring that the benefits of the reforms were spread around and creating new middle classes with stakes in the new socio-economic orders thereby contributing to the social and political entrenchment of the transition. In the event, the populations in all the new market economies displayed a spontaneous enthusiasm for doing business (see Osborn and Slomczynski 2005). As soon as it became possible, thousands of new businesses were registered across the whole of East-Central Europe, most of which, it appears, never began trading (Welter 1997). However, those that genuinely started-up immediately became the main source of new jobs in their countries (see Biesbrouck and Bilsen 1996; Bilsen and Konings 1996; Konings et al. 1995). Ever since the early-1990s it has been considered desirable to ensure that young people, the upcoming first post-communist generations of adults, experienced at least some of the early benefits of change. The age group has borne more than a fair share of the pain of 'the transition', evident in the high rates of youth unemployment – still around 30 percent in most East European countries. Yet ever since 1989 young people have been the most pro-reform age group. Large proportions are attracted by the prospect of business success. And very large numbers have been making serious attempts to do business (see Genov 1996; Machacek 1996; Roberts and Jung 1995). Should these young people be encouraged and, if so, exactly how? In the West young people's chances of succeeding in business are inferior to those of other age groups.

1 The research cited extensively in this paper was funded by the UK Overseas Development Administration (ODA) (grant number R6665). ODA funds supported this study and the preparation of the primary reports on the findings. However, the views and opinions expressed in this document do not reflect ODA's official policies or practices, but are those of the author alone.

This is particularly so for the young unemployed (Kellard and Middleton 1998; Metcalfe 1998). Does all this apply equally in the new market economies?

The evidence introduced below is mostly from interview surveys in the late-1990s with a total of 400 self-employed young people (aged up to 30) from four transition countries (Bulgaria, Hungary, Poland and Slovakia) Fifty young entrepreneurs were interviewed in each of two regions (one relatively prosperous and the other relatively depressed) in each of these countries. The intention was that the respondents would represent East-Central Europe's better established young entrepreneurs. Of all the young people in East-Central Europe who have made a serious attempt to do business, probably no more than one in five has reached the point of having business as a main and continuing occupation (see Roberts et al. 1997, 1998; Roberts and Tholen 1998). All the respondents in the survey had reached this stage. In fact business had been the main way in which they had earned their livings since leaving school. In total they had been self-employed for 41 percent of their working lives. All the businesses were officially registered, had turnovers of at least USA $1000 a year, and usually well in excess of this. The sex balance was fixed by quota: females always comprised 30 percent of the respondents. The methods of sample selection, and the interview schedules were standardised. Everywhere the fieldwork was conducted by specially trained teams of local investigators. The interviews sought biographical information focusing on how and why the businesses had been created, the successes and obstacles that had been encountered, the respondents' views on the advantages and disadvantages of being self-employed, the sources and types of assistance that they had received, the businesses' current condition, the proprietors' lifestyles and socio-political outlooks, and their future business intentions. The core questions in the interview schedules were closed and fully standardised so as to facilitate inter-country and inter-region comparisons, but the follow-ups were open-ended and allowed the young self-employed's own perceptions and concerns to be expressed. The samples of young entrepreneurs were not meant to be statistically representative of all the businesses in the localities. The main considerations in sample selection were to ensure that matched methods were used in all the countries and regions, and that all the main types of reasonably successful small businesses and their young proprietors should be adequately represented.

This study of the young self-employed was conducted alongside studies of the young unemployed in the same regions, and some of the findings from the latter study are referred to for comparative purposes in what follows. Among other things, this permits an assessment of the prospects of solving youth unemployment in East-Central Europe by transforming those concerned into proprietors of successful businesses. And all these findings are set in the context of evidence from studies of the transitions into employment of representative samples of young people in East-Central Europe and the former Soviet Union that are still ongoing.

2. The businesses and their proprietors

All the businesses in the study of the young self-employed had been created since 1988. Their new-ness was in fact their most distinctive and definitive characteristic.

A half of the firms had not existed at least until 1994. The young people who were interviewed, the creators of these businesses, were genuine pioneers, real entrepreneurs. They were creating not just new enterprises but wholly new business sectors in their regions, and new ways of earning a living in their countries. It is true that a quarter of the respondents had at least one sibling who was also self-employed as a main occupation, and between 5 percent and 27 percent in the different countries had parents who had embarked on this new kind of career, but in all the countries the majority were the first, and, as yet, the only business people in their families.

In this chapter the terms 'self-employed' and 'entrepreneur' are used inter-changeably. In the course of the fieldwork we encountered cases of pseudo self-employment (where the individuals were really working for an employer – a hairdresser for example – but were being treated as self-employed for the purposes of avoiding tax and specific employment regulations) but none of these individuals were included in the study. All the samples were running businesses of which they were sole or joint proprietors. It is possible to be enterprising (entrepreneurial) outside of self-employment. One can display enterprise during a career as an employee. One can also be an unpaid or paid social entrepreneur (setting up and running a not-for-profit organisation). However, in the study reported here all the businesses were profit-seeking.

None of the respondents were former directors of state enterprises who had transformed old social capital into new economic capital via 'honest robbery' privatisations. This has been an important route into business among older age groups in Eastern Europe (see Alanen 1998; Clark 1998, 2000; Nikula 1998; Stoica 2004), but young people's routes have necessarily been rather different. Nearly all of the respondents had created wholly new enterprises and had been reasonably successful in so far as business had become their main occupation, and they had all registered their companies. Most young males in East-Central Europe appear to have made a serious attempt to 'do business', but of all who have tried only a small minority, usually between 7 percent and 9 percent of the age group (lower proportions than among adults) have become self-employed as a main occupation on a continuous basis. Where the proportions have been higher this has usually been because the depressed local economies have forced larger numbers into 'survival self-employment' (see Roberts et al. 2000). The self-employed young people who feature in these passages had all been relatively successful, but even so there was a huge gulf between their enterprises, nearly all of which were still micro and fragile, and the small-to-medium-sized league. Fragility has been, and remains, a general feature of the new market economies' new businesses (see Barkhatova et al. 2001).

Most respondents' businesses had been created with few assets apart from the proprietors' enterprise. Many respondents explained how they had saved, and some explained how they had spent periods working in other countries, in order to raise start-up capital. They had made the effort because, 'I wanted to make money, to become rich... to achieve financial security... to be independent... to manage my own time... to earn rewards proportional to my efforts... so that I could rely on myself and be responsible for my own life.' Some had made very rapid and substantial strides. One young man explained how, 'I started with just enough money for equipment and materials. My brother helped me but it was difficult at first.' By 1997 this Trencin

(Slovakia) furniture manufacturer had five employees in a rented workshop. 'When I left school I took a job in a state book store and I also began selling books on the street.' By 1997 this young man was the sole proprietor of two bookshops in Szabolcs (Hungary), had a 50 percent interest in two others, a total stock valued at $20,000, and was branching into publishing. A young man in Velingrad (Bulgaria) who had faced unemployment had turned a talent for woodwork into a business and by 1997 had equipment worth $30,000 in a workshop behind his mother's house. A young woman in Velingrad had spotted a market gap, opened an estate agency with a loan of $50 from her father, and by 1997 employed a full-time broker plus casual assistance and was handling around two properties per month.

As already explained, most of the businesses were really micro rather than just small. A quarter of the proprietors were simultaneously students (usually enrolled on a part-time basis at a university) or employees in public sector or other private enterprises. They felt that they needed fallback options should their enterprises fail. Only just over a half of the businesses had any employees. None could offer job security to employees, let alone careers. The number of staff 'on the books' fluctuated according to the volume of business. Nearly all the enterprises were low-tech. A half were equipped with PCs and two-fifths of the proprietors had mobile phones but none were making anything so sophisticated. The modal annual turnover was in the region of 10,000 USA $. The incomes being drawn by the proprietors were usually around $3000 a year irrespective of a business's size and profitability. Wherever possible earnings were being ploughed back or saved towards a long-term project such as purchasing a flat. Contrary to their public image, most of the young self-employed could not be described as rich, and few had extravagant, extravert lifestyles. There was a glaring contrast between the public image and reality of being self-employed. All of our respondents were aware of this.

> Businessmen are considered dishonest. In fact we are mostly honest. People talk about mafia but this is simply because they are not used to private enterprise (metal goods producer, Trencin, Slovakia).

> We are supposed to be the new rich, driving Western cars and living in Dallas-type houses. A loan of $5000, two or three successful deals, and you are supposed to be able to visit restaurants every night, and have beautiful women. The image is different from the reality. People do not realise how hard it is necessary to work, or for how many years, before you can stabilise a business (garage owner, Vas, Hungary).

The young entrepreneurs' lives were governed by a work ethic. A third regularly worked for over 60 hours per week. Complaints about having insufficient time for themselves, and for their friends and families, were widespread. They were certainly more prosperous than most other members of their age group. Cars and satellite or cable television were normal possessions. However, a third had not spent a single night away on holiday during the previous year and the same proportion had not been to a restaurant or bar during the previous four weeks.

The business people were from a variety of backgrounds – virtually all sections of the local populations, though not exactly pro-rata. Some had parents who had been school-teachers, professors, chemists, telephone exchange managers and accountants, but others were the children of bus drivers, car mechanics, carpenters, farmers, cleaners and clerks. In all the countries over three-quarters were workers' children. Many had attended lycees and universities but nearly a half of the samples (48 percent) had completed their full-time education at elementary, or at vocational or technical secondary schools. Some had found the road into business easier than others, but the young entrepreneurs were from all sections of the local populations. Most were not from privileged backgrounds. Success in business (if achieved) meant upward mobility for the vast majority.

Most of the young people could be described accurately as artisans. Approximately three-fifths were operating businesses that matched or overlapped their specialities – the occupations for which they had been prepared in education. Young people who had been trained as tinsmiths, carpenters, motor repairers and so on had based businesses on skills that they had acquired initially in education, and then developed, in most cases, in their subsequent jobs. Retailing, and other forms of buying and selling, were the kinds of business most likely to attract individuals with no special training or qualifications in the field. In some of the new market economies, though not those in the study reported here, 'trading' has been the normal route into business (see Bahtijarevic and Poloski 1999). The traders who were interviewed in this study included young people who had been trained in accountancy, forestry and social care. Some young people had switched because there were few opportunities for self-employment in their original trades. This was why a trained lathe operator was running a transport business. Another individual had left his profession because, 'You can't live on teaching'.

3. Routes into self-employment

There had been three main routes into self-employment. Only a minority of the respondents had completed their education and had then become self-employed immediately. When they had done this the individuals had usually begun developing their businesses while at secondary school or university. Three-quarters had made initial transitions into employment in state or private companies. Some had made fairly smooth transitions into self-employment because, by that time, they already had all the necessary skills, market information and even customers from their previous state or private sector jobs, or from their own enterprises in the countries' second economies.

Many had been pushed towards self-employment because they had left school and had then been unable to obtain jobs or because the state enterprises where they were working had contracted or closed. This had been route number one into self-employment; as an alternative to unemployment.

> I was a skilled worker in a state firm but the salary was too low. So I went to another state firm where the job was better paid but then the business went into decline. So I began doing odd jobs on my own account (carpenter, Vas, Hungary).

I got married and had a child. My husband's salary was not enough. He went to work abroad for a year and when he came back we decided to open a video shop. We had inherited land and we built the shop ourselves. This took a year. Then we bought 400 second-hand cassettes and waited for our first customers. Now we buy new cassettes every week. Our greatest difficulty was with the building though we did have some help from relatives. Also I remember that we had problems with the baby. We had to move her from one grandmother to the other, then to an aunt at one time (Plovdiv, Bulgaria).

Several respondents explained how starting a family had created a need (for money) that could only be addressed by starting a business. Working abroad had been a quite common way of raising start-up capital.

It must be emphasised that very few of the respondents who had followed 'route one' had experienced prolonged unemployment. Most had ventured into business as an alternative to becoming unemployed, rather than as an escape from unemployment. In this respect the findings are in line with Western experience which suggests that self-employment will rarely be a successful solution when targeted at the chronically unemployed. In Britain it has been estimated that less than five percent of the unemployed take this route, and their businesses have above average failure rates. Projects aiming to transform the unemployed into self-employed persons are likely to succeed only when recruits are heavily screened, and even then they are likely to need ongoing training, advice and counselling (Kellard and Middleton 1998; Metcalf 1998). This is not the way in which youth self-employment will solve East (or West) Europe's youth unemployment. It is more likely that the new businesses that enterprising young people establish will create jobs that the young unemployed can then fill. However, a problem with this solution, encountered time and time again in the parallel studies of the young unemployed, was that the young people were out-of-work because they had no intention of repeating experiences in jobs with marginal micro-businesses where earnings were low and unreliable, likewise the hours of work, and where conditions at work, and their treatment by the employers, were often appalling (see Machacek and Roberts 1997).

Route two into self-employment had been via employment in other people's small private enterprises. Those who had worked in such businesses had often realised that they could do everything necessary to work on their own accounts and obtain the benefits that their employers were reaping.

I went to work for a private firm that ran into financial problems. It was long hours for hardly any salary. So I went to work in Germany for a month. I came back and got another job with a private business but I stayed for only six months, then I started my own firm. By this time I had all the skills. And I had earned enough in Germany to make this possible (furniture manufacturer, Trencin, Slovakia).

I spent three years in a private firm. Then I realised that I could earn much more working for myself. I earn three times as much as when I was an employee (metal goods producer, Trencin, Slovakia).

Many respondents had been assisted by their families (see below) and a smaller number had, in effect, been set-up. This was route three, the smoothest of all the routes into entrepreneurship.

At 19 I decided that I had reached the age when I had to provide for myself. You cannot rely for everything on your parents at that age. My mother had been running a business for six years and I started helping with stocking and selling in the shop. After a year I registered my own company. My greatest problem at the beginning was waiting for the local council to provide a site for the shop which I now rent from them (Velingrad, Bulgaria).

After school I joined the family business in wood processing and furniture. I wasn't interested. I wanted to build something myself. I asked for my share of the capital and participated in the privatisation of state storehouses for fruit and vegetables. Now I have 26 employees, an annual turnover of $3.5 million, and last year my profit was $140,000. I am satisfied. I have demonstrated that I can be successful alone (Plovdiv, Bulgaria).

There were other cases where a daughter had begun selling clothes that her mother made, and where the son of a builder had begun trading in construction materials. Other young people had taken-over businesses that their parents had launched. Some owed their business careers to marriage which had been followed by invitations to join the in-laws' businesses. Many others had received assistance from their families, usually money (see below), but this was different from being able to take over, or being set-up with the assistance of an existing family enterprise.

4. Commitment

Two-fifths of the respondents had some experience of unemployment but, as explained above, these episodes had usually been brief. The samples had been unemployed for only eight percent of their working lives. Most of the young people had been attracted (pulled) into self-employment rather than pushed by circumstances, the absence of any alternatives. A half had aimed to become self-employed, eventually, when still in education. So when interviewed most felt that they had already fulfilled, or were en route to fulfilling, their career aspirations.

I know that where I am is not a real career. Firms are going bankrupt all the time but I really want to stay in this business. I have no regrets. I often meet former colleagues who are still with the state firm. What I'm doing is better in terms of job satisfaction and financially (pizzeria proprietor, Szabolcs, Hungary).

Most of our respondents were highly committed to their businesses. A few were continuing only because the alternative was unemployment, but the majority had learnt about the advantages of independence and were more than willing to tolerate the disadvantages of sole responsibility and heavy workloads. Most wanted their children to become self-employed. The self-employed's own careers in business had been short, but nevertheless, the vast majority had become thoroughly committed to business as a long-term way of life, rather than simply as a temporary means of earning a living.

5. Doing business

Most of the young people's businesses were 'fiddling' in some way or another but none of the young people who we interviewed could be described as mafiosi. In most cases 'businessman' (or woman) was not really an appropriate description. They were tradespeople and professionals who were practising independently. Two-thirds were sole proprietors. However, a third admitted to having given gifts (wine, office desks, air conditioners and so on), or to having made under-the-counter payments to policemen, state officials, or managers of state enterprises, usually to speed up registration or an application for a licence, or to obtain supplies without filling-in all the forms, or to expedite imports or exports, or to strengthen a tender. A similar proportion (approximately a third) said that some of their business was in the second economy thereby avoiding taxation and other charges. We must assume that the answers received to these questions were often under-statements. The cash payments (bribes) that were reported ranged from $5 to $3500. Just over a quarter (27 percent) said that they had used family influence, and just over a half (51 percent) said that they had used friends' connections to assist in their businesses. Bulgaria was the country where unofficial payments were most common, but there, as elsewhere, the respondents' experiences varied greatly. One individual in Velingrad claimed to have paid over $3000 in total when registering his business and gaining all the necessary permissions whereas another business in the same region had paid a lawyer just $8 and 'he took care of everything'. Evidence from parallel studies of the young self-employed in Armenia, Georgia and Ukraine found that unofficial payments were far more common, the norm, usually considered essential in order to stay in business, in these ex-Soviet countries (see Roberts et al. 1998; Roberts and Tholen 1998).

Most of the business people were trying to minimise their tax liabilities. This was why some were determined to keep some of their business off-the-record. One business in Slovakia had a turnover of 10 million crowns but declared profits of only 2000 crowns. In Bulgaria one proprietor explained that such tactics were necessary, 'because the tax laws don't recognise all the expenses that businesses incur. For example, the cost of office equipment cannot be offset'. There was a consensus in all the countries that taxes on businesses were far too high.

> If I paid taxes on everything I would go bankrupt. My customers would be unable to afford the goods (Poland).

> There's a profit tax of 43 percent and a payroll tax of 48 percent. That's why there's so much casual, off-the-record employment (Slovakia).

All the entrepreneurs were determined to keep their liabilities to a reasonable level, if possible (see also Aidis 1997; Isakova 1997). A common tactic was to under-report any employees' earnings, sometimes to the lowest level that was legally permitted. This, presumably, was why tax rates had to be fairly high. Throughout the 1990s and into the 21st century business people in Eastern Europe have continued to complain about having to operate in unpredictable and, in many respects, hostile environments (see Manalova and Yan, 2002).

However, as previously indicated, in many respects the image and the reality of youth self-employment were at loggerheads. And by the late-1990s the days when East-Central Europe was part of a 'wild east' seemed long gone. Business had become a basically legitimate, respectable way of earning a living. The 'bribes' that had been paid by respondents were usually akin to the gift giving and business entertainment that goes on in Western countries. Everywhere business people use influence and connections, and seek to minimise their tax liabilities. None of the self-employed believed that a bribery culture served their own interests. They wanted laws to be enforced more strictly. They would have preferred not to be outlaws, operating partly in the second economies, but felt that they could risk playing by the rules only if the playing field was levelled. They wanted business to become fully legitimate and respectable, as they believed it was in the Western countries that they admired. 'Laws should be enforced. We have laws but they are not respected due to lack of effective control. The consumers should be protected then businesses will also profit.' Contrary to popular conceptions, East-Central Europe's new business classes are probably more sensitive than any other sections of the populations to the disadvantages, and are the most anxious to drive out corruption from business affairs.

6. Political orientations

Our respondents were not just supportive but enthusiastic about their countries' new market economies though there was quite widespread nostalgia for the old way of life. As many as two-fifths believed that the quality of family life had been superior prior to the reforms.

> We used to gather in the evening, watch TV together and talk about movies. Now we talk only about business. We discuss prices, plan deals and judge competitors. We've no energy for anything except money.

> We did not have to worry about jobs. We had no worries. There was no unemployment. There was peace in the family and greater confidence in the future. We were more equal and life was more peaceful. People shared the same values. Now love is running away from people's hearts.

However, even those who were most nostalgic acknowledged that the old system had gone for ever and that there could be no turning back. Many were worried about the commercialisation of life in general but on balance four-fifths preferred the market. They valued the freedom and open-ness, people being able to choose for themselves in work and politics, about what to buy, and being able to develop a preferred way of life.

> People used to be limited in their activities. We could not work creatively. We could not have quality holidays. Men of initiative had no chance.

Life is now more difficult but it is much more interesting. The old life was monotonous. There was censorship and nothing to buy. There were queues everywhere. We had no prospects and had to be content with small salaries.'

7. Assistance

The governments in all the countries in this study had batteries of policies and measures to encourage business starts and SMEs. They all had tax concessions, grants, loans and employment subsidies, always available on some sort of selective basis. State-funded training centres invariably had enterprise modules or entire courses within their programmes. All the countries had business support or advice centres, some high profile, others low profile. In some regions there were 'incubators', and the high profile examples always had joint funding from the central and local or regional governments, usually augmented by EU and sometimes other contributions from outside the countries, and some had space for NGOs either on-site or within the support portfolios (see National Agency for the Development of Small and Medium Enterprises 1997; Organisation for Economic Cooperation and Development 1995, 1997; Upper Silesian Agency for Development and Promotion 1996). Meanwhile, most of East-Central Europe seemed to be awash with new NGOs many of which were seeking to promote private enterprise. 'On paper' there appeared to be a wealth of assistance for the young (and older) self-employed (see Bozhikov 1997; Kabakchieva 1996; Kaminisky et al. 1997; Kovatcheva 1998; Kovatcheva and Roberts 1997; Kuti 1996; Kuti and Sebesteny 1997; Laczko 1993; Nikolov 1996; Stubbs 1997).

Table 3.1 Sources of assistance

	Advice	Information	Contacts	Money	Main assistance
	%	%	%	%	%
Family	60	42	40	64	71
Friends	49	47	47	12	20
Banks	5	7	2	15	1
State	6	18	3	9	–
Voluntary organisations	1	2	1	2	1
Other					8
N=	400	400	400	400	400

Yet the biographies of the self-employed who were interviewed, and their own assessments of the support that they had received, showed that the role of state agencies and programmes had been modest, and the role of NGOs had been minuscule, especially when compared with the assistance provided by friends and families, and, in the eyes of our respondents, their own efforts. Just over 70 percent named their families as their main source of assistance (see Table 3.1). Nearly two-thirds had received financial assistance from their families when starting-up. Friends were next on the list as sources of assistance. They had been less likely to loan or give money than advice and information. The young people were mostly running their businesses without any of the support services that Western companies take for granted. Most respondents did not use banks. Their business was almost always on a cash basis. Credit was rarely sought, expected or offered. Some of the young business people were emphatic that they did not want to use banks; 'I couldn't afford the interest charges'. Some who had sought assistance from lawyers, accountants, marketing firms and suchlike made scathing comments about 'pseudo-agencies' with 'trashy staff' (see Lloyd-Reason et al. 1997).

All studies of new businesses in the new market economies have stressed the importance of 'social capital' (see, for example, Andrle 2001; Batjargal 2003, 2006; Clark 2000; McMylor et al. 1998; Stoica 2004). This applies equally to the proprietors of large and small enterprises. Those with large enterprises are likely to value their links with state officials, maybe politicians, and financiers, and other business people (see Rehn and Taalas, 2004). Proprietors of small companies name families and friends. Having a wide network of weak contacts appears more valuable than a smaller number of strong ties. Young people who set-up in business need information from their friends or families about their markets – for supplies and products – and advice on how to deal with state officials. If they need financial help they rarely look beyond their families; going elsewhere is likely to prove too expensive.

The relatively small proportions who had been assisted by NGOs and state services (compared with those assisted by friends and families) should be set in the context of the limited use that was being made of all formal sources of assistance. This perhaps makes it less surprising that no-one named a state agency or programme as his or her main source of support and only one percent named an NGO (see Table 3.1). In market economies, and especially in emerging market economies, it is probably only to be expected that most assistance to businesses will be from private sources. It is probably more meaningful to dwell on the absolute, not the relative proportions who had been assisted by state agencies and NGOs.

Almost a fifth of the young entrepreneurs said that they had received some useful information (fewer mentioned advice) from a state source, and almost one-in-ten reported having received some financial assistance. There is likely to have been considerable under-reporting here. Information made available to the public at large was likely to have been regarded as just part of the context rather than a benefit to a particular enterprise. General tax concessions were likely to have been regarded in this same way. In any case, the young entrepreneurs themselves were arranging their most significant tax breaks through double book-keeping.

With NGOs there was a similar contradiction to the one noted with state assistance. No more than two percent of the self-employed samples in any of the research regions reported any kind of assistance (information, advice, contacts or money) from an NGO. There were some variations by country, region and socio-demographic groups but the beneficiaries were negligible within them all. All the countries were apparently packed with NGOs, but very few were reaching the young self-employed. This was despite youth being a popular target group in some of the countries. Most of the relevant NGOs were primarily concerned with youth's education, religion or politics, or poverty relief, rather than with employment issues. They were rarely regarded as a credible source of help. Those with foreign roots were likely to be held in some suspicion, partly because they were foreign, but also because, in many instances, any assistance would be wrapped in a religious or political message.

Discussion

Today Eastern Europe has swathes of small enterprises but few can be described as sturdy pillars of the new market economies. Their proprietors are more likely to have lofty aims and hopes than business development plans, and they often take huge uncalculated risks with their own and their families' savings (see Balaton 1998). Transnational companies are more likely to create their own offshoots than to deal with local SMEs (see Hardy 1997; Lloyd-Reason et al. 1997). Local firms are vulnerable to external competition (see Tibor 1997). Few trade outside their own areas. They lack the resources and the know-how to penetrate national let alone international markets. They are too small to self-generate the capital needed to make these quantum leaps. Many of the businesses are not even using banks. Their proprietors may be energetic but they are rarely innovative in the senses of introducing new technologies, products or production methods (see Wawryniak 1998). These businesses are not quality employers. As explained earlier, a reason why youth unemployment remains so stubbornly high across Eastern Europe is that the young people prefer to remain 'in transition' to settling in the new jobs in the *de novo* private businesses that have replaced public sector employment.

Rather than indiscriminately encouraging more and more young people to try to clamber into East Europe's small business sectors (already far more try than can hope to succeed), assistance will be better directed towards existing entrepreneurs with the potential to develop quality businesses. Today, approaching the third decade of 'the transition', it is more difficult than in the 1990s for new start-ups to succeed whatever the age of the entrepreneurs. In the 1990s there was a once in a lifetime window of opportunity. Novice business people entered virgin markets. There were no established competitors. It was possible to succeed with little more than hard work and effort, a modicum of skill, plus helpful friends and relatives. Today the threshold for market entry is higher, There are well-established local businesses. Moreover, international companies now trade in all sectors in the new market economies. Of course, there are always niches within which new businesses can succeed, and among the many who try to start-up, some young people will find these niches. Market selection will do this job better than any government agencies or NGOs. Assistance from NGOs and government agencies will be most effective if targeted at modestly successful young entrepreneurs whose businesses have the potential to grow into sturdy SMEs. This is the way in which jobs will be created by local companies that will employ the young people who are currently unemployed. Assistance (advice and finance) needs to be delivered locally, by local actors, but a problem is that local NGOs and government agencies alike rarely have sufficient know-how and relevant experience to be credible let alone effective in this role.

If they are to assist the development of small businesses, the Eastern NGOs and state services must acquire business know-how. In some cases the Eastern NGOs' Western counterparts can be an ideal source. There are already inter-country links between Chambers of Industry and Commerce. These could be used to disseminate know-how from Western Chambers with experience of assisting the formation and growth of small companies. And there are other Western NGOs with valuable expertise in assisting young people's business starts. The UK has probably the world leader in its field, the Prince's Youth Business Trust (see BMRB International 1997) which has an exemplary record of identifying young people from disadvantaged backgrounds with the potential to succeed, and nurturing their enterprises into self-sustaining growth or stability. Neither this example nor other Western NGOs may wish to internationalise their case loads, but they would be ideal mentors for Eastern NGOs with similar missions, reliable funding and the right local contacts. Governments will be able to use their unique capacities to broker such 'marriages', and thereby contribute to the deeper integration of an enlarged European community.

Bibliography

Aidis, R. (1997), 'Neisas is a woman: gender and entrepreneurship in Lithuania', paper presented to *Third International Conference on SME Development Policy in Transition Economies*, Wolverhampton.

Alanen, I. (1998), 'Why did decollectivization destroy the chance to form a broadly based middle class in rural Estonia?', paper presented to conference on *The Middle Class as a Precondition for a Sustainable Society*, Sofia.

Andrle, V. (2001), 'The buoyant class: bourgeois family lineage in the life stories of Czech business elite persons', *Sociology*, 35, 815-833.

Bahtijarevica, F. and Poloski, N. (1999), 'Individual characteristics of entrepreneurs in countries in transition – the case of Croatia', in Faculty of Economics, University of Split, *Enterprise in Transition*, Split-Sibenik, 1999, 457-460.

Balaton, K. (1998), 'Patterns of organisational changes in Hungary in the period of transformation', paper presented to *14th EGOS Colloquium*, Maastricht.

Barkhatova, N., McMylor, P. and Mellor, R. (2001), 'Family business in Russia: the path to middle class?' *British Journal of Sociology*, 52, 249-269.

Batjargal, B. (2003), 'Social capital and entrepreneurial performance in Russia: a longitudinal study', *Organization Studies*, 24, 535-556.

Batjargal, B. (2006), 'The dynamics of entrepreneurs' networks in a transitioning economy: the case of Russia', *Entrepreneurship and Regional Development*, 18, 305-320.

Biesbrouck, W. and Bilsen, V. (1996), *The Importance of Small and Medium Sized Enterprises in Restructuring with an Application to Poland*, Working Paper 54/1996, Leuven Institute for Central and East European Studies, Catholic University of Leuven.

Bilsen, V. and Konings, J. (1996), *Job Creation, Job Destruction and Growth of Newly Established Firms in Transition Economies: Survey Evidence from Bulgaria, Hungary and Romania*, Working Paper 59/1996, Leuven Institute for Central and East European Studies, Catholic University of Leuven.

BMRB International Limited (1997), *Prince's Youth Business Trust (PYBTI Scheme)*, Research Report 5, Department for Education and Employment, Sheffield.

Bozhikov, P. (ed.) (1997), *The Third Sector in Bulgaria: Statistical Barometer*, Foundation Eurica and National Statistical Institute, Sofia.

Clark, E. (1998), 'New capital for old: the social construction of private business in the Czech Republic', paper presented to *14th EGOS Colloquium*, Maastricht.

Clark, E. (2000), 'The role of social capital in developing Czech private business', *Work, Employment and Society*, 14, 439-458.

Genov, N. (ed.) (1996), *Human Development Report - Bulgaria 1996* (Sofia: United Nations Development Programme).

Hardy, J. (1997), 'Cathedrals in the desert? Transnationals, corporate strategy and locality in Wroclaw', paper presented to Regional Studies Association conference, *Regional Frontiers*, Frankfurt-Oder.

Isakova, N. (1997), 'Small business and foreign aid in Ukraine', paper presented to *Third International Conference on SME Development Policy in Transition Economies*, Wolverhampton.

Kabakchieva, P. (1996), 'The role of non-profit non-governmental organisations in the enhancement of social integration in Bulgarian society', in D. Minev, M. Zheijazkova and P. Kabakchieva (eds.), *Poverty Level and Fragmentation of Bulgarian Society. The Role of NGOs in the Enhancement of Social Integration* (Sofia: Bogeta).

Kaminski, R., Kowalski, R. and Wegsierski, J. (1997), 'Recent experiences of the creation and functioning of rural organisations to support SMEs in Poland', paper presented to *Third International Conference on SME Development Policy in Transition Economies*, Wolverhampton.

Kellard, K. and Middleton, S. (1998), *Helping Unemployed People into Self-Employment*, Research Report 46 (Sheffield: Department for Education and Employment).

Konings, J., Lehmann, H. and Schaffer, M.E. (1995), *Employment Growth, Job Creation and Job Destruction in Polish Industry. 1988-91*, Working Paper 38/1995 (Leuven: Leuven Institute for Central and East European Studies, Catholic University of Leuven).

Kovatcheva, S. (1998), 'Third sector in post-communist Bulgaria and its support for young people in the labour market', *Slovak Sociological Review*, 30, 297-310.

Kovatcheva, S. and Roberts, K. (1997), 'Youth labour markets in Bulgaria', in Z. Sevic and G. Wright (eds.), *Transition in Central and Eastern Europe, Vol 1* (Belgrade: YASF/Student Cultural Centre), 237-247.

Kuti, E. (1996), *The Nonprofit Sector in Hungary* (Manchester: Manchester University Press).

Kuti, E. and Sebesteny, I. (1997), 'Nonprofit sector in Hungary in the early 1990s', *Hungarian Statistical Review*, 4, 97-107.

Laczko, F. (1993), 'Social policy and the third sector in East-Central Europe', in S. Ringen and C. Wallace (eds.), *Societies in Transition: East-Central Europe Today* (Prague: Central European University).

Lloyd-Reason, L., Marinova, M. and Webb, T.J. (1997), 'Building business support in East-Central Europe: a Bulgarian perspective - policy issues and recommendations', in Z. Sevic and G. Wright (eds.), *Transition in Central and Eastern Europe, Vol 1* (Belgrade: YASF/Student Cultural centre).

McMylor, P., Mellor, R. and Barkhatova, N. (1998), 'Familialism, friendship and the small firm: survival, protection and informal relations in the new Russia', paper presented at *International Sociological Association Congress*, Montreal.

Machacek, L. (1996), *Slovak Youth Attitudes Towards the Market Challenges, 1993-1995* (Bratislava: Institute of Sociology, Slovak Academy of Sciences).

Machacek, L. and Roberts, K. (eds.) (1997), *Youth Unemployment and Self-Employment in East-Central Europe* (Bratislava: Slovak Academy of Sciences).

Manalova, T.S. and Yan, A. (2002), 'Institutional constraints and entrepreneurial responses in a transforming economy', *International Small Business Journal*, 20, 163-184.

Metcalfe, H. (1998), *Self-Employment for the Unemployed. the Role of Public Policy*, Research Report 47 (Sheffield: Department for Education and Employment).

National Agency for the Development of Small and Medium Enterprises (1997), *State of Small and Medium Enterprises in the Slovak Republic 1996*, Bratislava.

Nikolov, S. (1996), *A View into the World of Foundations* (Sofia: OSF Press).

Nikula, J. (1998), 'Position, skills and capitals - routes to entrepreneurial middle class in rural Estonia', paper presented to conference on *The Middle Class as a Precondition for a Sustainable Society*, Sofia.

Organisation for Economic Co-operation and Development (1995), *Labour Market and Social Policies in the Slovak Republic* (Paris: OECD).

Organisation for Economic Co-operation and Development (1997), *Entrepreneurship and SMEs in Transition Economies* (Paris: OECD).

Osborn, E. and Slomczynski, K.M. (2005), *Open For Business: The Persistent Entrepreneurial Class in Poland* (Warsaw: IFiS Publishers).

Rehn, A. and Taalas, S. (2004), '"Znakomstva I Svyazi" (Acquaintances and Connections – Blat, the Soviet Union, and mundane entrepreneurship), *Entrepreneurship and Regional Development*, 16, 235-250.

Roberts, K., Adibekian, A., Nemiria, G., Tarkhnishvili, L. and Tholen, J. (1997), 'The young self-employed in Armenia, Georgia and Ukraine', paper presented to *International Institute of Sociology World Congress*, Cologne.

Roberts, K., Adibekian, A., Nemiria, G., Tarkhnishvili, L. and Tholen, J. (1998), 'Traders and mafiosi: the young self-employed in Armenia, Georgia and Ukraine', *Journal of Youth Studies*, 1, 259-278.

Roberts, K., Clark, S.C., Fagan, C. and Tholen, J. (2000), *Surviving Post-Communism: Young People in the Former Soviet Union* (Cheltenham: Edward Elgar).

Roberts, K. and Jung, B. (1995), *Poland's First Post-Communist Generation* (Aldershot: Avebury).

Roberts, K. and Tholen, J. (1998), 'Young entrepreneurs in East-Central Europe and the former Soviet Union', in T. Lines (ed.), *Transition to What? Restarting*

Development After Communism, Institute of Development Studies Bulletin, 29, 3, 59-64.

Stoica, C.A. (2004), 'From good communists to even better capitalists? Entrepreneurial pathways in post-socialist Romania', *East European Politics and Societies,* 18, 236-277.

Stubbs, P. (1997), *Soviet Reconstruction and Social Development in Croatia and Slovenia: The Role of the NGO Sector,* Occasional Paper in Social Studies, Leeds Metropolitan University.

Tibor, A. (1997), 'Are all necessary efforts made in the transition countries to help SMEs catch up?' paper presented to *Third International Conference on SME Development Policy in Transition Economies,* Wolverhampton.

Upper Silesian Agency for Development and Promotion (1996), *Regional Development Strategy. Materials of the International Symposium, 18-19 April 1996,* Katowice.

Wawrzyniak, B. (1998), 'Innovative practices of Polish firms: regional perspective', paper presented at *14th EGOS Colloquium,* Maastricht.

Welter, F. (1997), *Small and Medium Enterprises in Central and Eastern Europe Trends, Barriers and Solutions* (Essen: Rheinisch-Westfalisches Institut fur Wirtschadtsforschung).

Chapter 4

Increasing Youth Employment Opportunities by Assisting Business Start-ups: The Experience of the Hungarian LiveWire Foundation

Péter Szirmai

1. Historical background

During the 40 years of Socialism, with its centrally planned command economy (between 1950 and 1990), unemployment was, officially, an unknown phenomenon in Hungary. There may have been what was called "indoor unemployment", while society at large was characterized by a restricted labour market. After 1990, Hungarian society was not ready to handle the high level of unemployment that arose, and the problem was especially acute for the younger generation.

An aside on the concept of youth

Even though the word "youth" is used in the title of this essay, there is still no objective, uniform definition of the concept of youth. In this field, one encounters a large variety of approaches. There are differences in the definitions used for the purposes of official statistics not only from country to country, but even within the same country. The definitions applied vary from one discipline to the next, and according to the purposes for which they are intended.

In Hungary, for example, the legal approach is that those under the age of 18, in other words those with a limited legal capacity, are classed as "youth". In the case of juvenile crime, for example, the youngest age at which one can be indicted for a crime is eighteen. Labour statistics, at the same time, also use the age group 19 to 24 as the definition of youth, since an increasing proportion of this age group is still in education. They are not yet wage-earners, i.e. they have not yet entered the labour market. In this essay, which is approaching the topic on a theoretical plane, the same age group definition will be accepted.

At the same time, when *LiveWire* Foundation, the case-study to be discussed below, organized the provision of assistance to young entrepreneurs, the age limit for its eligible target group was set at 30 years. Over the past five years, however, in line with the initiative of its English umbrella organization *Youth Business International*

(YBI), the age limit has been raised to 32 years of age (see www.youth-business. org).

In a research project in 2001, in which the various programmes providing support to youth enterprises in Hungary were investigated and their utilization and efficiency evaluated, it was found that in the field of agriculture, the Ministry of Agriculture and Rural Development set the age limit at 42 (!) years. This was the upper age limit for eligibility for supporting the launch of *youth* enterprises (see Szirmai – Fernbach 2001).

Unless otherwise indicated, the concept of youth will be used in this essay according to the definition of the LiveWire Foundation, i.e. those aged 32 and under.

2. The Political system change

After the change of the political system in the 90s, the appearance and oppressive progress of unemployment among the youth created a complex, multifaceted challenge in Hungary. On the one hand, it was clear that the young were overrepresented among the ranks of the unemployed. The proportions are shown in the table below:

Table 4.1 Unemployment rate in age groups 15-19 and 21-24 between 1992 and 2001

Age Group	1992	1993	1994	1995	1996	1997	1998	1999	2000	2001
15-19	27.0	33.3	29.8	31.1	30.4	28.8	24.8	23.4	23.7	21.2
20-24	14.0	17.0	16.0	14.7	14.5	13.0	11.1	10.6	10.4	9.5
Total	17.5	21.3	19.4	18.5	18.0	15.9	12.6	12.4	12.1	10.8

On the other hand, this growth took place despite the fact that in the period in question the number and proportion of those escaping unemployment by going into education increased significantly. The number of those in higher education approximately tripled in the period.[1]

Youth unemployment poses another problem, too. As has been observed in Western European and US experiences, a society which is unable to offer prospects other than unemployment for the youth as they enter the labour force, thus sending them the message that they are not needed, results in a generation beset by health problems. They are vulnerable to mental problems, which can lead to serious family

---

1 This high number will certainly fall in the coming years, for there is a demographical trough in Hungary, which results in the fact that this is the third year when the number of those entering into higher education (18-year-olds) exceeds the number of 6-year-olds starting their elementary studies. (Both groups contain some 100,000 young people.)

problems and a higher incidence of deviant behaviour, drug and alcohol problems, as well as delinquency in the studied age group. Indeed, one can say that youth unemployment not only brings about cases of individual tragedy, but also unbalances society as a whole.

As mentioned above, the problem was unexpected and unusual in Hungary, though it was known already in 1990 that several market economies had faced such challenges in the recent past. For example, between 1968 and 1984 the unemployment rate among teenagers (age group 15-19) grew from 12.7% to 18.9% in the US, from 7.3% to 30.7% in France, from 7.0% to 22.8% in the UK and from 12.4% to 26.6% in Italy[2] (Gazsó-Laki 2004).

The LiveWire Foundation in Britain made an important contribution to the fight against youth unemployment. Through its advisory network, the Foundation helped young entrepreneurs to develop their ideas and work out a business plan. This know-how was imported to Hungary in 1991, when – with the support of the company *Shell AG* –the Hungarian LiveWire Foundation was established (HLWF). The experience of the Hungarian LiveWire Foundation will be treated in the second part of the chapter, while the first part will describe the contextualities of youth unemployment in Hungary.

3. The history of the recent past – uneven development

One problem in Hungary – as in many parts of Europe – is that socio-economic development is not at a uniform level throughout the country; in fact significant regional differences can be observed. These differences are usually considered natural between separate countries with their own borders (therefore no one is surprised by the differing statistics on development – or from another point of view, unemployment – when Sweden and Greece are compared with each other). That regional differences exist within a country is also generally accepted, provided there are clear historical roots (as in, for example, the traditional lagging of southern Italy behind the developed northern regions).

Regional differences were historically and culturally less encoded in Hungary, and it was only after the 90s that we had to acquaint ourselves with the idea – in fact not only an idea, but a tragic social fact – of Hungary having significant regional differences.

The extremely uneven distribution of the GDP (GDP per capita measured at purchasing power parity) among the regions and the counties reveals the inequalities very well. For example, in 1999 the leading position belonged to Budapest, the capital of Hungary, where per capita GDP reached $20,400. Szabolcs-Szatmár-Bereg county (together with Nógrád county which was almost on the same level), where the per capita GDP was less than $6,000, ranked last. It has to be mentioned that the exceptional GDP of $20,400 in Budapest is followed by a much lower rate even in supposedly developed counties ($14,000 in Győr-Moson-Sopron, $12,600 in

---

2 Knowing the challenges and the statistics, it seemed reasonable to use the experience of developed economies when searching for a solution.

Vas and $12,200 in Fejér). Another gap exists in the ranking before the counties with a GDP of $8-10,000 ($9,600 in Zala, $9,500 in Tolna, $9,200 in Csongrád, $8,700 in Pest and $8,500 in Veszprém). They are followed by the less developed regions with a $7-8,000 in average and finally – as mentioned already – by the two counties at the end of the list with less than $6,000.

It is hardly surprising that this GDP-ranking demonstrates a similarity with the ranking on the basis of unemployment, and of youth unemployment within that. It is essential to highlight that a country like Hungary, with a relatively small area (93,000 km²) and 10 million inhabitants, can show huge, fourfold regional differences. The regional differences in income have an impact on economic activity and inland revenue, and also affect the life opportunities of the local people and the future of the younger generation. This it was seen as extremely important to create an organization based on the model of the British LiveWire, which would not work exclusively in the capital, nor limit its activity to one or another less developed county. Rather it would operate as a national network, and therefore be able to create opportunities for the youth of all counties. According to the original idea, providing equal opportunities must include giving young people access – through the network and with the help of information technology – to the national market, which may be more developed than the county average. It should be said that this idea proved impossible to realize – micro businesses mainly produce their goods for or deliver their services to the local market, and other research has shown that the businesses are strongly integrated into the local network of family, neighbourhood and social relationships, and in the network of demand determined by them (see Szirmai 2003, 122-129).

We also have to highlight another fact. The research of Ferenc Gazsó and László Laki (see Gazsó – Laki 2004, 28) indicates that the majority of the Hungarian entrepreneurs, and the sub-set of young Hungarian entrepreneurs, must be classed as self-employed when applying the classification criteria of developed countries. Their predicament is seen as very insecure even in developed countries, since the deterioration of economic conditions has a direct and immediate impact on the sustainability of their "workplace" and their related subsistence. It must be highlighted that there is an interrelation between the number of self-employed people and the level of economic development of a country: their proportion is higher in poorer, but lower in richer countries. In 1999, the proportion of the self-employed was 10% in German and 11% in both France and Sweden, while the figures were 19% in Spain, 25% in Portugal, and 32% in Greece (see Laky 2001, 43). In the light of this data, we have no reason not to classify our country as a less developed market economy.

3.1. Ethnic, social and industrial considerations

Although present research places the demographic approach in the centre and examines youth unemployment and the possible ways to combat it, it should be mentioned briefly that many unfavourable factors have an influence on youth employment in Hungary. Among these factors there are many that have a cumulative impact or, in other words, intensify the negative tendencies. Let us take the example of the biggest ethnic minority, the Roma, whose number exceeds half a million.

Their proportion is usually higher in the less developed counties, and there are more children and consequently a higher number of young people than within the non-Roma communities. At the same time, their level of education is typically low, which results in a disadvantage on the labour market (see Laki, Szabó and Bauer 2001).

It is interesting to note that textbooks from the 1980s – and this has been my experience not only in Hungary but all over Europe – defined Hungary as an agrarian or an agro-industrial country. The basis of this definition was the large proportion of those working in agriculture (35-40% in the 1960s). However, in the following period the proportion of agricultural employees experienced a rapid fall, partially due to "socialist industrialization" that resulted in new towns based on heavy industry "growing out of the ground". At this time there was a general increase in urban population and the rate of employment. In 1990, 17.5% of employed people were still working in agriculture. Within ten years this rate had fallen to nearly one third: only 6.5% were employed in agriculture in 2001. Meanwhile, the employment rate in the service industries grew from 46% in 1990 to 60% in 2000. It is interesting that in the 1990s the proportion of industrial employees did not continue to increase, but in fact decreased from 36% to 34%. These figures reflect an important developmental dynamic, with the Hungarian employment structure showing characteristics that are increasingly similar to those of the developed Western European countries (Szirmai-Fernbach 2001).

It should be noted that the formal statistical approach has its limits. In Hungary, a large proportion of the economy operates unseen, in the shadow of offical statistics. This is also indicated by the fact that while only a small percentage of the employed people as described above work in agriculture, the actual proportion of people producing agricultural products to supplement their pensions or their income from "primary employment" in the industrial sector or in the building-trade is much higher. According to the "lifestyle and time balance 1999/2000" analysis based on data from the KSH (Hungarian Central Statistical Office) the number of families involved in small-scale agricultural production fell significantly from 1,400,000 in 1991 to 960,000 in 2000. However, this latter number is exactly four times the 240,000 employees who officially work in agriculture. Agricultural production contributes to the subsistence of an even larger segment of society, since the prevalence and weight of the self-employment on a national scale justifies our contention that even the data of 960,000 is skewed, i.e. less than the real figure.[3]

3.2. Social inequalities according to a sociological approach

Socialism, the planned economy and the centralized, totalitarian structure can be described as a sort of modernization attempt.[4] Similarly, the change of regime – that

---

3 There are many reasons why someone might not admit to a supplementary or other income from agricultural production, but there is no imaginable situation wherein someone who has nothing to do with agriculture would have said that his income comes from or is supplemented by agricultural production.

4 One can think of what Winston Churchill said of Stalin when he died: "the greatest genius of the 20th century, who took over his country with a wooden plough and passed it

is, the change-over from the despotic, paternalist political system to a democratic structure – represented a drive towards modernization on the part of Hungarian society. Some aspects of this modernization have already been mentioned (for instance, the changes in the employment structure), but some other economic aspects cannot be included within the framework of our present study because of its necessarily limited scope,[5] and some of these aspects are subject of continuous discussion in the sociological literature.

The central question of this discussion is whether the relative differences have increased or decreased (more precisely: to what extent have they increased and changed compared to earlier periods). The famous sociologist Tamás Kolosi published the findings of his research in 2000 (Kolosi 2000). His work reveals that although the differences increased, the average moved upwards and the social structure remained significantly tilted toward the centre, i.e. the middle segment is still the largest.

Kolosi tried to schematize society along several variables of inequality, and for each variable he gave a ranking from 1 to 5 depending on an individuals circumstances, from the most disadvantageous to the most advantageous. The five variables are the following:

- Education
- Position in the division of labour
- Income
- Financial lifestyle
- Cultural lifestyle

With this measuring technique, the group that gets the maximal 25 points (5*5) is in the most advantageous position, while, of course, the most disadvantaged group receives only 1 point in each dimension, making 5 points altogether. The researchers analysed this point-based breakdown, created status groups and identified 9 different groups (see Table 4.2 below, based on 1999 data) (Kolosi 2000, 170-197).

The people who drew up this model thought that society was characterized by a 5-level stratification. The "upper middle class" is at the top of the hierarchy with more than 20 points, and 6% of the population belongs here. (To this group belongs – or out of this group emerges – the "elite" or "ruling class" of the present day, which represents an estimated 1% and is not specified because of the lack of data.)

The status group with 16-20 points forms the second stratum of the hierarchy, representing 24% of the population. The "lower middle class" is situated in the

---

over with a nuclear bomb."

5   Two decades ago Hungary exported lightly processed goods and mainly agricultural goods. 75% of its markets were part of the COMECON market, automobile and modern electronics manufacturing did almost not exist at all. 90% of the markets of today's Hungary can be found in the developed countries. The manufacturing of automobiles and automobile parts is significant, a considerable proportion of the country's export represents modern technology and the percentage of the export of the agricultural goods – especially of those processed on a low level – has reduced in a great extent.

middle stratum with 13-14 points, and at 12% represents little more than one tenth of the population. The status group with 10-12 points is the fourth stratum of this model, and represents 30% of society. On the lowest of the five strata are the people with a social status that can be called disadvantaged, who represent 29% of the population and have – far below the next level up – a maximum of eight points.

Table 4.2 Status groups in 1999

Name	Average status value points	Percentage in the population
1. Upper middle class	22.7	5.6
2. High status, lower, middle income group	18.8	7.1
3. "Elite of workers" – developing middle class	16.4	11.7
4. Cultural middle class	16.2	5.1
5. Lower middle class	13.1	12.1
6. Comfortably housed lower group	11.7	9.7
7. Lower group with good income	10.6	9.6
8. Declining and returning people	12.4	10.3
9. Disadvantaged status	7.7	28.8

The top of the above model – in common with the previous one – is very "narrow": it consists of the 1% "elite" and a 5% "upper middle class". They are followed by the "middle classes", much talked about, but whose proportion does not exceed 25% of the population. Two large groups can be found under them: the people with a disadvantaged status (29%) and the other group just above them who are either not disadvantaged, or merely partially disadvantaged (declining), but who do not belong to the "middle class" either (30%) (see Szirmai 2002/a, 53-55).

3.3. Youth unemployment

Natural processes probably partly explain the fact that youth unemployment is higher than the average unemployment rate. Those who are already employed, who are already integrated in the labour market, have gained the experience to safeguard their own interests more efficiently than those who just want to start work. Employees can also form trade-unions to represent their interests. One of the reasons why first-job employees are less efficient and focused in fighting for their interests is that they often consider other entrants to be competitors or adversaries. Consequently solidarity among them is rarely stronger than shared opinions.

On the basis of the data introduced above (see Table 4.1), it can be seen that young people are overrepresented among the unemployed and that three further factors should be highlighted. In 1992 the unemployment rate among 15- to 19-

year-olds rose to 27%, and among 20- to 24-year-olds to 14%, although only a few years earlier all young people in this age range were able to find a job. Thus the phenomenon – as has already been mentioned – was unexpected, and society was not prepared for it. The second factor that has to be emphasized is that – although the figures show some improvement since the mid-1990s (unemployment reduced between 1996 and 2001 from 30% to 21% among the under 19s and from 14.5% to 9.5% within the 20 to 24-year-old age group) – this decrease remained lower than that in the overall rate of unemployment. Thus it can be concluded that the state of the labour market for young people is still cause for concern, and no improvement in their relative situation has been observed. The third thing to mention is that the unemployment rates are still high even after this decrease (think of the figures for 15- to 19-year-olds, of whom one in every five is unemployed), and this calls for an urgent solution, particularly if one remembers the psychological and socio-psychological context discussed above.

It is not surprising that young people experience and conceptualize changes mentioned so far. In the 1980s the young people questioned in the frame of public opinion polls almost never indicated unemployment as one of the problems of their age group (rather the unresolved and insoluble problem of housing). According to research by Ferenc Gazsó and László Laki (Gazsó-Laki 2004, 110-111) today unemployment is the foremost factor among those given.

One of the characteristics of the ranking of the age group problems considered important by young people is that it is reflects the most important structural changes of the new society that has evolved since the change of regime and its consequences, all of which shape the individual, family and social situation as well as the general condition. Out of the structural factors observed, the ones that formed the thread of the web of problems were those upon which the most basic elements of social life depend: "unemployment", the difficulty and the unpredictability of finding a job (47%), the "low level of income" in Hungary (34%), the unresolved problem of housing (32%). The determining role of these factors has an irrefutable role in securing the individual and family subsistence, in the cost and standard of living and in integration into society. Unemployment – as has been mentioned – can divide society into two parts even at this age, making it clear which people are capable or incapable of finding their own way on the labour market either at the time or in the longer term.

Besides this cruel and unambiguous selection, the difficulty of breaking into the market or achieving a long-term, secure presence on it is detrimental to the life of others as well, it can confound their efforts, restrict their prospects or even prevent them from entering the market. Likewise a number of subsistence problems are related to salaries and earnings, and both personal and family incomes. The lack of these or their being at a low level does not only mean shelving long-term aims (such as starting a family) and has a limiting effect on, for example, housing and education, it can also lead to the failure to satisfy basic needs (e.g. clothing, eating, and heating) (Laki-Szabó-Bauer 2001).

We have not mentioned the impact of technological development among those factors revealed by polling the youth public opinion. A reason for this is that the impacts are not unambiguous, and they do not always point in the same direction.

The technical specifications of accommodation (whether they are built of stone or brick clay, supplied with water, connected to the sewage system, supplied with electricity, equipped with household and electronic appliances) is related directly to the social structure, but achievements of modern technology do not correspond with the social hierarchy to such an extent. Just 20 years ago having a phone could be an important indicator of the social status, whereas nowadays the majority of families own a technical appliance enabling communication (mobile phone). The differences in the possession of numerous other goods are not that visible either (e.g. automobiles). Of course, there is no need for an extraordinarily exacting sociological and methodological system to identify the 20% of the population who split off the main social current. Those who are a little above them and the members of the lower middle class, on the other hand, do not differ as visibly from the majority than they did a few decades ago. The major factor of the split off is integration into the labour market. As is shown in the case-study below, the HLWF was created in recognition of this.

Table 4.3 "What do young people consider to be the most acute problem?"
(in % on the basis of comparative evaluation of the questions)

1. Unemployment	47
2. Lack of money, low salaries	34
3. Unresolved problem of housing	32
4. Poverty and social insecurity	14
5. Increasing drug use	13
6. Growing social inequality	9
7. An empty future	8
8. (Financially) limited opportunity to continuing studies	7

3.4. Social and governmental efforts for solving the "youth problem"

It has almost become a commonplace in sociological literature that the group that is the main loser following the economic and political changes in Eastern Europe is the young. Recognition of this was followed by practical steps, even though the criticism can be made that these steps were very ineffective. They were typically without any strategic prospects and have been limited to the four-year cycles of the individual political party terms of office. By way of illustration, it is worth noting that the foundation of the Hungarian National Institute for Youth Research in 2000 was quickly followed by its termination in 2003, as a consequence of the change of government following the general election of 2002.

The tasks and activities of this centre can be summarized as follows:

- concentrating on, coordinating and supporting research projects dealing with children and young adults of Hungarian citizenship living in Hungary or belonging to the Hungarian minority abroad;
- systemising and disseminating the results of the youth research projects of various workshops, and in connection with this aim:
- setting up a youth database;
- establishing a research centre where researchers can access the results of the most important Hungarian and international youth research projects;
- conducting its own research as a function of social changes and financial possibilities, as well as the expectations and decrees of government and civil society;
- carrying out regional research projects, as far as possible with the involvement of the regional youth offices;
- on the basis of the results of the large-sample study, conducting targeted research projects at the regional level, with the help and cooperation of the regional youth offices;
- conducting continuous supplementary research projects at the national level on the basis of the findings of the large-sample study;
- supporting and implementing the youth research efforts of various workshops;
- publishing a scientific journal dealing with the issue of youth research (Bauer-Szirmai 2001).

The importance of such a research institute probably does not need to be discussed at length. Its link to political regimes, however, proved to be an obstacle to carrying out long-term, longitudinal, comparative research projects, and even though in the short period of its existence it brought to light important information in the field of research into the young, its research programme remained incomplete.

Apart from this very illustrative example, one could enumerate a number of initiatives, campaigns and political endeavours aimed at improving the status of young people and their integration into the labour market. Despite this, research has shown that in Hungary after the change of the political system, the organizational, institutional and personal framework for youth employment has not been established. The reasons for this include:

- the uncertainty of the central administrative institutions;
- deficiencies in the legislative requirements;
- the deficiencies in the professional standards of necessary personnel (the lack of professional standards for Hungarian youth work, the lack of training programmes);
- the haphazard, uncertain nature of the budgetary conditions (instability of funds).

In the current system of local government, the emphasis has been on following examples rather than following norms, establishing self-sufficient institutions that are independent from others rather than looking for opportunities for cooperation, and on a departmental approach to public policymaking rather than enforcing an interdepartmental or holistic approach in the field of the youth work carried out on the micro-regional level. Instead of creating institutions, local governments were busy establishing "interest reconciliation forums".

4. The struggle to overcome the paternalistic heritage

The Socialist era in Hungary can be best characterized as a "paternalist system". From the point of view of our narrower topic, it meant that the state took upon itself the handling and solution of the youth problem, and reciprocally, the citizens also primarily considered this set of issues to be a state matter. So entrenched was this attitude, that after the change of political system (i.e. after the free, multi-party system of election in 1990) the various networks set up to promote entrepreneurship and enterprise (such as the Hungarian Enterprise Development Foundation in 1990 and the Hungarian Chamber of Commerce and Industry in 1994) were established primarily (although not exclusively) from state money and Phare grants (Szirmai-Csapó 2005, Szirmai 2002/b, 12).

In discussing youth unemployment, it would be a mistake to ignore the foundation and activities of the various foreign NGOs that also stimulated the development of civil society both across Eastern Europe and specifically in Hungary. These organisations helped many civil projects to overcome initial difficulties, and then provided them with the necessary conditions for survival. Particularly noteworthy are the activities of the Soros Foundation, US AID, CIPE and the British Know-How Fund. Their activities, including publications, conferences and other events, were very important for ensuring that the change of the system is not restricted to the upper realms of politics. At the same time, it is obvious that on their own they could not possibly have provided the solution to such fundamental social problems as youth unemployment. This is why it appeared self-evident in the early 1990s that civil initiatives are also necessary in order to change the situation for the better. The Hungarian LiveWire Foundation (HLWF) set itself this very objective. The following section will provide a brief analysis – in the form of a single case-study – of the experience of the HWLF.

5. A Brief History of the HLWF and its Work

The target group of the foundation is young people between 18 and 32,[6] i.e. the age group overrepresented in the unemployment statistics. During the 12 years since the foundation was established, nearly 10,000 young people have got in contact

---

6 At the time of the launch – following the English conception – the age group between 18 and 30 was defined as young. Later on, experience led to the age limit of the supported group (the young) being raised to 32.

with LiveWire's advisory network. This meant that it was possible to supply them with information materials dealing with basic issues of enterprises, offer them consultations, and answer their questions as to how realistic their ideas were and how they could be developed. The intention and the result of such meetings was to encourage young people to start preparing a business plan. Roughly a quarter of the young people passing the first consultation went on to prepare their own business plans.

In order to encourage young people to develop their business ideas, the foundation holds an annual competition entitled "Young Entrepreneur of the Year" in which the entrants' business plans are evaluated and ranked. Since the start of the foundation, 12 such competitions have been organized, in the course of which – with counting with 100-120 participants per year – a total of some 1400-1600 business plans have been created. It is important to note that the jury consists not only of bankers and successful entrepreneurs, but also other young people who were shortlisted in previous competitions and have grown to take part in the evaluation process as entrepreneurs. Furthermore, valuable prizes and awards are supplemented by offers from young entrepreneurs (some of whom are not actually that young anymore) whose business start-ups were also supported by the HLWF foundation. The young winners happily receive a briefcase from a leather company, a bunch of flowers from a small company dealing with flower arrangement, or sweets from a confectioner.

Awards from sponsors, such as mobile phones, computers, software or discounted or free advertisement places in a business journal, also aim to help young entrepreneurs in their early days. In general, the publicity of the competition provides a great support to the participants, giving them a starting push to enter the market as well as providing them with good examples. Indeed, presenting alternatives and future prospects, showing that these young people have a future other then being unemployed, is one of the major positive effects of the foundation's work. In light of feedback received, the overall beneficial effect of the foundation is far greater than the couple of thousand young enterprises showing up in the statistics would suggest.

During the first years the main purpose was to set up a network and get the foundation acknowledged. From 2000 onwards, with the financial help of H.M. Prince Charles, it has become possible for young entrepreneurs to apply for micro-credit. The amount of the micro-credit may vary between HUF 100,000 and 1,000,000 (EUR 400-4000). The results of this initiative will be discussed later. A voluntary advisory service is available, which covers the whole country and consists of highly qualified lawyers, accountants and managers, who help the young applicants in converting their business ideas into business plans free of charge. All the 50-60 activists of the advisory network perform this charity work for free. Not surprisingly, many of them are also active in other organizations such as the Lions Club, the Hungarian Business Leaders Forum or the Hungarian Foundation for Enterprise Promotion. In their professional lives they work as accountants, entrepreneurial advisors and businesspeople. This increases their ability to help, as the role and importance of the advisory network lies not only in transferring information; these professionals are also in a position to help the youth find their feet in the business world. They introduce young people to the business community, entrepreneurial organizations and chambers of commerce of the given region, and can often help them in identifying their market. They support the new enterprises of the young businesspeople not only by transferring knowledge, but by sharing their personal experiences as well. The fundamental elements of the methodology followed by HLWF can be summed up as follows:

- Nation-wide network of highly qualified advisors.
- Understandable business planning guides worked out by top experts in the field.
- Marketing for communication with the target group.
- Customized counselling (linking consulting and counselling).
- The "Young Entrepreneur of the Year" competition, with regional and national finals, attractive awards, and favourable press coverage.
- Offering micro-credit for enterprises that lack sources.

5.1 Follow-up, maintaining contact with young people

In 2001, the young people who had been in touch with the Foundation were interviwed by the Hungarian LiveWire Foundation in the framework of a follow-up research. Almost 10% of them, a relatively large sample of 140 young entrepreneurs, were questioned about their situation, aspirations and opinions. A series of detailed, focussed and in-depth interviews, which addressed 30 people out of these 140, was part of the study. First of all, one of the findings of the research was that that the survey, the renewal of contact, and the Foundation's attention received a very warm welcome from young people. There exists a strong need for assistance that does not end with simple, one-shot counselling, but for a support that is ongoing and that helps them feel themselves part of a community.

Within our research, the young people who had started their own business with the help of LiveWire formed a separate sample group, and the roughly 70 people who ultimately did not try to set up a business were also studied. Those who realized their business ideas mainly based their choice on their existing professional knowledge. Those who, in the end, chose not to give it a try, justified their decision by citing the lack of market demand, and often said they lacked expertise in a particular field. The importance of professional knowledge when starting up a business turns our attention to the education system. It is not only knowledge that has to be instilled in young people. Abilities and skills have to be developed in order to enable them to become successful entrepreneurs. This is exactly what the Hungarian LiveWire Foundation does – although not as a part of the state training and education system. It shows how to be a successful entrepreneur by providing support materials for distance learning and practical examples. Therefore, it would be misleading to measure the success of the Foundation solely on the basis of the number of young people becoming entrepreneurs with the devoted help of the team. Sometimes the foundation saves someone by advising a person that he or she should not start a business that would be doomed to failure. Teaching the basics of commercial thinking and tricks of the trade in order to teach a young person when not to start a business is another success of the Foundation.

Don't just look for a job! Create one for yourself!

This is the slogan with which young people who are considering starting up a business are welcomed. In the follow-up study mentioned above, it was found that the larger part (53%) of young people who start a business operate as private entrepreneurs. Another 38% of them have set up limited partnerships.[7]

The start-up capital required is one of the most important considerations for young entrepreneurs not only when choosing the legal form of their company (this is why more than 90% of them choose the forms with the lowest capital requirement), but also when defining the range of activities. This is why half of the young people are active in the service industry and tend to run businesses that can be started with a minimal capital investment.

Obviously someone starts a business to ensure a better income for himself. However, according to the results of our survey this is not the only aspiration of young entrepreneurs. Seventy of them gave the following answers to the question of why they had started a business (not only one but more answers could be given to the question):

Table 4.4 Reasons for starting a business

I think that I can achieve a better standard of living than if I were to work as an employee	61.4 %
I wanted to be independent	41.4 %
I am continuing the family tradition, the family business	5.7 %
I didn't find a job after finishing my studies	4.3 %
I found my previous job boring	1.4 %
Other answer	17.1 %

Most of them explained that since they had been running their businesses the main change in their lives was that they had to work much more than before. This was also confirmed by other findings of the study that revealed that working hours are often much longer than eight hours a day. It seems that young people "burn the candle at both ends" and though they do not think about it yet, they will not be able to continue this constant rush forever.

---

7 The limited partnership (Bt. in Hungarian) is the cheapest and simplest company from a legal point of view. It consists of at least one general partner who has unlimited responsibility for the company's liabilities, and of at least one limited partner who is responsible only to the extent of his stake, and not for any other liabilities of the company. There is no legal requirement concerning minimum start-up capital or other requirement that can be difficult to fulfil when setting up a fully limited company (Kft.).

5.2 Summarising, the clients of the HLWF

A number of years ago, a survey was conducted to find out who the clients of the Foundation were. The major findings were as follows:

- Clients are young people under 32 who typically work at least eight hours a day in their enterprises. In their view, the biggest change in their lives is that they have worked more since they became entrepreneurs.
- Most of them started their businesses seeking better living conditions compared to those offered by working as an employee. Another major motivator is their ambition to be independent.
- Half of those running an active enterprise started business with less than HUF 100,000 (EUR 400). Fourteen percent of them chose a business field where a large sum of starting capital was not needed.
- The support of friends and family members is vital for their success. Besides their financial help, their encouragement also means a lot. They can even support the young businessperson in acquiring entrepreneurial skills (legal, marketing, accounting etc.).
- There are major differences between the two groups of young people studied in the survey in terms of business planning and preparation for starting an enterprise. Of those with an active enterprise, the majority worked out a business plan before starting their businesses (70%), and their purpose was, besides taking part in the HLWF, to make sure their ideas are viable. In contrast, the proportion of those making business plans in the other group was only 60%, and their main goal was to participate in the HLWF. Out of those with an active enterprise, 44% took part in a training program, while their proportion in the other group was only 28%.
- Both groups ranked family first in their list of values, though for those with an active enterprise family seems more important (the average is lower (1.8) compared with that of the other group (2.17)). Honesty, friendship and money are more important for those who either have no active enterprise yet or no longer have one (in all cases the average is lower). For those with an active enterprise learning is more important than money. In the other group money "outranked" learning.
- The majority of those running active businesses have found their place, with nearly half of them saying that their enterprises improved their own and their family members' living standards. Furthermore, a significant majority of them (94%) intend to continue their business activities, or said that if they had to make a decision, they would choose entrepreneurship again (about 80%). Many of them are planning further enlargement of their enterprises (78%).
- Existing as an entrepreneur is also an attractive alternative for those without an active enterprise; 71% of them said they were toying with the idea of running a business in the future.
- Among the most frequent wishes of those with existing enterprises were: "consumers, market, connections" (46%); "a positive change in the legal and economic political background" (37%); "capital, money, financial background"

(29%); "professional acknowledgement, success" (21%). Among their three major wishes, a large number of those asked indicated changes relating to their private lives, their families and living conditions (26%). Almost all without an active enterprise listed "capital, money, financial background" (97%), besides "consumers, market, connections" (49%), "good workforce and colleagues" (31%), "facilities, office, site" (21%). These wishes generally cover factors that are inevitable for starting up a business. In this group the proportion of those hoping for change in their standard of living and private lives was significantly lower (4%).

6. A critical overview: what HLWF has achieved and not achieved

As discussed above, HLWF was established as a non-governmental initiative to deal with real-life social problems. Still, when its now 15-year history is reviewed, it is clear that it has been able only to partially fulfil its original objectives.

6.1 The levelling out of regional inequalities, or the infiltration of regional inequalities into the work of HLWF

The scarcity of available funds, as well as the original concept of the founders both forced the Foundation to set up a very strictly cost-efficient operating model. This meant that the Foundation could not establish a national network of full-time employees, but rather that it has primarily relied on volunteers. Such an arrangement certainly had advantages (staff members motivated from within are more reliable and can be expected to give better quality work than those working for hire; the volunteers from the individual regions often represent the most active business layer from other points of view; the volunteer helpers are more client-centred, meaning that they focus on the actual needs of those turning to them for help, and they are not interested in providing strictly formal assistance etc.). However, it inevitably has disadvantages as well (a team that can be put to work rather unevenly; formal requirements are more difficult to define; the time that volunteers can set aside for this work is subject to fluctuation).

Valuable assistance in their work came from the national networks mentioned earlier, such as the Hungarian Chamber of Commerce and Industry, which was present in each county, or the Hungarian Enterprise Development Foundation, which also had a nationwide network of offices. With careful organizational work, the colleagues were identified in these networks who considered the enhancement of the efficiency of their work important enough to merit joining the HLWF network (it should be stressed here that the annual budget of HLWF never exceeded 25 million HUF, or 100,000 EUR, while the national organizations mentioned typically had a budget 50 to 100 times as high).

Unfortunately, however, the tendency towards the automatic reproduction and reinforcement of regional inequalities was also felt in the work of HLWF. Finding volunteer colleagues proved to be most difficult in the poorest and least developed regions, because it was here also that the networks of the Chamber of Commerce or the Enterprise Development Foundation were least organized. This meant that it was in these regions that the target group was reached least effectively, and also, conversely, the majority of the beneficiaries of the various programmes were from the capital city. The level of activity in the developed regions was always higher than in less developed ones.

6.2 Deficiencies in social equalization

Comprehensive organization was (would have been) an aim and mission of HLWF. It is certainly not the case that there have been only failures in this field, as quite a number enterprises launched from under the wings of HLWF originated in less educated, poorer strata of society, among them ethnic minorities. It was more typical, however, that the staff of HLWF found common ground more easily and quickly with the children of urban middle-class families, with similar backgrounds to their own, than with those from the lower strata of society. Such people were often quite alien to them, especially if they had dropped out of school, suffered from parental neglect, or had problems with drugs. No formal refusal of consultation was ever made; in fact, as mentioned earlier, from the mid-1990s, an important role was played among the supporters of LiveWire by H.M. Prince Charles and his umbrella organization *Youth Business International*. He visited the HLWF Foundation on several occasions, and it is obvious that he was better able to make a connection with youth enterprises if the young people concerned spoke English, understood his questions and were able to respond to them.

In view of the fact that the problem of unemployment has never been limited entirely to the lowest strata of society, it is not necessary to overplay the deficiencies of HLWF in this respect. However, the requirements of a critical analysis demand mention of the fact that neither regional equalization nor socially comprehensive operation achieved the levels originally set as targets.

6.3 Micro-credit – the Financial Programme for Supporting the Young (IPTP)

The designation of the Programme Under the Hungarian laws regulating financial institutions, giving credit is the exclusive right of financial institutions. Therefore the HLWF itself cannot give credit, neither can it launch a programme – not even in cooperation with a bank – promoting a "HLWF credit". That is why the programme has been designated as a supporting programme.

However, the IPTP can be defined as a cash-flow based credit. The supporting character of the programme means that it maintains contact and establishes a relationship with clients (young people) with whom banks would not ordinarily enter into a partnership. Reasons for the lack of bank support are the inexperience, the inadequate business expertise, and the lack of collateral and financial means in general of young people, which results in banks considering them too high a risk. Another reason is the related high transaction costs, which can seem unaffordable high if one considers the relatively small amount of credit required. The IPTP accepts and tries to deal with these risk factors, invests a lot of energy into the preparation and understanding of the business plan, supports the young person by providing an advisor in order to make his or her business successful. With this help, and the maintenance of the relationship, the programme greatly increases the payback ratio and eliminates the failures.

Credit Reference The HLWF gives loans like a bank, therefore basic regulations governing the procedure and conditions for a loan are set out and documented. When evaluating the prudence of a business operation, the main criteria are how realistic the enterprise is and what level of profit can be expected, not the financial standing and funds of the applicant.

What is special about the IPTP credit manual is that it is not secret. It is not a confidential internal bank document, but a public set of rules that can be studied by young people while planning their business. On the one hand, it is very useful for them to be familiar with it and to evaluate themselves beforehand by following the guidelines of the manual, which all helps them to decide if it is worth applying for a credit. On the other hand, the credit manual serves as a guideline for the credit evaluating board and the advisors in defining what they can – indeed what they *must* – require from the applicant before offering credit, and which are the factors that fall outside their objective considerations.

The manual regulates in detail the rights and obligations of all participants in the procedure, and enables the young entrepreneur to prepare himself or herself for receiving the credit, since by reading the manual the young person can learn what he can expect and from whom, and who should provide what in order to get a positive decision on the credit application.

Credit Evaluation Board Credit applications (applications for support) are submitted to the Foundation by the young applicants, who are offered consultations with the help of which they can change and improve the submitted application. The application is reviewed and evaluated by a credit manager and then transferred to the evaluation board. The board consists of bank managers, advisors, entrepreneurs, even former winning applicants, and a representative of the bank that would issue the loan. The loan is a cash-flow based one, thus the provision will be the equipment bought from the sum borrowed and the envisaged income of the enterprise.

The evaluating board is continuously in a "dual tie". On the one hand, the advisory board requires of them to approve the issuing of support (credit) to those who will actually pay it back, so that the credit fund does not run out too fast. One the other hand, society expects that it should be available to young people, who start risky businesses but will have a chance to safeguard their standard of living and make a success of their business venture. If they are too "strict" (i.e. there are a lot of rejected credit applications), society will disapprove, whereas if the number of failed and liable businesses grows, then the leaders of the Foundation are unsatisfied. These conflicts are resolved in due course, and young people are able to access the necessary financial support.

Advisors, Mentors One of the major features of this cash-flow based credit is that the connection between the bank and the applicant does not end with the signing of the contract, as the young borrower has to stay in touch with a designated mentor, and inform him or her on the business progress of the enterprise. This serves the mutual interests of both parties: the success of the young person means that he or she will be able to pay back the loan to the bank. In the event of a successful cooperation in which the young businessman has paid back the principal and the interest by the end of the credit period, the mentor receives premiums, thus has a vested interest in the success of the business.

This form of remuneration paid to the mentors raises conflicts all the time. It may happen that although a mentor works a lot with a "problem entrepreneur", the enterprise cannot be saved and will have problems paying back the loan. In such a case, regardless of how much energy the mentor invested the job, he will not receive remuneration. On the other hand, there are also "lucky mentors" who only have to visit their entrepreneurs once every three months, confirm with pleasure that the business has grown, check the statements of the instalments paid, and soon he can go to the pay office to pick up his mentor's fee, even though in reality he has invested very little time and energy into the mentorship. In my view this conflict is unresolvable, because any form of radical restructuring of the support system that would seek to "eliminate" these difficulties would only create a worse situation than the present one.

Figures and Experience As mentioned earlier, the financial support program was launched at the end of 2000, so it has only a short history. Thus far, 55 credit transactions have been made, out of which only one business has demonstrably failed.[8]

An important lesson is that the number of requests for a delay of payment, re-scheduling of repayment, or suspension has been relatively high. If the mentor or the credit manager thinks that the young businessperson will be able to continue paying the instalments, and his or her financial problems are no more than temporary, or they have someone to help them out, the request will be granted. Nearly half of the applicants have experienced temporary financial problems which prevented them from paying the monthly instalments. At present three or four enterprises are about six months in arrears, and a greater number are overdue by one or two-months.

Overall, the experiences of the IPTP have been very favourable and the willingness to repay the credit is good. Although the program is adapted to the usual practice of Hungarian entrepreneurial credit, and the rate of interest is lower than in the case of entirely market-based loans, the support itself is made unique by the involvement of the mentors and by the fact that this source of credit is accessible to those entrepreneurs who really need it. With the help of the credit evaluating board, the bank considers the risk acceptable and assumes a portion of the risk. The HLWF is able to reduce the risk and the transaction costs to an acceptable level thanks to the organizational solutions that are presented here.

---

8 Two young persons, who had just left a foster home at the age of 18, decided to start an enterprise in their profession. However, as a result of a difficult start-up, one of them got seriously ill and died. The company went bankrupt and could not continue paying back the loan. Most of the collateral was lost, and the sum outstanding could not be collected.

7. Network System of the HLWF

To reach the target groups more efficiently, the Foundation maintains contact with the following institutions:

- Labour market centres
- Unemployment offices
- Schools
- Entrepreneur education programs (e.g. Young Enterprise, Junior Achievement)
- Budapest Young Entrepreneur Centre
- Business incubators
- Hungarian Chamber of Trade and Industry
- Hungarian Foundation for Enterprise Promotion
- Other supporters – offering awards for the competitions

This high degree of social embeddedness constitutes the major value and virtue of the support activity. However, at the same time it also carries a danger, as external factors independent of the work of the organization can have a significant effect on the success of the foundation. For instance, when the cancellation of compulsory chamber membership led the national chamber network into a crisis, it also set back the work of the HLWF in several regions. Likewise, the poor performance of the national network of the Hungarian Foundation for Enterprise Promotion also had a negative effect on the performance of the HLWF.

8. Concluding remarks

The experience of the HLWF foundation show us, that in the fight against young unemployment, business education (transfer of entrepreneurial knowledge) and business development is a more efficient tool than any other subsidy, which makes participants sooner or later concerned to sustain the out of work situation. We can state that program participant not only establishing jobs for themselves, rather for their community, in this way they help to overcome unemployment problems in their society.

References

Bauer, Béla and Péter Szirmai (2001), *Az ifjúsági vállalkozások a kormánypolitikában* (Youth enterprises in government policy) (manuscript, Budapest).

Gazsó, Ferenc and László Laki (2004), *Fiatalok az újkapitalizmusban* (Youth in the neo-capitalism) (Napvilág Kiadó, Budapest).

Kolosi, Tamás (2000), *A terhes babapiskóta* (The pregnant sponge-finger) (Ozirisz Kiadó).

Laki, László, Andrea Szabó, and Béla Bauer (eds.) (2001), *Ifjúság 2000 gyorsjelentés* (Youth 2000, Flash report) (Nemzeti Ifjúságkutató Intézet (Budapest: National Youth Research Institute), also 2004 (2005).

Laky, Teréz (2001), *A munkaerő keresletét és kínálatát alakító folyamatok.* (The processes forming the demand and supply of the labour force) (Budapest: Országos Foglalkoztatási Hivatal).

Szirmai, Péter and Zoltán Fernbach (2001), *Fiatal agrárvállalkozókat támogató program az EFBM területén, kutatási zárójelentés* (A programme supporting young agricultural entrepreneurs in the field of EFBM, final report of research project) (manuscript, Budapest).

Szirmai, Péter (2003), *The Capital-less Capitalism: Review on Hungarian Small Enterprises in Knowledge Transfer, Small and Medium-Sized Enterprises, and Regional Development in Hungary* (edited by Imre Lengyel) (University of Szeged: JATEPress), 122-129.

Szirmai, Péter (2002a), *The Missing Keel* (Thoughts on Hungarian small enterprises), (Hungarian Chamber Horizon, 2002/01), 53-55.

Szirmai, Péter (2002b) *Vállalkozásoktatás és helyreállítási periódus* (Entrepreneur education and the period of restoration) (Vezetéstudomány), 33:1, 12.

Szirmai, Péter and Krisztián Csapó (2005), *A Hungarian Experience of Entrepreneurship Teaching: Fostering Student Enterprises* (ISBE 2005 conference, Blackpool, 02.11.2005).

Internet-based references

The website of YBI: http://www.youth-business.org/

PART 2
Youth Entrepreneurship at Work:
A Comparison of New Member
Countries and Accession Countries

Chapter 5

The Strata of Young Entrepreneurs in Post-socialist Hungary: Chance or Illusion?

Mihály Laki

One of the favourite topics of debate in Hungarian politics is whether the young generation is among the winners or the losers of post-socialist transition. The representatives of the prevailing opposition (and influential intellectuals with critical attitudes towards post-socialist transition) focus on the high and growing *unemployment* of the young generation. Their argumentation is correct: the rate of unemployment in the group of the 20-24 year old Hungarians was 13.4% in 2004 and 17.5% in 2005. This number was much higher than the 6.1% and 7.0% yearly total average rate of unemployment in the same years and increased faster than the average (in 2005 by 4.10%) (Munkaerőpiaci tükör 2006, 18). One third of the 15-29 year olds was unemployed once or more in his/her life. Moreover, 42% of the respondents was afraid of being unemployed (Ifjúság 2004, Gyorsjelentés, 33). According to a recent survey, young Hungarians are aware of this problem. In 2000, 47%, and in 2004, 19% of them, defined unemployment as the most serious problem of the young generation (Ifjúság 2000, Gyorsjelentés, 65).

The representatives of the prevailing government (and influential intellectuals supporting the capitalist development of the country) emphasise the fast growing level of education and skills of the young generation. Their argumentation is correct as well. Since the collapse of socialism the number of higher education students increased very fast. In the school year of 1989/90, there were 72,381 and in 2005/6 there were 231,482 registered university and college students in Hungary (Munkaerőpiaci tükör 2005, 316).

Because of this development the level of education is much higher among the young generation than in the population at large. Other indicators of skill and knowledge show similar tendencies. The share of those who have a foreign language exam certificate was 23% in the group of 20-24, and 20% in the group of 25-29 years of age in 2004. On the other hand, only 4% of the 40-44 year olds has this type of certificate (Az idegennyelv 2004, 27). Young people use computer and internet more often than the Hungarian population at large (Gyorsjelentés 2001, 65). In spite of their divergent interpretations, the participants of the recent political debate agree that entrepreneurship may improve the position of this better educated but less employed part of the population. They conclude similarly: one of the important tasks of central and local governments is to support (to discriminate positively) the young entrepreneurs.

In this chapter, we shall analyse the probability and the feasibility of this attractive but trivial programme of Hungarian politicians and opinion leaders. A short overview of the development of private small businesses in post-socialist Hungary will help us to define the most important characteristics which improved the *probability of success* of Hungarian entrepreneurs in the post-socialist transition. Based on this analysis we will try to separate those subgroups of the young generation the members of which have or had any chance to establish and to manage successful (mainly small) businesses.

1. Prehistory

When and where communists came to power the whole economy was nationalised in a short period of time. Small businesses in towns and peasants' farms in the countryside were collectivised as well. Small nationalised units were concentrated (centralised) into big state-owned companies or huge co-operatives. There were only a few exceptions. The majority of the agricultural sector in Poland, a more than marginal part of the service sector (and a few small industrial firms) in the GDR (during the period of 1949-1972) and in Hungary remained in private hands.

The share of legal small businesses measured by indicators of labour statistics (Table 5.1) shows that a remarkable minority of the Hungarian population was involved in different forms of private sector activities. The sector's share in GDP was less impressive. It was only 3% in 1989, in the last year of the socialist system in Hungary. The extension of the private legal sector measured by share in physical assets was marginal as well. It was only 0.7% in 1989 (Laki 1998, 61).

The main reason for the permanent existence of this small private sector was the bad performance of the state sector. There were several signs that, since the beginning, the robust and highly centralised Stalinist command economy had worked in a very inefficient and chaotic manner. Controversial plan targets, lack of managerial skills and inefficient investments disturbed inter-firm relations and, as a consequence of these negative tendencies, permanent shortages of goods and services characterised the everyday life of the socialist economy (Kornai 1982).

According to the results of the social science of late socialism, only a small minority of those involved in this discriminated private economy showed entrepreneurial skills and motivations (Laky 1984; Vajda 1987). The majority of them belonged to the subsistence economy or shared its efforts between the private and the state sector. That is the reason why about 34% of private craftsmen were collaterally employed by the state in the last years of socialism. The owners of 1.5 million household plots were members of agricultural cooperatives as well. Many ventures, such as economic partnerships and registered private firms were dependent on symbolic (and at times parasitic) relationships with the large state-owned firms or semi-nationalised co-operatives. In connection with this strategy, the majority of private entrepreneurs *minimised the size of the firm and the volume of investment* as well. However, in spite of all the distortions caused by the system the private sector served as a pre-school for thousands of entrepreneurs in the post-communist era.

Table 5.1 Persons and firms active in the legal private sector in 1989 in Hungary

Branch	Number of persons	Number of firms
Craftsmen (industry, construction and services)		174,837
part time (having a job at the state sector)		54,446
Tradesmen in retail trade		39,612
Household and auxiliary plots		1,435,000
Members of economic partnerships	184,000*	
Economically active population 4,822,700		

* in 1987
Source: Statistical Yearbook of Hungary (1987), (1990).

The group of people involved in these registered private activities of the socialist economy was dominated by middle-aged urban males. The share of educated persons, with university or secondary school degrees, was higher than the average. Engineers and skilled workers were over-represented in this group as well (Vajda, 1987). It looks surprising but the share of communist party members was higher in this group than in the adult population at large.

2. Fast growth and radical changes of the private business community after 1989

The number of economic units grew extremely fast in the first years of post-socialist transition in Hungary (Table 5.2). Because of this development there are more than 1.2 million (mainly private-owned) economic organisations in Hungary in 2005. The population of the country is about 10 million – it means that less than every tenth Hungarian citizen is registered as a private entrepreneur. The favourable atmosphere created by the abolition of negative discrimination concerning private business, the radical deregulation and the small business protection policy of the new (freely elected) government were the main reasons for this development (Hanson and Heller 1993).

Part of the newly established small businesses were not conventional enterprises. Because of efficient tax avoiding tricks (details of which are not the topic of our chapter) owner-managers of several big or medium-sized private companies forced the workers to change their legal status. Working in the same workplace with unchanged technical conditions, they made contracts with the company as licensed entrepreneurs. Other popular subtypes of short-term single issue enterprises emerged in the first years of post-socialist transition as well. Because of the temporary reduction of imports, many companies were founded as well. After managing a few transactions these 'single issue businesses' ceased to exist.

We have to add here that a remarkable part of the registered enterprises is not active. No input and output was observed and declared by 20-30% of the economic organisations and therefore no tax was paid by them.

Table 5.2 Number of popular forms of economic organisations

	Company Limited		Individual Proprietorships	
	number	prev. year =100 %	number	prev. year =100%
1989	17341		320619	
1990	26807	154.6	393450	122.7
1991	43439	268.0	510459	129.7
1992	60762	164.0	608207	119.1
1993	86867	142.9	715105	117.6
1994	121128	139.4	778026	108.8
1995	106245	87.7	791496	101.7
1996	125940	118.5	745247	94.2
1997	147388	117.0	659690	88.5
1998	162588	110.3	648701	98.3
1999	165307	101.7	660139	101.7
2000	171495	103.9	682925	103.3
2001	177424	103.4	698001	102.1
2002	186744	105.2	708513	101.5
2003	197667	105.8	716729	101.2
2004	214151	108.3	717323	100.1
2005	228586	106.7	710838	99.0

Source: Statistical Yearbook of Hungary.

These distinctions and considerations reduce the number of the *de facto* existing enterprises but the numbers of active ones, compared to the data of 1989, show that the Hungarian business community has extended with hundreds of thousands of new participants since the collapse of the old regime.

The overwhelming majority of the newly founded and *de facto* existing enterprises remained very small. The number of the active individual proprietorships was 456,077 in 2004 and 99.6% of them employed 10 or fewer persons. The other group of economic organisations – called companies and partnerships (joint stock companies, limited liability companies, limited partnerships and co-operatives) – is dominated by small companies as well. The share of enterprises employing less than 10 persons was 96.7% in this group of economic organisations (Table 5.3).

Table 5.3 Companies and economic partnerships by size in 2005

Number of employees	Number of firms	%
500 or more	426	0.09
250-499	518	0.11
50-249	4823	0.96
20-49	10695	2.15
10-19	19102	3.84
1-9	270389	54.30
0 or unknown	191989	38.55
Total	497942	100.00

Source: Statistical Yearbook of Hungary.

The emerging society of entrepreneurs was dominated by 35-45 year old males. Town-dwellers were over-represented among them. As in the socialist period, they are relatively better educated than the population at large. The frequency of former communist party membership is above the average as well (Laki-Szalai 2004).

3. Privatisation

The huge wave of start-ups has contributed to the change of the ownership structure as well. The share of the state sector has diminished very fast since 1990. Sixteen years after the collapse of socialism the Hungarian economy is *dominated by the private sector* (Table 5.4).

The privatisation methods used by the Hungarian governments (namely the dominance of privatisation for sale method) gave strong preferences to the big and influential foreign investors. In connection with these applied methods of privatisation the permanent increase of the share of companies with dominant foreign owners was observable within the private sector. Foreign-dominated companies controlled more than half of the total subscribed capital in 2001.

There is no causal or functional relationship between size and ownership but we may observe strong tendencies. Foreigners, or the Hungarian state, are the dominant owners of big companies in the majority of cases. Typical owners of the medium-sized and big companies are Hungarian companies.

Hungarian private persons are the dominant owners of micro-, small- and medium-sized companies. In other words: small business is dominated by private persons, big business is controlled by multinationals or by state-owned companies, and the third sub-sector between the two is dominated by Hungarian companies which are usually founded by Hungarian companies or by groups of private persons.

Table 5.4 The distribution of the subscribed capital of enterprises with single and double entry in 1992-2003

	THE DOMINANT OWNER IS					
Year	State	Hungarian	Hungarian	Foreigner	Other	Total
		private person(s)	company			
1992	52.1	10.2	0.0	11.4	26.2	100.0
1994	44.5	10.7	17.6	17.8	9.5	100.0
1995	25.7	11.5	19.1	26.8	17.0	100.0
1997	13.5	10.5	22.6	35.0	18.4	100.0
1998	12.0	10.7	25.6	40.3	11.3	100.0
1999	9.2	9.1	20.6	51.6	9.5	100.0
2000	7.9	9.2	18.0	58.5	6.4	100.0
2001	7.7	8.8	17.0	60.1	6.4	100.0
2002+	12.3	13.9	24.5	40.2	9.9	100.0
2003+	13.3	12.9	22.0	44.2	7.7	100.0

+ The share of the subgroups has changed since 2000 because of the modifications in data collection.
Source: A kis és középvállalatok helyzete 2003, 57-58.

4. Career paths of the successful Hungarian entrepreneur-capitalists

There are remarkable exceptions in this *dual structure*. The second and third columns of Table 5.4 consist of medium-sized and big companies owned by Hungarian private persons or by shareholder companies with a Hungarian majority. The majority of these companies were able and willing to grow. The analysis of the history of such companies and of the career path of their owner-managers may help us to induce the most important *preconditions* of successful entry and activity of young entrepreneurs to the Hungarian market.

The number of interviews we have made in this group of Hungarian owner-managers was not enough to fulfil the requirements of representativeness. We produced a realistic sample, in which only the main branches of the Hungarian economy are represented. The majority of 48 owner-managers involved in the sample were male. (We had interviews with only three female owner-managers.) Thirty-seven of the 48 interviewed were highly educated (they finished university or high school), moreover two of them have a Ph.D. degree as well. The interviewed are owners of companies located either in the capital or in the countryside. The majority was born in villages but, typically, lives in Budapest now. Concerning their age, the majority was older than 40 on the day of the interview. The frequencies of these indicators are similar to those published by other Hungarian researchers (Kolosi-Sági 1997; Szalai 1997; Róbert 1999).

According to their knowledge, skills and social connections, similar owner-managers arrived from different directions and in a different manner to this social group. In the following parts of the chapter we distinguish the life periods in which owner-managers accumulated knowledge, skills, and personal connections, and the cross-roads (or revolutionary changes) when their path of life changed dramatically. With regard to the latter, we attached great importance to two turning points, i.e., the decision to accept or to refuse communist party membership, on the one hand, and the decision to remain in or to leave the state sector, on the other. These two strategic decisions deeply influenced their career in socialism and afterwards.

5. Accumulative periods

The interviewed owner-managers, *without exception*, spent some time as employed in the state-co-operative sector of the socialist economy. Therefore, *a part* of their knowledge, skills, and social connections was accumulated there. Their age and the extension of time they spent in the school system influenced not only the length of their presence but the *extent* of knowledge and skills accumulated in the socialist sector. The majority of the interviewed owner-managers passed more than the half of their working days in the socialist period which refers to the importance of socialism (and of the socialist sector) in the accumulation of skills and knowledge they have. Only 6 of the interviewed 48 started his or her career after 1980. It means that they passed less time in the socialist than in the post-socialist economy.

Table 5.5 consists of all the working places in the socialist sector occupied and mentioned by the interviewed persons. It shows that these owner-managers – like the majority of those employed in socialist Hungary – worked for big- and medium-sized state-owned companies with the highest occurrence (these companies predominated the socialist economy). They very often found jobs in the much smaller co-operative sector as well. Members of this group (which was characterised by a higher than average level of education) were present in great numbers at research institutes and at the institutions of higher education. *But they were markedly underrepresented in party and state organs and the large companies with exceptional status.*

Those who worked in the socialist sector in one company only are of the *insider-type*, while those who worked for more companies are characterised by *a company change type career path.* Those who have got higher and higher positions in the organisation(s) are characterised by an *upwardly moving,* and those who remained on the same level belong to the *horizontal* type career path.

A significant majority of the respondents (26 out of 48) belonged to the group of the upmoving company changers. It means that those who have started up and managed the majority of the large and medium-sized private companies involved were (according to the rules of the socialist economy) successful, and within the socialist sector, mobile.

Table 5.5 Working places in the state-co-operative sector before 1989 (mentioned by the interviewed)

Working place by size and/or sector	Number
Big state-owned companies with exceptional status (citadels of the labour class)	5
Big state-owned companies	32
Medium-sized state-owned companies	26
Agricultural industrial or consumption co-operatives and their joint venture companies	16
Small co-operatives	12
Banks and other financial organisations	1
Research institute, university, model farm	15
Non-productive sector (education, mass media, culture)	12
Total	129

Table 5.6 The highest position in the socialist sector

Position	Number
Staff (subordinate)	11
Foreman low ranking product manager	5
Middle ranking manager	20
General manager chairman director	12
Total	48

Another success indicator used by us is the highest position or rank in the state-co-operative sector of the socialist system. This indicator shows that the interviewed persons performed quite well. The majority of them left the sector as a middle-ranking manager or as a top leader of a state-owned company (general manager, director) or of a co-operative (Table 5.6).

The structure and the amount of accumulated knowledge, skills and personal relationships differ remarkably concerning the function of organisational units within the company. Table 5.7 informs us of the distribution of all the working positions in the state co-operative sector mentioned by the persons interviewed. The relatively high number of staff (subordinate) positions agrees with our earlier statement about the occurrence of the up-moving careers. A high number of respondents started on the low levels of the hierarchy and moved up to higher positions later. *The respondents managed a lower level unit of the company's organisation or they were members of the top management of a state-owned company or of the co-operative in about two-thirds (64) of the higher positions (104).* The occurrence of the so-called functional positions (like finance book-keeping or research) was much less. It is not surprising that working positions in the non-economic spheres were mentioned less frequently.

Table 5.7 Labour positions in the state-co-operative sector in the period of socialism (mentioned by the interviewed)

Labour position	Number
Worker, administrative employee	26
Subordinated engineer, agronomist, technician	
Economist, research worker	37
Manager of a unit within the company +	36
Manager or deputy manager of the company	
(incl. co-operatives and small co-operatives)	28
Head of department of sale, procurement or marketing	9
Head of department for organisation	2
Head of department of finance planning or book-keeping	4
Head of technical development or R and D	5
Quality control	1
Small enterprise for R and D	3
Party worker	3
Employed by the state administration	3
Teacher journalist adult educator	7
Total	164

+ Units organised for doing the main activity of the company (workshop, plant, factory, management of construction, store, network of shops, service plant).

6. The turning points in the path of life

The interviewed owner-managers with several similarities concerning their life story and skills made sharply different decisions at *the turning points* of their path of life. The acceptance or refusal of communist party membership was an exceptional event and an extraordinary momentum in their life. Those who refused or avoided joining the HSWP expected a moderate career path only.

The share of party members was much higher among these interviewed than in the adult population. Party membership was declared by more than one-third of the group (18 of the 48).

Another important turning point was when the persons interviewed decided that they would go to the private or remain in the state co-operative sector of the socialist economy. The share of those who worked in the state-co-operative sector alone was quite big till the end of socialism, and only after 1989 they went to the private sector. But those who, mainly in the first part of the eighties, went over to the legal private sector or kept their job in the state-owned companies or institutions but were active in the private sector *collaterally*, were a slight majority.

These strategic decisions made by our interviewees exercised mutual influence. The majority of the former party members worked only in the state-co-operative sector before 1989 (Table 5.8). The majority of those who left the socialist sector before 1989 were non-party members. Those who spent longer time in the state co-operative sector (mainly party members) occupied higher and decisive positions in the company hierarchy more often than those (mainly non-party members) who left the state-co-operative sector partly or totally.

Table 5.8 Party membership and sector changes

	Career types		
Party membership before 1989	state-co-operative working places only	collaterally working in the state and private sector	before 1989 joined the private sector
Total			
Party member 18	11	5	2
Non-party member 30	12	5	13
Total	23	10	15 48

7. Special/ exceptional skills and knowledge

We have seen that the life stories of Hungarian owner-managers contain many common elements: the majority of them is characterised by higher education qualifications. They accumulated knowledge and skills in:

- managing organisational units;
- comparing costs and benefits;
- company planning;
- mobilising market relationships.

These elements of their human capital increased the probability of success. But we may argue that there are several thousands of Hungarians with similar combinations of accumulated knowledge, but without a significant amount of accumulated wealth or capital. But a more detailed content analysis of the interviews showed that a decisive part of our sample of owner-managers have learned and accumulated special, and in the post-socialist environment, very useful experiences.

1. Because of the slowdown of the Hungarian economy and of Comecon trade, a growing number of the state-owned companies could not sell their products or services. The top managers (who remained in duty till the end of the socialism)

of these companies or co-operatives were forced to learn some elements of *crisis management.*

2. In the period of radical reforms of the eighties, the legislation abolished or weakened the strict size limits of the private enterprise. High ranking reform-minded officials of the communist party used the party-controlled mass media and sent entrepreneurship-supporting messages to the public. In this changing socio-economic environment several private entrepreneurs *modified* the well-prepared former business strategy. Instead of "classical" local market-oriented small businesses, they created sophisticated *networks of formally independent, privately owned economic units.* These structures of legally independent units were practically medium-sized private companies. There were a lot of cases in which these networks competed successfully on the national or the international market.

8. Different ways of property acquisition

These private entrepreneurs of late socialism, as well as managers of state companies and co-operatives, who often accumulated special skills of crisis management, discovered at the end of the eighties, in a very early period of the fast and radical social changes, that the socialist system collapsed and *therefore the formulation and implementation of a radically new life strategy was unavoidable. They understood that a revolutionary and very exceptional historical period was coming.* Analysing the interviews, we might observe different start ups and acquisition strategies:

1. A separate group is formed by those who mobilised some private capital and a significant amount of preferential loans, and in the course of privatisation became the main and/or decisive owner of the company in which they were employed.

2. Another group of property acquirers consists of those who – using their accumulated money or assets or the accumulated money of others – bought, and later sold for a third party, companies or shares of companies which were tendered by the State Property Agency for privatisation.

3. We may classify those who *established a new private company* (or companies) before or after the collapse of the socialist system in a separate group. The invested money, and therefore their own share, was not significant in these cases. They had, or acquired, a relatively modest amount of money or physical assets which were necessary to start up a small or micro business.

4. There is the group of those who *combined the above-mentioned methods of property acquisition:* they established new companies and took part in privatisation projects as well.

The differences concerning the methods of property acquisition and of company establishment related mainly to the different career paths and property-acquiring strategies which were chosen at the turning points of the life path of the respondents. The refusal or acceptance of party membership, the timing and radicalism of departure from the state-co-operative sector and, in connection with these two factors, their highest position and rank in the organisational structures of the state-owned companies and co-operatives, deeply influenced their chances and methods in property acquisition in the post-socialist period.

The *former party members acquired property mainly by the privatisation of their working places.* Members of this group included those who established new companies and participated in privatisation projects too. The correlation is working inversely as well: *the majority of non-party members were not involved in privatisation but founded new companies.*

The remaining in, or the departure from, the state co-operative sector also influenced the method of property acquisition. Those who remained in the state co-operative sector till 1989 acquired assets by participating in privatisation more often than those who left the sector earlier (or worked parallely in the socialist and in the private sector). On the other hand, the share of those who established new companies is higher among those who left the state co-operative sector earlier.

It is not surprising then, that mainly party members and deputy general managers who remained loyal to 'their' companies (and to their positions, of course), after the collapse of socialism, usually acquired property as 'privatisers'. On the other hand, mainly non-party member subordinates and lower rank managers who moved into the private sector earlier usually acquired property by funding new companies.

Table 5.9 Main methods of acquisition

Turning point indicators	Privatisation	Founding of new companies
Party membership	rather party member	rather non party member
Rank or position	rather top manager	rather staff member
Sector changes	rather remained in the socialist sector till 1989	rather moved into the private sector before 1989

Based on this very simple statistical analysis of a small sample of the persons interviewed (keeping in evidence the mixed cases), we summarised the characteristic linkages and common occurrences in Table 5.9.

9. Old and exceptional managerial skills in a new environment

Not only their methods and chances of property acquistion were different but the owner-managers with different origins applied different methods in the *operation* of their property as well. The main task of those who acquired property by privatisation was crisis management and the reconstruction of stagnating or declining medium-sized and large companies. Those who established small private companies were forced to produce the financial and market conditions for the extremely fast growth of their businesses.

The connection between past experiences and the future is exceptionally clear here. The same set of skills helped them to adapt to the changed circumstances and new conflicts of the subsequent period of gradual economic stabilisation which did not automatically conclude in preferable conditions for entrepreneurship. But for these people, steady shortfall of capital, frequent constraints in liquidity, uncertainties in the legal embedding of business, etc. have been difficulties resembling 'old' crises in a new shape, hence, they have been responding with 'old' forms of manoeuvring – though also in new shapes. In other words, their most appropriate reaction to all these challenges has been to mobilise the above-described skills in crisis-management, and simultaneously, to adapt these with invention and flexibility to the radically changed conditions of the present.

10. The chances to be a young entrepreneur in the 21st century

According to the strong anti-capitalist sentiments of the Hungarian public (Angelusz-Tardos, 1997), there is a popular *mono-causal explanation* for the emergence and the recruiting of the new entrepreneurial-capitalist strata of the post-socialist Hungarian society. We may interpret these beliefs in the following manner: the members of the *nomenclature* (as participants of a conspiracy, see Tellér, 1999) or only those following the logic of spontaneous development (Staniszkis 1991; Hankiss 1989) were able to convert their political privileges and influence into economic power in the turbulent circumstances of the post-socialist transition. Privatisation combined with state capture and corruption was the dominant method of this transfer.

This argumentation coincides with the popular opinion that the young generation missed the train of privatisation, therefore – except for a few – they are among the losers of the post-socialist transition. The political implication of this argumentation is that *positive discrimination* of the huge strata of losers, including young people with entrepreneurial aspirations, should counterbalance the disadvantages caused by the 'unfair' recruitment of the strata of new capitalists. There are elements of our short history on Hungarian private entrepreneurship which fit into this mono-causal explanation.

Table 5.2 shows that the number of limited companies and individual proprietorships increased much faster in the period of 1989-1996 than in 1997-2005. *The growing risk of market entry* contributed to this radical modification of the trend. In the first years of the transition the main competitors of the new entrants were the nearly collapsed state-owned companies. In the second period, the late-comers competed not only with earlier established small and medium-sized Hungarian private companies. Huge and very aggressive multinationals, the market share of which continuously increased, entered the Hungarian market as well (Table 5.4). We have to add that the transfer of state-owned companies into private hands ended in the first years of the new century, therefore the property acquisition by privatisation is now practically impossible. It is therefore not a surprise that according to the last international comparisons Hungary – where the entrepreneurial inclination was very high in the first year of transition (see Lengyel 1997-1998) – is not among the forerunner countries concerning entrepreneurial activities (Szerb-Márkus 2006).

The modified life strategy and changing aspirations of several young Hungarians strengthened this development. The share of 20-24 year olds who were registered in higher education was 24% in 2000 and increased to 38% in 2004. We may observe similar tendencies in the group of 25-29 year olds where the share of the registered in high education increased from 4% to 12% in this period (Gyorsjelentés 2000, 2004). The share of entrepreneurs (young people with licences) remained 8-9% in these age groups in the meantime. With other words: a growing share of the young generation tried to avoid unemployment by going into or remaining in the educational system instead of starting a business. (The picture is, in reality, more complicated because half of university students have second jobs.) Based on a recent study, we may recognise that the future plans of Hungarian university students show similar tendencies (Szerb-Márkus 2006). The majority of them would like to be an employee of a company or of a governmental institution. Only 12.4% of the questioned university students mentioned that he or she has entrepreneurial plans or expectations for the future such as working for the family-owned company, buying or franchising a company, buying shares of a company, being self-employed, or starting a new business (Szerb-Márkus 2006, 8).

11. State promotional programmes

In the first years of post-socialist transition, when the number of business start-ups, and therefore the number of companies, increased extremely fast, it seemed obvious that this process would, spontaneously, partly counterbalance the negative effects of unemployment without the strong and permanent support of the central and local governments.

The development of *the education of business skills and knowledge* illustrates well these beliefs and hopes of the first stage of the post-socialist transition. Instead of central or local governments, the representatives of civil society discovered how important it is to teach business skills and knowledge in the attempt to counter unemployment (Darázs-Szomor-Szűcsné-Varga 2004). In the first years of the post-socialist transition voluntary/private non-profit organisations like the Young Enterprise Foundation, the Junior Achievement Foundation Hungary, the SEED Foundation for Small Business Development, and the National Association of Teachers of Business Skills introduced and implemented teaching programmes of business skills in secondary schools. These programmes were not supported by the state at that time. The second stage started in 1995 (This was the first year when the growth of the number of new business starts slowed down!) when the law on the National Core Curriculum defined the teaching of these skills and knowledge as a compulsory part of the curriculum of secondary schools (Darázs-Szomor-Szűcsné-Varga 2004, 1).

The teaching, at universities, of business skills and knowledge started with spontaneous actions too, as a part of the Hungarian universities and colleges of natural or human sciences recognised the growing demand for this kind of skills and knowledge. The government declared the importance of these courses and disciplines a few years later (Szerb-Márkus 2006, 11). The support for the young generation's business start-ups showed similar tendencies. Especially non-profit or civil organisations played a decisive role in supporting the business start-ups of the young generation in the first years.

12. Concluding remarks

This short presentation shows that the politicians, and therefore, the Hungarian state (especially in the period of the decline of the entrepreneurial inclination) recognised not only the growing unemployment of the young generation but the importance of these support programmes and activities as a tool for increasing the chances of employment. *But the philosophy of the state support is not clear.*

If the successes of the new capitalists are *only* the result of their social status in the communist past (the fact that they were members of the nomenclature), the task of the central or the local governments is to support *all those* who were excluded from the strata of the privileged.

In the previous parts of the chapter we tried to deny the validity of the mono-causal explanation. We agreed that party membership and a higher position in the management of state-owned companies increased the probability of successful property acquisition. But we have found other events, accumulated skills, knowledge and routines in the life stories of Hungarian owner-managers of small and medium-sized companies which influenced the chances of successful property management as deeply as party membership or a position in the decision-making bodies of a state-owned company or co-operative.

From the point of view of the designers of support programmes, this *multi-causal explanation* of business success is not so favourable. Instead of supporting, as much as possible, talented and ambitious young applicants as losers of the post-socialist developments, they have to evaluate *the differences* of the applicants measured by accumulated knowledge, skills, location, and money available. Based on the results of such a complicated process of evaluation, they have to rank the aspirant entrepreneurs. They have to take into account the great social and cultural differences within the young generation. They have to take into consideration that the rate of unemployment of young people is much higher in the villages than in the large towns. It is higher in the Eastern than in the more developed Western regions of the country and higher in the less educated groups than in the more educated ones.

We assume that those who show more similarities to the above described group of successful owner-managers – who are better educated and accumulated some sort of managerial experiences and those who are able to mobilise saved money or other family assets – have better chances to enter the market and therefore to belong to the entrepreneurial society. There are several signs that the designers and managers of support programmes have different values. If they are ready and able to support the disadvantaged, they have to ignore the above-mentioned factors of probability of success. But they have to take into consideration that these different values do not only regard different success indicators, but may modify the costs and benefits of the program as well.

References

Angelusz, Róbert and Tardos, Róbert (1997), 'Az átalakulás és a közvélemény arcai', *Társadalmi Szemle*, Nr. 3., 3-23.

Az idegennyelv-ismeret Magyarországon (2004), *Jelentés az országos nyelvtudásfelmérés kvantitatív szakaszáról* (Budapest: Medián).

Darázs, Dóra, Szomor, Tamás, Szűcsné, Szabó, Katalin and Varga, Zoltán (2004), 'Gazdasági ismeretek oktatása a fővárosi iskolákban', *Új Pedagógiai Szemle* Nr.2.

Fueglistaller, Urs, Klandt, Heinz, Halter, Frank (2006), 'International Survay on Collegiate Entrepeneurship', University of St. Gallen, European Business School.

Gray, Cherryl W., Hanson, Rebecca, Heller, Michael (1993), 'Legal reform for Hungary's Private Sector', *Acta Oeconomica*, Vol. 45 (3-4), 269-300.

Hankiss, Elemér (1989), *Kelet-európai alternatívák* (Budapest: Közgadasági és Jogi Kiadó).

Ifjúság, Gyorsjelentés (2001) (ed.), *László Laki, Andrea Szabó, Bauer, Béla* (Budapest: Nemzeti Ifjúságkutató Intézet).

Ifjúság, Gyorsjelentés (2005) (ed.), *László Laki, Andrea Szabó, Béla Bauer* (Budapest: Nemzeti Ifjúságkutató Intézet).

Kolosi, Tamás and Sági, Matild (1997), Az új tőkésosztály megitélése in', *A tulajdon kötelez. Az új tőkésosztály társadalmi szerepéről ed. Hankiss, Elemér – Matko, István* (Budapest: Figyelő).

Kornai, János (1992), *The Socialist System. Political Economy of Communism* (Princeton/New Jersey: Princeton University Press).

Laki, Mihály (1998), *Kisvállalkozás a szocializmus után* (Budapest: Közgazdasági Szemle Alapítvány).

Laki, Mihály and Szalai, Júlia (2004), *Vállalkozók vagy polgárok? A nagyvállalkozók gazdasági és trársadalmi helyzetének ambivalenciái az ezredforduló Magyarországán* (Budapest: Osiris Kiadó).

Laki, Mihály and Szalai, Júlia (2006), 'The puzzle of success: Hungarian grand entrepreneurs at the turn of the millennium', *Europe Asia Studies*, Vol. 58. No. 3, 317–345.

Laky, Teréz (1984), 'Mítoszok és valóság', *Valóság*, January pp 1-17.

Lengyel, György (1997/1998), 'Entrepreneurial inclination in Hungary, 1988-1996', *International Journal of Sociology*, 27 (4), Winter 36-49.

Munkaerőpiaci, Tükör (2006) (ed.) Károly Fazekas, Jenő Koltay (Budapest: MTA Közgazdaságtudományi Intézet).

Róbert, Péter (1999), 'Kikből lettek a vállalkozók? A vállalkozóvá válás meghatározó tényezői Magyarországon a kommunizmus előtt, alatt és után', *Közgazdasági Szemle* Nr.5, 403-428.

Staniszkis, Jadwiga (1991), 'Political capitalism in Poland', *East European Politics and Societies*, Vol. 5. No. 1, 127-144.

Szerb, László and Márkus, Gábor (2006), 'Karrierelvárások és vállalkozóvá válás az egyetemi hallgatók körében Magyarországon, nemzetközi összehasonlításban', mimeo.

Szirmai, Peter (2006), 'Increasing Youth Employment Opportunities by Assisting Business Start-ups (the Hungarian experience)', mimeo.

Szalai, Erzsébet (1997), 'Kaleidoszkóp. A nagyvállalatok, a nagyvállalati vezetők és a nagyvállalkozók megújulási készségéről', *Közgazdasági Szemle* No. 12, 1075-1090.

Tellér, Gyula (1999), *Hatalomgyakorlás az MSZP-SZDSZ koalíció idején* (Budapest: Kairosz Kiadó).

Vajda, Ágnes (1987), A kisiparosok és kiskereskedők mobilitása I-II, *Statisztikai Szemle*, No. 4., Nr. 6.

Voszka, Éva (2000) ,Tulajdonosi szerkezet és vállalatirányítás a magyar nagyiparban Közgazdasági', *Szemle* No. 8-9, 549-565.

Chapter 6

Supporting Youth Entrepreneurship: The Case of Poland

Aleksander Surdej

Introduction

Post-communist transformations can be described as policy-induced, multidimensional social change accelerated by the impact of economic openness and globalization. This policy was initiated in Poland in the late 1980s, first as economic reforms within the socialist system, then as transformations towards market economy (Kolodko 1999).

It should be stressed that the socialist economy in Poland, like in Hungary, was not a monolithic state-owned economy as the socialist state allowed for a relatively broad scope of private economic activities. Thus, for instance, private farmers retained approximately 80 percent of land and private firms played a significant role in retail trade and construction. Yet, these private economic activities used to have a supplementary role to the state sector: the socialist ideology and the government control of the economy limited their growth possibility.

From the mid-1980s onwards, the socialist state started to loosen the control of economic activities and even encouraged the growth of small enterprises. As a result the number of private companies increased by almost 0.2m to reach 0.572 by 1988 when on 23 December 1988 the parliament passed a "revolutionary" law on economic activities proclaiming the freedom of enterprise and simplifying administrative requirements for business activities. Only in 1989 the number of enterprises increased by 50 percent in response to the changing economic policy and announced gradual political democratization – thus, to an extent Poland was prepared for the launching of economic transformations towards market economy.

The programme of postcommunist economic transformations, the so-called Balcerowicz plan, launched in January 1990, was not, despite claims to the contrary, comprehensively designed and precisely implemented, but rather it was based on some rather crude policy concepts and general ideas about the direction of changes. One of the dominant assumptions was the belief in the need of shock therapy characterized by a broad scope and rapid pace of economic changes which would set off the process of "creative destruction". Initially the government policy was thus conceived as "negative" consisting of *not-impeding* and *not-acting* and the idea of building an adequate institutional and legal framework for the market economic came to the attention of policy makers only in mid-1990s.

Throughout the 1990s the central organizing idea of economic and social policies consisted of moving responsibility for one's life and wellbeing from the state and other collective bodies to individuals. Politicians kept repeating that individuals and families are expected to take advantage of new opportunities and chances, and to cope with emerging challenges and threats. In a typical formulation it used to be stressed that democratization has granted political and civil freedoms and economic liberalization has opened opportunities to start own business.

What was however neglected is that new opportunities could not be and in fact have not been exploited by all members of society since taking advantage of new opportunities required experience, specific skills, initial resources or, at least, a good position in the facilitating network of incumbent managers or policy makers (see the phenomenon of the *nomenklatura* as a capitalist class examined by Maria Łoś and Andrzej Zybertowicz, Los and Zybertowicz 2000). Researchers have confirmed that in general the opportunities offered by post-communist transformations have been better exploited by people, who were well-educated, entrepreneurial, with higher professional skills and who were relatively young (Domanski 2002). Conversely, costs like unemployment, poverty and marginalization have fallen with some regularity on the poorly educated, with low skills and living in rural areas. In addition, in the late 1990s researchers have discovered to their surprise that economic security is higher amidst the elderly than among the young. This has been the result of the fact that the bulk of social transfers was directed to the elderly who also benefited from the generous system of pre-retirement and that the young were vulnerable to the threat of unemployment, low pay and work in precarious employment (Marody 2003).

Gradually social researchers have confirmed with empirical data that several social groups did experience problems with adapting to and coping with radical changes in the socio-economic conditions of their lives. Research has allowed to distinguish "three kinds of Poland", that is three important social categories of Poles differentiated according to their sources of income and subsequently to economic opportunities. There were: "the entrepreneurial Poland", "the Poland of dependent workers" and "the Poland of welfare recipients" (Hausner and Marody 1999). Although these types of income groups are encountered universally, the Polish peculiarity is their socio-economic characteristics and low inter-type mobility. Thus, "the Poland of welfare recipients" is composed chiefly of people from rural areas, villages and small cities, that is, people with low skills, low educational attainments and low professional and geographical mobility, although they are not very old, being often slightly above 50.

At the end of 1990s, and in the beginning of 21st century, Poland experienced a parallel dramatic increase of unemployment and the coming to the labour market of the young born in the baby boom years of early 1980s. Such conditions made youth, as will be shown later, one of the social groups most vulnerable to labour market exclusion. In such a situation the attention of policy makers has been directed towards the search of ways to facilitate labour market participation and to increase the entrepreneurial activities of the Polish youth.

1. Labour Market Changes in Poland in 1990-2005

From the beginning of the 1990s the Polish labour market has undergone deep transformations exemplified by such indicators as the total number of employees, the unemployment rate and the rate of employment. The whole postcommunist transformation period can be divided into three main subperiods with regard to the basic characteristics of the labour market.

Table 6.1 Economically active persons by employment status (in thousands)

	1990	1995	1998	2000	2002
Public sector	8,243.4	5,623.1	4,671.3	3,988.5	4,182.0
Private sector	7,902.0	9,506.0	11,249.8	11,170.7	9,876.0
Employers and self employed	4,990.4	5,261.5	5,648.0	5,578.6	5,421.6

Source: Yearbook of Labour Statistics, 2001; GUS, Warszawa, 2001 and 2003.

The initial period of economic transformation, dating from 1990 till the end of 1994, was characterized by the declining number of employed and the rate of employment together with the sharp rise of unemployment. The main cause of such changes were bankruptcies and the restructuring of state-owned enterprise which used to massively shed the labour force. The private sector grew rapidly but was still unable to absorb redundant workers from the public sector. As a result, the rate of labour market participation of the population between 15-64 fell by several percentage points amounting to 68.4 percent and the unemployment rate reached 14.8 percent.

Fast economic growth in the years 1995-1998 led to the improvement of the labour market situation. The number of employees increased to 14.8m persons and the unemployment rate decreased to 10.8 percent, but nevertheless the labour market participation rate fell to 66.1 percent.

The third period began at the end of 1998, when, despite a still relatively high rate of economic growth, the employment trend got reversed. During 1999, the number of employees decreased by 0.7m, the employment rate grew to 16.4 percent and the labour market participation rate decreased to 54.9 percent. The labour market situation got stabilized in the subsequent year, but it deteriorated later with the economic slowdown which started in 2000 and lasted till the end of 2002. Between 2000 and 2002 the number of employed declined by 0.76m, the number of unemployed increased by 0.6m, the labour market participation rate fell by 3.5 percent and the unemployment rate reached 20.1 percent in early 2003 (MGiP, 2005). The return on the path of faster economic growth in 2003 did contribute to the gradual fall of the unemployment rate which fell to 19.5 percent in September 2003, 18.9 percent in September 2004, 17.6 percent in September 2005 and to 15.3 percent in September 2006.

Although the labour market situation in terms of unemployment rate was similar to the EU-15 average in 1998, it has deteriorated since and turned unemployment into the main socio-economic problem of contemporary Poland, placing the country at the bottom of the European league of employment. In addition, it became obvious that Poland would not reach the labour market participation rate set in the Lisbon Strategy in the foreseeable future.

The economic analysis shows that some important features of the Polish labour market, such as an early economic desactivation, a low average level of human capital and a large share of employment in agriculture have a structural character, that is, their change requires a long period of time and long-term oriented policy measures.

As economic theory and empirical evidence show age is one of most important factors influencing the economic behaviour of people and their position on the labour market. It is a general regularity that labour market opportunities are the worst at both ends of the age structure. In the beginning of the economic transformation Polish decision-makers focused their attention on the problem of the low adaptability of older people to new economic circumstances. Thus, older people (aged 55 and over) were encouraged to leave the labour market, to go on early retirement or to take so called "bridging pensions" (*emerytury pomostowe*) in the hope that this would "free the place for the young". As a result an average age to go on retirement amounted in the mid-1990s to 55 for women and 57 for women (Cain and Surdej 1996), thus almost 5 to 8 years before the statutory pension age. Although between 1997 and 2001 the total number of inactive in the age group 55-65 did not increase, the share of economically active in this age group decreased from 35 to 31 percent. The low rate of labour market participation in the age group 55-65 has resulted in a relatively low unemployment rate characterizing this group. Thus, for instance, in 1998 despite an 18 percent unemployment rate, the unemployed accounted only for 2 percent of the economically active people in the age group 55-65. The phenomenon of low labour market participation of older people has persisted till now despite the general improvement of the labour market situation.

Table 6.2 Number and age structure of unemployed in 2004 and 2005

Age groups	Number of unemployed			
	December 2004		June 2005	
	in 1,000	%	in 1,000	%
Total	2.999.6	100.0	2.827.4	100.0
18-24	728.2	24.3	650.0	23.0
25-34	844.7	28.2	794.9	28.1
35-44	628.5	20.9	585.3	20.7
45-54	681.8	22.7	666.5	23.6
55-59	101.3	3.4	113.9	4.0
60–64	15.1	0.5	16.8	0.6

Source: GUS Statistical Yearbook, 2006.

In the beginning of the 1990s, in contrast to older workers, the young aged 18-35 were believed to be the socio-demographic group having least difficulties in getting jobs, promotion and higher wages. This belief seemed to be confirmed by the economic developments until mid-1990s. But, the economic slowdown of 1998-2001 and in parallel the inflow on the labour market of numerous cohorts born in the baby boom years in the beginning of the 1980s (the cohorts of baby boomers are more numerous, by 200,000, than the cohorts of "normal" years) has drastically worsened the labour market situation of the Polish youth. Although the labour market situation started to improve from 2003 onwards, in 2004 the unemployment rate of youth was still more than double the total unemployment rate, amounting to 41.1 percent according to the BAEL measure (*Badanie Aktywnosci Ekonomicznej Ludnosci* – Research of Economic Activities of Population).

The labour market situation of youth has worsened further due to the effects of demographic change. Demographers agree that in the long run Poland faces risks and challenges which are similar to those encountered in other European societies – that is, the ageing of the population and by 2030 the reduction of the population. This trend has been amplified by the lengthening of life expectancy. After a temporary decline in the beginning of the 1990s, an increase of life expectancy has been registered. In 1990 the life expectancy at birth was 66.50 years for male, and for women 75.50, in 2000 it was for men already 69.72 and for women 77.91. Polish demographers have calculated that as a result the share of people over 65 which amounted to 12.3 percent in 2000 is going to increase to 14.7 percent in 2015 and to 21.2 percent in 2030 if the current fertility rate remains unchanged (Strzelecki 2003).

The combination of demographic and conjectural factors did produce the tightening of labour market conditions for youth. Thus, between the end of 1998 and mid-2004 the number of working young people fell by 0.49m, whereas at the same time the number of unemployed in this age group increased by 0.3m and the number of economically inactive went up by 0.215m. The analysis of labour market changes in the years 1997-2001 proves that the Polish youth was particularly vulnerable to adverse economic developments. The BAEL research data show that in 1997 the flows of the young between 15 and 24 from unemployment to work was easier than for the group of old between 25 and 34, but in 2001 the tendency reversed and the very young faced more difficulties in transiting from unemployment to work. It seems just justified to say that difficult labour market conditions favor prime-age workers at the expense of the very young.

It is also worth stressing that a large part of the Polish youth has displayed increasing educational aspirations by prolonging their education to the tertiary level in the expanded sector of paid higher education institutions. This phenomenon has led to the increase of the number of students from approximately 0.4m in 1991 to 1.9m in 2006 and to the increase in the share of students in the age group 19-24 from approximately 12 percent to almost 50 percent.

**Table 6.3 Employment rate according to the level of education
(average for 2000-2004)**

Level of education	Unemployment rate (%)
Higher	6.7
High	19.2
Vocational	22.5
Elementary and lower	24.3

Source: Zatrudnienie 2005, MGiP, Warsaw, p. 66.

A large part of this increased motivation to study might be explained as a rational adaptation strategy since the data that show that the level of education is negatively correlated with the incidence of unemployment. But empirical evidence points also to the threat of being overqualified for jobs which are available, or misqualified as matching jobs and formal qualifications has become difficult in modern economies. Thus, for instance, graduates of management or marketing studies face problems with getting a job in line with their specialization as more than half of all Polish students study these specializations.

With the increased number of persons with a higher education diploma it has been recognized that the threat of unemployment is related less to the lack of appropriate level of education than to the lack of job experience. In 2002 the government started a programme called "First job" (described at some length later). Young people in turn have started to mix, whenever possible, education and work and Polish universities have started to develop work placement offices and to help students to get their first job experience as early as possible.

2. Youth Unemployment in Rural Poland

Analyzing the phenomenon of unemployment in Poland one cannot omit the situation in the country side since almost 40 percent of Poles live in rural areas. It has been estimated that open unemployment in the country side amounts to 0.8-1m persons, but besides people registered in labour offices as unemployed there are as much as 0.9m persons who should be counted as in hidden unemployment, that is *de facto* idle, not working people who nevertheless are not registered since they are part of farmers' families (Kolarska-Bobińska, Rosner and Wilkin 2001). This high number of unemployed and underutilized, low productivity people would be further augmented if we add people who are likely to quit farming as the size of farms, at present on average smaller their Western European counterparts, would come closer to the EU average. It is expected that in the near future the employment in agriculture might decrease by 2.1m persons.

Unemployment in rural Poland will continue to rise until 2010 because the working age population in Poland has been growing from the late 1990s yearly by

250,000 persons and 2/3 of this growth is concentrated in rural areas. After 2010 the working age population in Poland will stagnate and then decline.

Income and living conditions in rural Poland and small cities are worse than in large cities. Not surprisingly thus less than 40 percent of young people living there declare their plans to stay in the country side. Others want to leave for cities or to emigrate abroad.

The changes of the employment structure in Poland are especially difficult as there is a shortage of low cost apartments in cities and most jobs available are poorly paid. Against such background it is not surprising to observe a large emigration of young people after Poland's accession to the EU in May 2004. As of Fall 2006 it is estimated that after accession to the EU approximately 0.8m Poles emigrated to the EU countries. Half of this number went to work in Great Britain. According to the available data approximately 80 percent of the emigrated is below 35. Many of them have higher education diplomas and accept skill downgrading in exchange for any job with salaries higher than in Poland. This wave of emigration has reduced the scale of unemployment, but on the other hand it might exacerbate demographic problems Poland would face if a high share of the emigrants stay abroad for all working life.

3. The Shadow Economy and Youth

The analysis of economic activities of Poles will be incomplete, if no attention is paid to the size of the shadow economy in Poland. The shadow economy emerged in Poland in the 1980s, but its nature and characteristics were changing over years, shaped by post-communist economic transformations. Throughout 1990s the shadow economy has been present in almost all areas of economic activities in Poland.

Employment in the shadow economy, named also informal employment, is most of the time a precarious employment as people are not protected by the labour law or collective agreements and they are not building up their future economic security by contributing to the system of social security.

Table 6.4 Estimation of shadow economy in creation of GDP in 1995-1997

In %	1995	1996	1997	1998	1999	2004
GDP without shadow economy	100	100	100	100	100	100
GDP with shadow economy	116.6	115.9	115.2	115.3	114.5	113.5

Source: Grabowski (2002) and Ministry of Finance, Warsaw.

The estimations of the size of the shadow economy in Poland vary between 12 and 27 percent (Schneider and Enste 2002), although the true share likely oscillates around 13-14 percent. Some authors argued (Kloc 1998) that the shadow economy and informal employment of the 1980s and early 1990s were indispensable for individuals' wellbeing (if not for their survival), but it is surprising to realize that the size of the shadow economy in Poland has stabilized at a relatively high level. High unemployment has been the main cause for people to get involved into informal employment. Relatively high tax rates have been the main motive for businesses to employ unregistered labour and to perform unregistered business operations.

National statistical office (GUS) reports that in mid-1990s 2.5m people were employed in the shadow economy, which amounted to 16.4 percent of registered employment. 14 percent worked for officially registered private entities, while 70 percent were employed by households and 12 percent were self-employed. For 1.1m unregistered employment was the main source of income, while for 1.4m it was an additional source of income.

The research data shows that almost all age groups and socio-professional categories participate in the informal economy. But, research shows that informal employment is more frequently encountered among men than women, and that 45 percent of the informally employed is not older than 34. The 1999 GUS study concludes that informal employment is usually short-term, casual, and that it is an additional form of employment. Only 4.2 percent of respondents conceive it as a stable, main source of work (GUS 1999). Informal employment in Poland seems to be a diffused, but "shallow" phenomenon.

Table 6.5 Shadow economy employment by socio-professional structure in 1995

Socio-economic category	Share (in %)
Employed	57
Unemployed	16
Pensioners and retirees	11
Students	9
Farmers	4
Economically inactive	3

Source: Kloc (1998), 45.

Informal employment has been a shelter for youth searching for jobs and income. But, the jobs available there have been predominantly low paid and casual, not offering stable employment and good income prospects.

4. Development of Small and Medium Sized Enterprises in Poland

The fast growth of small private companies in the first years after the start of postcommunist transformations can be considered one of the greatest successes of Polish reforms. The fast recovery from the deep economic recession of the period 1990-1991 was in large part due to the outburst of entrepreneurship of many Poles. These years were also the years of so called "small privatization", that is the privatization of retail trade and economic facilities owned by Polish communities (*gminas*). Small privatization was an important leverage in the process of accumulating capital and increasing the scale of business activities, but in general the initial economic growth was dominated by micro-enterprises employing between less than 10 employees (Grabowski 1996). At the end of 1996, there was in Poland approximately 2.4m small and medium sized enterprises and they accounted for 40 percent of the GDP. These companies created 1.5m new jobs in the period from 1990 till 1994 (Woodward 1999).

The second half of the 1990s strengthened the position of Polish SMEs, but their development was not very spectacular neither in quantitative, nor in qualitative terms. In 2004, the SMEs accounted for 47.9 percent of GDP, whereas small enterprises, that is enterprises employing less than 50 persons accounted for 38.3 percent of the Polish GDP. This share has been relatively stable as for several years it used to grow or fall within a range of 0.5 percent.

In 2004, there were 3.67m enterprises registered in Poland, of which 94.96 percent are micro-enterprises, 99.03 percent small enterprises and 99.91 percent medium and small sized enterprises. They employed approximately 68 percent of all employed outside agriculture, forestry and fishery.

The development of SMEs in Poland has followed some universal patterns. They are concentrated in economic areas with low capital requirements: almost 45 percent functions in trade and reparation sector or real estate and business and educational "knowledge" services.

In addition, they display a relatively high birth and death rates as yearly approximately 8-9 percent of SMEs cease their activities, whereas approximately 9-10 percent are newly registered, which leads to an average rate of growth of approximately 2 percent.

The duration of enterprise life differs according to the sector of activity. In such sectors like tourism and real estate services there is a relatively high number of new entrants and a relatively high number of exits. A higher level of stability characterizes businesses active in manufacturing or transportation.

In addition, Polish SMEs tend to be concentrated in wealthier regions (in the richest regions more than 10 percent of the population owns their own firm, in the poorest approximately 7 percent). This fact contradicts hopes of some policy makers that SMEs might act as a cushion against such social problems like unemployment and poverty severely affecting the poorer regions of Poland.

The growth of Polish SMEs has been limited by the fact they finance their investments in approximately 70 percent from their own sources and only for 25 percent from commercial loans, the rest coming from public grants (PARP 2005). This ratio points to the existence of several factors both on the side of entrepreneurs and financial sector which reduce ability and possibility to use external financing. One of the most important factors is the unwillingness of entrepreneurs to transform their businesses from family activities into impersonal, statute-based commercial undertakings.

Table 6.6 Size distribution of registered enterprises in Poland, 1991-2004

Enterprise by size	Number of enterprises					% share in 2004	Ratio (1991=1.0)
	1991	1993	1995	1999	2004		
Total	502,275	1,988,079	2,099,577	2,904,700	3,670,915	10.00	7.3
SME (<251)	494,211	1,980,705	2,093,148	2,894,477	3,665,158	99.84	7.41
0-50	469,436	1,957,209	2,069,930	2,868,072	3,635,129	99.02	7.74
51-250	24,775	23,496	23,218	26,405	30,029	0.82	1.21
>251	8,064	7,374	6,429	6,223	5,757	0.15	0.71

Source: Reports on the State of SMEs in Poland, various years, PARP Warsaw.

The general data about the state of SMEs in Poland do not allow to analyze new phenomena such as self-employment. Recently, self-employment has been recognized as a way to increase employment flexibility, to support entrepreneurship and to counter unemployment (Drozdowski and Matczak 2004).

Self-employment is defined in Poland as an intermediary form between dependent employment based upon an employment contract and proper business activities. From the legal point of view, there is little difference between self-employment and entrepreneurship since the self-employed can choose, like entrepreneurs, to function in one of two legal forms: as a sole owner company or as persons' labour based on civil legal contracts. In addition, the self-employed have been taxed like entrepreneurs and they have paid similar, reduced in comparison to dependent workers, contributions to social security.

Self-employed individuals are often suppliers or sub-contractors of their previous employers' and render services to them as a business entity. It is worth noting that many companies used to push out their previous employees to become self-employed in order to save on social security contributions. It has been estimated that approximately 14 percent of workforce in Poland is employed as self-employed (IAR 2006). In order to reduce the scale of this phenomenon the government has introduced legal changes which, from January 2007 onwards, would take away fiscal and social security privileges from those self-employed who perform their work in the facilities of the employer and under his supervision.

In response to surveys, the majority of Poles considers self-employment a viable alternative to classical employment, as something between entrepreneurship and employment. Declaratively self-employment is highly valued by young people and especially by high school graduates. But, young people tend to think about self-employment from two, somehow contradictory, points of view: as a desirable way to gain work autonomy and as a necessity due to the shortage of job offers. Such an incoherent attitude finds a confirmation in the data from the National Population Census in 2002 which show that among the self-employed there is only 4 percent of people in the age group 18-24. Self-employment seemed also not interesting for the young unemployed, since in the years 2000-2004 only 0.1-0.2 percent of the young unemployed quit unemployment to take a loan to start their own business.

The results of social research allow us to make some tentative generalizations about sources of the lack of interest among youth for self-employment. The main sources seem to be:

- lack of skills and courage to undertake their own economic activity, lack of business ideas and a high perceived risk of such an activity;
- fear of administrative difficulties in creating an enterprise;
- lack of financial resources;
- fear of taking loans and the perception that taking loans is especially risky for self-employed;
- barriers to taking loans due to complicated procedures and long waiting periods (Drozdowski and Matczak 2004).

It seems that two causes of the low level of independent economic activities among the Polish youth prevail. First, little knowledge and experience in implementing business ideas and fulfilling administrative requirements facing all business startups. Second, limited own financial resources and limited access to capital. They together produce the low level of self-employment and entrepreneurship among young Poles.

The analysis of social attitudes suggests that for many Poles self-employment and entrepreneurship are second-best solutions, that Poles undertake their own economic activities rather due to lack of other income alternatives and not as a result of their own choice or an attempt to be economically independent (Piech and Kulikowski 2002). Thus, the decision to undertake self-employed activities seems to be of a negative, defensive character: a reaction to a difficult life situation, an attempt to defend one's level of living and the reaction to the perceived lack of opportunities in the labour market.

A survey conducted by the Regional Labour Office in Poznan in 2002 shows for instance that no one of the high school graduates was interested in starting their own business, but almost one fourth declared that they would decide to launch their own business once the socio-economic situation in the country would improve. This conditionality has been confirmed by the fact that in 2004 28.2 percent of the newly founded firms was created by persons below 30.

Thus, starting their own business as self-employed or micro-entrepreneurs is potentially interesting for young people and might actually materialize when young persons gain practical experience and learn from practice that such barriers as fear of competition, fear of bureaucracy, or pessimism about the future socio-economic situation of the country are less important in reality (Drozdowski and Matczak 2004).

Thus, in the future, one could expect a growing interest in the start-up of private enterprises, so that entrepreneurship ceases to be an abstract option.

5. Public Policies towards SMEs

All post-1989 Polish governments have made public their will to conduct policies favorable to the development of entrepreneurship. But, it was rather a declarative support since in the beginning of the 1990s the development of SMEs was believed a natural process, the spontaneous rebirth of once suppressed private business activities. The breakdown of state-owned trading organizations, the "small privatization" of municipally owned facilities, and the opening of the economy did create a myriad of business opportunities. But, the spectacular numerical growth could not hide structural weaknesses of Polish SMEs: their slow growth in qualitative terms (in terms of innovativeness, investments in modern technologies and commitment to research and development) and the survival orientation of most entrepreneurs (Surdej 2003).

From the mid-1990s onwards, governments initiated policies to support the growth of SMEs. These interventions were aimed at the simplification of administrative and tax regulations, at facilitating the access to external finance by establishing the Credit Guarantee Fund in the National Economy Bank (*Bank Gospodarstwa Krajowego* – BGK) in 1995 and 49 Local Loan and Guarantee Funds (*Lokalne Fundusze Pozyczkowo-Gwarancyjne*); at supporting entrepreneurial activities by the development of a host of institutions which would strengthen the business environment. In 1996, the government via its specialized agency supporting entrepreneurship called PARP (Polish Agency for Entrepreneurship – *Polska Agencja Rozwoju Przedsiebiorczosci*) created an umbrella structure under the name of the National System of Services for Small and Medium Enterprises (KSE – *Krajowy System Uslug*). This network grouped in 2006 almost 200 organizations providing various kind of services for SMEs: from business services, training, information gathering to guaranteeing and issuing loans. The KSE acts as a self-regulatory body contributing, thanks to the system of accreditation, to the improvement in quality of services to SMEs.

Business support institutions function in Poland as general centers of business support (*osrodki wspierania biznesu*); as information centers (*osrodki informacyjne*), incubators of entrepreneurship (*inkubatory przedsiebiorczosci*), centers of innovation and technology, training centers and financial institutions. The institutional density and variety of the business environment is even higher when one adds the more than 250 business chambers and over 800 crafts associations and cooperatives (MGiP, 2004).

Table 6.7 Typical services offered by polish business support institutions

Informational services	Promotional services	Administrative services
Rules for running business	Organization of exhibitions and fairs	Preparation of business plans
Databases of businesses	Organization of foreign business trips	Preparation of loan application
Information about sources of financing	Organization of trips to fairs	Preparation of contracts
Information about fairs in Poland Information Polsce	Publication of brochures	Preparation of business offers
Information about public procurement	Organization of promotion in media	Sale of documents needed for foreign transaction
Information about custom duties	Publication of informational leaflets	Legalization of commercial documents
Information on foreign quality standards and norms		
Offers of cooperation with foreign partners		

Source: Own elaboration.

The quantitative growth and institutional differentiation of the business environment has become of crucial importance since with accession to the EU in 2004, the Polish government has gained significant resources from the European structural funds to support the competitiveness of SMEs. Although public aid to enterprises in Poland has been oscillating around 1.2-1.3 percent of the GDP, it has been directed to support large enterprises in the declining sectors like hard coal, steel industry and shipyards. No substantial funds were used to support of SMEs until the late of 1990s, the only exception being the Labour Fund. The Labour Fund and labour offices have been created to distribute unemployment benefits and to conduct active labour market policies like retraining or public works. At the turn of the century, the activation policies started to include support for self-employment and entrepreneurship among unemployed or redundant workers. Unemployed or persons waiting for dismissal (after receiving the note of dismissal) could take loans at a reduced interest rate of 50 percent of the market rate amounting to at maximum 20 months of the average salary to start their own enterprises. The results of this support are not fully documented, but the existing sketchy evidence suggests that taking loans has been considered risky and that the use of the instrument has been limited.

As already mentioned, public support for SMEs used to be rather declarative. Only with the accession of Poland to the EU the government made available 1.71 bl Euro (1.25 bl from European structural funds) for the years 2004-2006 to support the competitiveness of enterprises, including SMEs. The distribution of public resources has taken place in the framework programme called "Sectoral Operational Programme. Support for the Competitiveness of Enterprises" (SPO WKP). The main goals of the programme have been: a) the development of entrepreneurship and the rise of innovativeness by strengthening business environment, and b) the direct support of enterprises by investment subsidies (Case Doradcy 2005). The programme is in the process of implementation and it will not be fully completed before the end of 2008.

6. Support to Youth Employment and Entrepreneurship

Youth entrepreneurship became one of the main focuses of public policy at the beginning of the 21st century when it became evident that an expected 5 percent growth of the national economy would be unable to absorb the then unemployed and the expected inflow of the baby boom cohorts into the labour market.

Only then policy makers started to consider self-employment and entrepreneurship as options available to youth. At the most general level this meant promoting the positive image of entrepreneurship, as the social perception of the entrepreneur is in Poland quite ambiguous (Marody 2000). On the one hand, Poles tend to admire entrepreneurs as men or women of success, as wealthy persons, able to implement long term plans and work hard. On the other hand, they think that entrepreneurs consume ostentatiously and consider themselves better than others. In addition, an average Pole tends to think that entrepreneurs often do not respect laws, are rather dishonest and care more for their financial success than their employees. The majority of people also believes that entrepreneurs live from the work of others, which indicates a lasting legacy of the ideology of the recent past (ISP 2004).

The first programmes directed to support youth entrepreneurship were introduced at the beginning of the 21st and were financed from the pre-accession fund PHARE in 2001 and 2002. These were rather pilot programmes as the central focus of "the competitiveness segment" of PHARE was to support the investments and export capacities of Polish SMEs. The funding available in 2002 amounted to 58m Euro for all type of entrepreneurship-related activities.

Yet, the challenge had been identified and the government decided to start promoting and teaching entrepreneurship earlier by introducing the course named "Introduction to entrepreneurship" (Podstawy przedsiebiorczosci) in high schools from the school year 2001/2002, which is supposed to teach pupils entrepreneurial attitudes and give them basic knowledge about the functioning of the economy, the principles of working in teams and running small businesses. The introduction of such a course in high schools did require the preparation of teachers, textbooks and business cases. These preconditions have not yet been completed and timely support came in the form of European financed projects like "The Promotion of

Entrepreneurship among students of vocational schools" (Youngbusiness.net2), which have helped to strengthen the quality of entrepreneurial education.

7. From First Job to First Firm

Before 2000 youth was not the main target of labour market policies. But, as the large wave of graduates started to complete high schools, the government began to design and implement programmes which would support the entry of the young into the labour market.

In 2002 – the peak year of the entry of baby boom cohorts – there were 0.694m young people of nineteen-years old, approximately half of them continued education, but together with earlier cohorts the government expected that 0.52m persons would look for a first job. Fearing that most of these persons would become unemployed, the Ministry of Labour and Social Policy designed a programme called "First Job", which was supposed to protect high school graduates against unemployment. The programme was supposed to increase the likelihood of young graduates to get employment by offering employers the refund of social contributions for the first 12 months of employment. In addition, the government introduced the programme of refunded traineeships for high school leavers and made loans available to entrepreneurs employing high school graduates. The programme "First Job" contained also some instruments supporting self-employment among youth such as subsidized loans for start-ups, the temporary suspension of social security contributions or "tutoring" of young self-employed. In 2002 and in 2003, the programme "First Job" absorbed 1bl PLN from budgetary sources yearly. The preliminary evaluation of this programme has pointed to the existence of a difference of preference between youth and employers with young people preferring being employed with subsidized social contributions and employers preferring subsidized traineeships.

"First job" was a large scale policy intervention. Only in 2002 subsidized work was taken up by almost 119,000 people. In addition, in the same year 'public intervention' jobs were taken up by 51,000 people (30 percent more than in 2001) and 'public works' jobs were taken up by over 33,000 unemployed people. Other types of support for youth searching for their first job consisted of vocational training courses and of vocational counseling. In 2002, more than 68,000 unemployed people participated in training, 44 percent more than in 2001. After completing the courses, more than 20,000 of these people commenced employment. It is worth noticing that the effectiveness of the training depended on its subject. More than 50 percent of participants found jobs after completing courses in occupational health and safety, and in tourist services, but only 16 percent of participants found jobs after completing courses in computer operation, 22 percent after courses in economics, and 22 percent after courses in commerce.

Additionally, in 2002, the Ministry of Labour and Social Policy started to implement 238 special programmes funded by the Labour Fund, their main objective being the 'vocational activation' of people belonging to risk groups in local labour markets. The programmes covered over 3,000 unemployed people (approximately 50 percent more beneficiaries than in 2001). Of these, almost a third was composed of women, almost half of them long-term unemployed, and more than a half were residents of rural areas. A significant proportion of the programmes' beneficiaries accounted for people aged up to 24, high school graduates and people, who did not hold any formal vocational qualifications.[1]

The programme "First Job" lasted till June 2004 when it was discontinued as the programme was deliberately designed to cushion the labour market entry of baby boom cohorts, but, in addition, it was discontinued because it was costly. To date no comprehensive evaluation of the programme has been performed and not much is known about the durability of its outcomes.

Although the programme "First Job" had an entrepreneurship supporting component, a major shift in the methods of supporting youth entrepreneurship came in 2005 with the launch of the programme named "First Firm". The programme's main goal is to reduce the barriers to youth entrepreneurship by spreading entrepreneurial knowledge, creating networks of consultants supporting young entrepreneurs and facilitating access to start up financing thanks to subsidized loans and loan guarantees. The programme offers various types of aid to young entrepreneurs by financing projects, which have been implemented by such business support institutions as business incubators or centers for entrepreneurship and innovation. Special attention has been paid to the increase of the volume of loans to young start-ups as in the past this instrument of support proved quite ineffective. The programme "First Firm" has been financed from the Labour Fund, the resources of the National Economy Bank (BGK), and the resources of the Polish Agency for Entrepreneurship (PARP).

The main aim of the programme has been to "make entrepreneurship" a realistic alternative for youth, which means supporting young people in their attempts to start their own businesses by giving them practical advice, helping them to overcome administrative barriers and to gain experience. Young entrepreneurs could count on limited financial aid and reduction of social contributions. It seems that the main focus of the programme is to offer young entrepreneurs real assistance in setting and conducting business and not just to provide them financial aid. This orientation entrusts business support institutions, which have been growing and maturing over last 15 years, with the task to select and tutor potential young entrepreneurs. The quality of this assistance has yet to be assessed.

A special segment of activities supporting youth entrepreneurship has been centered around so-called Academic Incubators of Entrepreneurship (AIE). The AIEs have to work with high school graduates to help them develop entrepreneurial ideas and start their own businesses. Potentially, AIEs can stimulate innovative business ideas created by young people. The government agency PARP is planning to allocate more financial resources from structural funds for AIEs in the programming period 2007-2013.

Parliamentary elections and the resulting change of the government in the fall of 2005 have led to significant changes in the personnel of the central government. Yet, regardless of its ideological color any government has to address the problem

---

1 Information taken from the webpage of the Polish Ministry of Economy and Work – accessed on 29.09.2006 - http://www.mgip.gov.pl/Serwis+Prasowy/Informacje+i+komunikaty/Program+Pierwsza+Praca+w+I+kwartale+2004+roku.htm.

of youth unemployment in such a way as to slow down emigration and to encourage youth's return to Poland after shorter or longer periods of working abroad. Improving conditions for business activities and supporting enterprises with funds and counseling seem to be the preferred direction of actions by the current government.

Conclusions

The examined changes in the economic situation and government policies have shown that subsequent Polish governments have slowly recognized the key role of entrepreneurship for youth life chances and Poland's economic development. Entrepreneurship seems to be the most promising road to reduce the weight of "the Poland of welfare recipients" on the economic development of the country. It is one of main factors of endogenous growth – the factor which helps to reduce the dependence of the local economic situation on the vagaries of international markets and foreign investors.

Although policy initiatives to support youth entrepreneurship have been stimulated more by demographic pressure than by the anticipation of policy problems, some types of ideas and programmes seem to have been well received and likely to remain for the years to come. This is first of all the idea of founding in each high school an Academic Incubator of Entrepreneurship and to give young graduates an opportunity to test their entrepreneurial ideas in such a supportive environment. Thanks to the higher institutional density and increased maturity of business support institutions it is also more likely that policies to offer real assistance and not just financial aid would prove effective and less prone to the exploitation by special interests. Finally, the accession to the EU has made additional resources available to the Polish government, which will fuel innovative public policies in the years to come.

References

Cain, Michael and Aleksander Surdej (1996), 'Facing the Pension Crisis: Current Problems and Future Perils in the Polish Pension System', *Emergo* 3:2, pp. 15-28.

Case, Doradcy (2005), *Evaluation of Progress of SPO WKP* (Warsaw: Fundacja CASE), September.

Domanski, Henryk (2002), *Polska klasa srednia (The Polish Middle-Class)* (Wroclaw: Wydawnictwo Uniwersytetu Wroclawskiego).

Drozdowski, Rafał and Piotr Matczak (ed.) (2004), *Samozatrudnienie. Raport z Badań (Self-employment, Research Report)* (Warsaw: PARP).

Grabowski, Maciej (1996), 'Zmiany w sektorze małych i średnich przedsiębiorstw' (*Changes in the Sector of SMEs*), in Krystyna Gawlikowska-Hueckel (ed.), *Zmiany strukturalne w polskiej gospodarce w okresie transformacji w latach 1989–1995 (Structural Changes in the Polish Economic in the period of transformation 1989-1995)* (Gdańsk – Warsaw).

Grabowski, Maciej (2002), 'The Informal Economy in the European Union Accession Countries: Size, Scope, Trends and Challenges to the Progress of European Union Enlargement', paper presented for the Round Table, Sofia, April 18-20.

GUS (Glowny Urzad Statystyczny) (1999), *Praca nierejestrowana w Polsce w 1998* ('Unregistered Work in Poland in 1998') (Warsaw).

Hausner, Jerzy and Miroslawa Marody (ed.) (1999), *Three Polands: The Potential for and Barriers to Integration with the European Union. EU-monitoring III* (Warsaw).

IAR (Informacyjna Agencja Radiowa) (2006), 'Samozatrudniajacy straca przywileje podatkowe' ('Self-employed will lose their tax privileges'), 13 November 2006.

ISP (Instytut Spraw Publicznych) (2004), *Swiadomosc Ekonomiczna Spoleczenstwa i Wizerunek Biznesu (Economic Awareness of the Polish Society and Business Social Image)* (Warsaw: Instytut Spraw Publicznych).

Kloc, Kamila (1998), Szara *strefa w Polsce w okresie transformacji* ('The shadow economy in Poland during transformation') CASE Reports, no. 13 (Warsaw: Fundacja CASE).

Kolarska-Bobińska, Lena, Andrzej Rosner, and Jerzy Wilikin (ed.) (2001), *Przyszlosc wsi polskiej. Wizje, strategie, koncepcje (The Future of Polish Countryside. Visions, strategies and ideas)* (Warsaw: ISP), 21.

Kolodko, Grzegorz (1999), *Od szoku do terapii. Ekonomia i polityka transformacji (From Shock to Therapy. Economics and Politics of Transformations)* (Warsaw: Poltext).

Kulikowski, Marcin and Krzysztof Piech (2002), *Przedsiębiorczość, szansą na sukces rządu, gospodarki, przedsiębiorstw, społeczeństwa (Entrepreneurship, a chance for the success of the government, enterprises and society)* (Warsaw: Instytut Wiedzy).

Los, Maria and Andrzej Zybertowicz (2000), *Privatizing the Police-State. The Case of Poland* (New York: Macmillan Press).

Marody, Miroslawa (2000), *Między rynkiem a etatem (Between Market and Job Post)* (Warsaw: Wydawnictwo Scholar).

Marody Miroslawa (ed.) (2003), *Wymiary życia społecznego (Dimensions of Social Life)* (Warsaw: Scholar).

MgiP (Ministerstwo Gospodarki i Pracy) (2004), *Przedsiebiorczosc w Polsce (Entrepreneurship in Poland)* (Warsaw: Czerwiec).

MgiP (Ministerstwo Gospodarki i Pracy) (2005), *Zatrudnienie (Employment)*, (Warsaw: MGiP).

PARP (Polska Agencja Rozwoju Przedsiebiorczosci) (2005), *Raport o stanie sektora MSP w 2004-2005 (Report about the State of SMEs in 2004-2005)* (Warsaw: PARP).

Schneider, Friedrich and Dominik Enste (2002), *The Shadow Economy, An International Survey* (Cambridge: Cambridge University Press).

Strzelecki, Zbigniew (ed.) (2003), *Problemy demograficzne Polski przed wejściem do Unii Europejskiej (Demographic Problems of Poland before the Accession to the EU)* (Warsaw: PWE).

Surdej, Aleksander (2003), 'SME Development in Poland: Policy and Sustainability', in Robert J. McIntyre and Bruno Dallago (ed.), *Small and Medium Enterprises in Transitional Economies* (New York: Palgrave Macmillan).

Woodward, Richard (ed.) (1999), *Otoczenie instytucjonalne małych i średnich przedsiębiorstw (Institutional Environment of SMEs)*, CASE Raporty nr 25, Warsaw: Fundacja CASE.

Chapter 7

Youth Entrepreneurship in Slovenia

Miroslav Glas and Blaž Zupan

1. Introduction

As the most developed transition country in Central and Eastern Europe (CEE), with a rather liberal economy as compared to other CEE countries and a favorable strategic position between East and West, Slovenia managed the transition problems quite efficiently. The policy of gradual changes helped the country to avoid stronger economic and social shocks although it also stalled some radical structural changes. The rate of unemployment has never reached the levels as experienced by other republics of former Yugoslavia and the social and individual welfare did not suffer any huge decrease in early 1990s, although the increased income and wealth differences produced some social and political tensions.

The structural changes in the Slovenian economy, also mirrored in society have hurt some strata of the Slovenian population and it is fair to say that youth suffered probably most due to unemployment and housing difficulties while pensioners enjoyed a high level of social protection due to their political influence as one of strongest layers of the elective body. The unemployment and housing problems both contributed to a sharp decrease in the fertility rate which has contributed to the ageing of the population as the potentially worst problem of Slovenia in the future.

While the development of SMEs from the early 1990s onwards started to fill the gap in the size structure of Slovenian economy, also contributing to the creation of new jobs, it has not been able to substitute for the loss of jobs in larger companies. Also, entrepreneurship during the first wave mostly attracted experienced employees and only more recently, young people have embarked on the entrepreneurial career. In the future, the share of youth among nascent entrepreneurs could be enhanced through entrepreneurship education and training as well as other forms of a more coherent assistance to start-ups.

2. Background: the performance of Slovenian economy

The Slovenian economy grew out of the long industrial and crafts tradition (see Glas 1998). Even during the socialist period, it depended less on large industrial conglomerates than other Yugoslav republics and the policy of dispersed local companies or plants of larger companies ensured also the relatively strong economic development in small towns and villages. This economy was a kind of a Yugoslav "window" towards Western Europe and joint-ventures and co-operation with a number of foreign companies prevalently from West Germany, resulted in higher levels of managerial knowledge and skills. This openness to the European market provided also the alternative to the lost Yugoslav market in the early 1990s, although some years were still needed to resume the production at the pre-1990 level, since tougher Western markets resulted in some loss of the GDP due to lower prices and the need to provide for improved quality and innovation in products during the 1990s.

The difference in the intensity of economic and social problems during the transition period between Slovenia and other CEE countries could be attributed to several factors:

1. Slovenia dissociated early from the former Yugoslavia, only suffering some two weeks of war acts, with minor loss of human lives and few physical destructions. It enjoyed the support of the EU countries, the preferential treatment in economic relations and the business resumed quickly (see Glas et al. 2001). Still, some activities, e.g. tourism and traffic, were severely hurt by the effects of the war in the nearby Balkan countries.

2. The strong tradition of crafts and small-scale private production generated a dynamic wave of new venture creation after the Company Law enacted in December 1988 allowed for the private and mixed ownership of companies. Other factors contributed to this "entrepreneurial wave" during 1990-1994:
   - low capital and legal barriers for new corporations,
   - slow start of the privatization process during the early 1990s encouraged many managers to quit and establish their own companies,
   - bankruptcies of large companies created market opportunities for new firms and a source for their resources.

3. Although slow at the beginning, the privatization process proceeded fairly smoothly. It has left a strong share of the quasi-state ownership through the Capital Fund to support the pension system and the Restitution Fund, but privatized firms started to focus soon on the issues of strategic development, some started to create employment and the process of concentration through the merger and acquisition deals enabled some firms to grow considerably and with ownership by Slovenians.

Admittedly, newly created businesses faced several obstacles, from the lack of financing, to difficulties in finding proper business premises to rent or buy, and the resistance of local bureaucracies to give up their power of interfering with business. It is difficult to provide a coherent picture of the new venture creation process and the restructuring of the economy due to a number of administrative and institutional changes, the new legal statutes of crafts and sole proprietors, and the increased capital requirements for incorporation. However, the almost fivefold increase in the number of registered incorporated businesses from 10.528 in 1990 to 48.158 in 1994 demonstrated the power of the entrepreneurial challenge and the strong motive to become an independent business owner-manager (Glas and Drnovsek 2000).

After 1994, the growth of new ventures slowed down dramatically:

- the first wave gradually exhausted the corps of entrepreneurial talent among employees, freed from the socialist limits on private ownership;
- the stronger competition from new ventures, imports and restructured larger companies reduced the number of promising market opportunities;
- legislation created a more unfriendly business environment through increased start-up capital requirements while the alternative status of sole proprietors offered an easier entry but assumed higher personal financial risks;
- the restructuring of some large companies and subsidiaries of foreign multinational firms created a strong challenge to small businesses.

The decade of 1996-2005 experienced a slow increase in the number of registered incorporated businesses, while the number of sole proprietors continued its slow but steady growth. New businesses filled some market niches, while others started co-operation among SMEs or with larger firms. However, it became increasingly difficult to identify an opportunity, even for experienced business people, and much more difficult for youngsters. Although the creation of new firms did not follow the chaotic pattern of some CEE countries, e.g. the Czech republic or Romania, with the increase in the number of businesses the average size of a business in Slovenia reached 6 employees/business, the average of the European Union.

Table 7.1 The number of registered SMEs in some CEE countries (1996) and Slovenia (1998)

Country	Number of SMEs	Country	Number of SMEs
Russian Federation	894,000	Hungary	519,502
Bulgaria[1]	600,000	Czech Republic	700,000
Romania[2]	439,627	Slovenia – Total[3]	118,881
Poland	1,057,102	• incorporated businesses	54,581
		• sole proprietorships	61,300

Notes
[1] Only 50% of the SMEs were really operating.
[2] Data are for 1994.
[3] In the middle of 1996, there were 52,193 registered incorporated businesses, but only 35,785 were really operating (68.6%), with the structure of 32,056 micro, 2,284 small, 1,099 medium and 346 large companies
Source: OECD 1998, 272; Glas 1999.

While there existed no thorough research on the origin and the profile of Slovenian entrepreneurs at that time, from different samples we could deduct that entrepreneurs were originating from various social and professional groups (Glas 1999):

- former employees of medium and large socially-owned companies establishing their own firms to capture business opportunities and to build on their skills, experience and networks;
- former top and middle managers seeking profit and possibilities to get richer through private firms avoiding the past problems of larger firms (debts, over-employment, pay practices discouraging creative and risk-taking individuals);
- successful craftsmen with established circles of customers and accumulated resources;
- graduates of government sponsored self-employment programs (Glas and Cerar 1997);
- "free-lancers" in professional services (accountants, lawyers, architects, business consultants) etc.

The studies as summarized in Glas and Drnovsek (2000) revealed that the dissatisfaction with a job in former socially owned enterprises and the desire for independence were leading reasons for Slovenians to establish a private business, and only dynamic entrepreneurs have put the need for achievement as the first motive (33%), followed by independence (30%). While research on the age of entrepreneurs when founding their business is lacking, the data regarding working experience before starting on their own shows a low share of youth among start-ups. In the group of dynamic entrepreneurs (see Glas and Drnovsek 2000), 83% had at least 5 years of work experience and 62% had more than 10 years experience. Average entrepreneurs were slightly less experienced, particularly women entrepreneurs with only 57% having more than 4 years of experience and 34% having ten years or more (Glas and Petrin 1998).

Recently, Kotar (2006) tried to establish the pattern of Slovenian entrepreneurship during the 1990s, with a sample of 49 dynamic entrepreneurs, 135 "ordinary" entrepreneurs and 135 people that never had their own business. Few businesses existed before 1990 and most were created during only four years, in the period 1990-93 (42.5%). Women owned 23.4% of businesses, the share commonly found in Slovenia (Drnovsek and Glas 2006), and 60.9% of businesses were considering themselves as family businesses (53% in Duh and Tominc 2006; 58.6% in Vadnjal 2005). Kotar confirmed the known fact that most entrepreneurs are still first generation entrepreneurs (72%), since only 10% had mothers and 28% fathers as entrepreneurs – parents could hardly be role models for their enterprising children, while 54% had relatives among entrepreneurs and even 90% had some entrepreneurial friends. Still, 76% of entrepreneurs in the sample thought they demonstrated entrepreneurial intentions early in their lives but the socialist economic system had prevented them from starting before 1990. Most entrepreneurs were learning-by-doing from their previous jobs: 39% have started businesses in the activities of former employers and 29% partly in the same activity. Most entrepreneurs did not start their business because of necessity, as a result of being unemployed: 71% have never been fired in their working lives and 28% have deliberately left the companies to start own business.

The worldwide recession at the beginning of the 21st century largely stopped the new venture creation process, but the revived economy also encouraged entrepreneurs to start new firms and the number of operating firms increased from 91,250 in 2002 to 97,134 in 2004 (for 7.8%), although the critics scorn this process for establishing mostly new real-estate firms because of new regulation, and some other service firms.

Table 7.2 The size structure of the Slovenian economy, 2004

Economic parameter	Size of businesses per employees					TOTAL
	0	Micro 1-9	Small 11-49	Medium 50-249	Large 250+	
Number of businesses	12,274	78,301	5,089	1,186	284	97,134
– share (in %)	12.6	80.6	5.2	1.2	0.3	100
Number of employees	0	156,927	98,409	122,927	199,462	577,725
– share (in %)	0	27.2	17.0	21.3	34.5	100
Employees per business	0.0	2.0	19.3	103.6	702.3	5.9
Sales revenues per business (000 €)	77	136	2,132	11,268	77,382	595
Value added per employee (€)	0	16,004	26,076	25,813	29,801	24,787
– share (in %)	0.9	17.5	17.9	22.2	41.5	100

Source: Rebernik et al. 2006, 15.

In terms of the number of employees per firm and size structure, Slovenia is approaching the situation in the European Union, with 99.7% of businesses being SMEs, employing 65.5% of all employees and generating 58.5% of added value. Still, there are some structural weaknesses of the Slovenian SMEs:

- the lack of stable, well-developed small businesses,
- low level of added value per employee as compared to the developed EU countries,
- low technology level, particularly in craftsshops (lack of capital),
- gap in R&D (research and development) and innovation,
- high share of SMEs with internet links but weak management information systems,
- focus on the local/regional market, only few "born globals",
- weak university/industry cooperation, particularly for SMEs,
- networking, clustering and other forms of more long-term collaboration mostly started only after the year 2000.

The level of formal education of entrepreneurs, while quite dissatisfactory during the 1990s, with the majority having only high-school (40-46% in different samples) has improved, and Kotar (2006) has found in her 2005 sample that 59.6% already had college or university education. However, it is important to stress the regional differences in the level of entrepreneurial activity: while the Central region as the most developed region had 64 businesses per 1,000 inhabitants, with 49 as the average for Slovenia, the least developed regions had substantially less, e.g. Zasavje (an old coal-mining region) only 31 and Pomurje (the North-Eastern part of Slovenia along the Hungarian border) as few as 32. In some regions, the entrepreneurial activity is still rather weak and the bleak prospects are probably tormenting youth as well.

Glas and Drnovsek (2000) concluded that Slovenian SMEs would need:

- less administrative procedures and bureaucracy (starting from the registration procedure and urban planning practices);
- a pro-business environment and tax incentives for new venture creation, new jobs, stronger R&D activities;
- entrepreneurship education and training promoting leadership know-how, marketing skills, internationalization of operations,
- more accessible financial funds, either debt or equity financing;
- creating entrepreneurial networks and business clusters to promote shared resources and experiences from different markets;
- enhanced co-operation between small and large companies,
- development of an entrepreneurship infrastructure to provide for "hard" and "soft" support to SMEs, in particular incubators and business zones.

Finally, membership of the EU has not generated increased competitive pressures on SMEs (see Glas 2005), the "China phenomenon" was felt more through price pressures.

From the existing research it is not possible to give a quantitative assessment of the impact of young entrepreneurs on the economic development of Slovenia. However, in some industries e.g. information and communication technologies and internet-based businesses, the share of young entrepreneurs has been very strong since educated youngsters more easily embraced new technologies and business models.

3. Unemployment and youth in Slovenia

The first period immediately after independence has not been easy for Slovenia since the war with the Yugoslav army came on top of other economic and social problems of transition. The war, although only a short two-week period of limited bloodshed, caused the breakdown of economic co-operation with companies from other republics and the virtual closing of a large part of the former Yugoslav market. A substantial part of Slovenian companies lost 30-60% of their supplies and sales since even the business with neighboring Croatia suffered from political tensions and some payment difficulties due to the new currencies and the consequences of problems with banking systems.

Figure 7.1 demonstrates clearly the acute problem of unemployment that resulted from the transformation process in early 1990s. Slovenia figured as a country with full employment up to the 1980s, with only some persons seeking their first job or changing from one to another job being unemployed – in 1980 there were only 12,227 registered unemployed persons (Statistical Yearbook of Slovenia 2005, 234). The number of registered unemployed persons at the Employment Services has risen dramatically during early 1990s to 137,142. Government decided not to impose legal barriers on lay-offs and it allowed companies to lay-off excess labor force that resulted in high open unemployment. Still, due to the social pressures and labor unions many managers were quite reluctant to use the path of radical restructuring through massive lay-offs and companies have sought "soft ways" to decrease the labor force ("hidden unemployment" in socially-owned companies was estimated to be 15% of employment), preferring early retirement, re-training etc., they mostly sought to restructure through gradual downsizing. The unfinished privatization and the "voucher model" favoring employees and retirees as majority owners discouraged foreign capital to become stronger player and to create new jobs. Contrary to some expectations women were not the first victims of unemployment since the burden of transition hit the man-dominated industries heavily and the increasing share of services allowed women to stay in jobs. However, persons seeking their first job filled the stratum of unemployed persons, most of them being young people who recently completed their formal education.

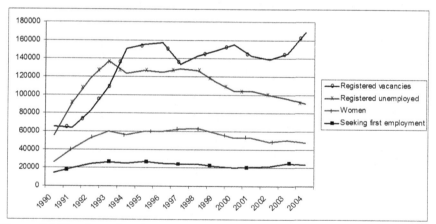

Figure 7.1 Number of registered vacancies and different groups of unemployed persons in Slovenia, 1990-2004

Source: Statistical Yearbook of Slovenia (various volumes).

The problem of unemployment would have hit the population harder in the absence of some social processes and economic and other policies favored by the government:

1. Slovenia opened vast *channels to early retirement* that has eased the burden of unemployment substantially but also created a strong stratum of retirees that will dominate the pension system for years to come. This process duly created the subculture of dependence, people opting for retirement instead of seeking self-employment or new jobs through re-training and other efforts. The pension system is offering handsome retirement packages and the number of retirees increased sharply from 356,274 in the year 1990 (17.8% of population) to 504,202 in 2004 (25.2% of population and 64.5% of persons in employment), increasing by 41.5% with the increase of further recipients of social transfers by 14.9%.

2. Both families and government encouraged young people to continue their education resulting in *the number of students* steadily increasing from some 35,000 in early 1990s to over 110,000 in 2005 (see Figure 7.2); this increase of students has worsened the student-teacher ratio and the financial resources allocated for higher education have not followed this trend of students' enrolment, creating financial pressure on higher education institutions. However, the government did not seriously consider enrolment fees for students as a new source of income for universities due to the opposition by students and the population at large. While new universities and higher education institutions were established in some regional centers, the structure of students changed substantially, with business and law attracting a larger share of students, creating an imbalance on the market for graduates, where the needs of the revitalized economy are increasingly inconsistent with the inflow of graduates, contributing to a rather new phenomenon of an increasing share of higher education graduates among the unemployed (see Figure 7.3).

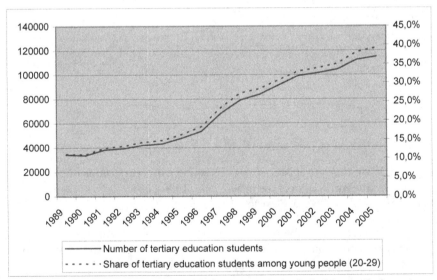

Figure 7.2 The number and share of young people included in tertiary education programmes in Slovenia, 1989-2005

Source: Statistical Office of RS.

The discussion about the number and structure of students/graduates is increasingly topical. In recent years, the share of the labor force with the lowest level of educational attainment decreased. This can be largely explained by early retirements of low-level qualified workers and the better qualification of new young entrants. Still, the slowly changed structure of the Slovenian economy is not demanding highly qualified and educated workers and it represents a structural weakness in the effort to create internationally competitive economy aspiring to get closer to the EU average.

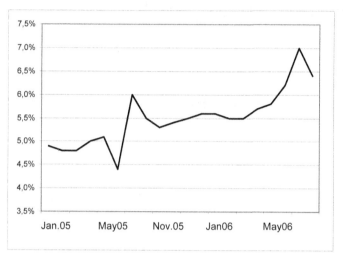

Figure 7.3 Registered unemployment rate among young graduates, January 2005-July 2006
Source: Statistical Office of RS.

3. While not many Slovenians *emigrated* during the last decade to the EU countries, the number of people finding full-time or temporary jobs, even jobs in the shadow economy in neighboring Italy and Austria greatly increased (there are no official statistics available). On the other hand, Slovenian government has chosen to waive job licenses to foreign citizens, mostly people from other republics of the former Yugoslavia in order to free these jobs to Slovenian citizens. However, in some sectors, e.g. construction and tourism, the shortage of Slovenian job seekers already demanded an increasing flow of less skilled workers from the Balkan area (88.1% of foreign workers in 2005) and increasingly from other countries, recent members of the EU, still mostly for short-term, seasonal work contracts.

4. Although changing, Slovenia is still a country with *strong family ties* and inter-generational solidarity. These ties have often eased the burden of unemployment by supporting unemployed members of the family for longer periods. These ties also extend to the situation where younger people tend to stay for longer periods with parents solving thereby the acute shortage of low-rent small apartments, but resulting in family-formation at a higher age

and lower birth rates. The number of marriages has dropped from 7,709 as the average for 1995-1999 to 6,558 in the year 2004 (for 14.9%) and the number of newborn infants declined to the lowest 17,106 in the year 2003 as compared to 18,102 as the average for 1995-1999 (for 5.5%), resulting in an acute demographic problem in Slovenia, only eased by net immigration flows.

5. The spread of the *grey economy*, already well-developed during the socialist period of 1980s, provided additional job opportunities, particularly for lower skilled workers and family members in family businesses as well as income sources for a large share of population.

Nevertheless, unemployment hit the population, which was not used to such a situation. Although the unemployment rates did not surpass those of some EU countries in the past, e.g. Ireland and Spain, it was an unexpected fact having a number of economic, social and psychological impacts on the welfare of different groups of the population.

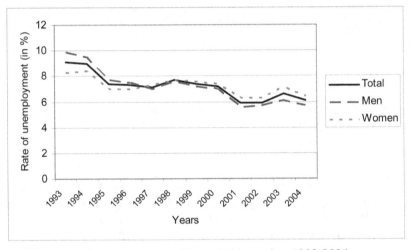

Figure 7.4 Rates of unemployment, Slovenia by gender, 1993-2004
Source: Statistical Yearbook of Slovenia (different volumes).

Figure 7.4 is already showing the period of decreasing unemployment where the gender structure is changing with women taking a larger share of unemployment in the second part of 1990s. During 2005, only 40.8% of newly employed persons were women. The declining labor intensive industries (textiles, leather etc.) contributed to this result. However, it is important that the rate of unemployment by age groups is showing dramatically different access of youth to employment.

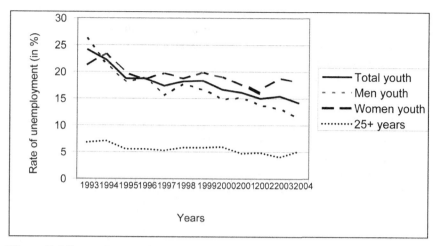

Figure 7.5 Rate of unemployment by age groups, Slovenia, 1993-2004
Source: Statistical Yearbook of Slovenia (different issues).

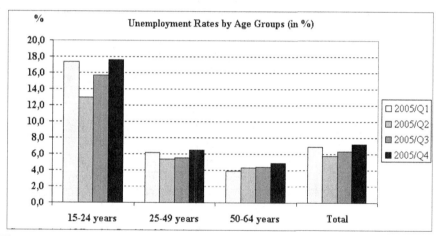

Figure 7.6 The rates of unemployment according to age, Slovenia, 2005
Source: Statistical Yearbook of Slovenia (different volumes).

Figure 7.5 is explaining two important facts: first, the level of unemployment of youth (aged up to 24 years) is drastically higher as compared to the adults (above 25 years) and, second, the situation is worsening for women where unemployment is almost persisting while declining for men. Figure 7.6 provides a clear picture of age-specific rates of unemployment and their seasonal changes that are also most expressed for young people according to their cycle of leaving formal education. We can summarize these findings in Table 7.3 that shows:

- systematic decrease in the number of unemployed after 1998, partly due to some changes in regulation that sharpened the conditions for the status of unemployed with the intention to encourage unemployed persons to search actively for a job;
- high share of aged under 26 years among unemployed persons, although decreasing due to the improved economic situation and declining share of younger generations in population;
- increased share of women among the unemployed persons due to structural changes in the economy and the effects of crisis in the sunset industries with a high share of female labor force;
- increased share of first job seekers pointing to the practice of companies to look for more experienced workers, particularly small and medium sized businesses;
- large share of older unemployed persons.

Table 7.3 Structure of unemployment in Slovenia, 1995-2006

Year/ month	Average number of registered unemployed persons	Average shares of characteristic groups of registered unemployed (%)					
		Aged under 26	First job seekers	Women	Unemployed for over 1 year	Without vocational qualifications	Aged over 40
1995	121,483	32.2	19.7	46.7	61.9	46.6	34.0
1996	119,799	31.4	19.4	48.1	56.1	47.0	36.6
1997	125,189	29.1	18.3	48.8	57.4	47.1	40.8
1998	126,080	26.3	18.1	49.9	61.7	46.9	46.0
1999	118,951	25.8	18.7	50.6	63.7	47.5	48.5
2000	106,601	23.4	17.9	50.7	62.9	47.2	51.7
2001	101,857	24.1	18.8	50.8	58.9	47.0	50.5
2002	102,635	24.0	19.6	51.2	54.4	47.0	49.4
2003	97,674	26.1	23.2	52.8	48.6	44.2	44.1
2004	92,826	26.2	25.2	53.1	46.2	41.6	42.8
2005	91,889	24.2	24.3	53.8	47.3	40.8	43.6
I-IX 2006	87,954	21.6	22.2	54.7	48.3	39.4	45.9

Source: Employment Services of RS, Annual Reports.

The lower birth rates are already having an effect on the labor market suggesting a further fall of labor supply, so a shortage of labor is anticipated in Slovenia around 2015 when unemployment levels will be insignificant (Kraigher 1995). However, young people are currently facing two problems:

- it is difficult for them to find their first job since companies prefer more experienced workers,
- employment is mostly offered for a specific time period.

In the period of transition from formal education to employment, there were usually three common paths:

a. scholarships: young people granted scholarships by companies were to a large extent also employed by these companies; they usually have to provide a period of (paid) work practice during summer holidays; other scholarships provided by the government did not ensure employment but applicants had more freedom to choose a job after finishing their education;
b. probation period, usually 4-12 months, provided a chance to employers to evaluate the new employee and to exercise their option not to continue with a full or part time employment in case of unsatisfactory performance of the employee;
c. apprenticeships give young people at the level of vocational school a chance to built on their theoretical knowledge through the learning-by-doing process and to develop a link to potential future employers. However, during the harsh period of transition, companies have cut the number of scholarships and they have extended less opportunities to develop experience by probation period or apprenticeships.

Due to the rigid regulation of employment, employers started to exploit the possibility of the time-limited labor contracts that should be rather an exception but developed into a common practice. Slovenian employment regulation makes it difficult for an employer to lay-off workers with lower performance in case of unlimited full-time employment, so employers exploit the facility of contractual employment. In the year 2005, among 136.950 newly employed persons, 76.6% were employed as temporary employees on time-limited work contracts (Employment Services 2006). Such a solution, besides providing a lower level of economic and social security to employees, also extends to further problems:

- employers are less inclined to invest into education and training for these groups of employees; these employees themselves are also less probable to engage in long-term programs of education;
- without long-term employment, it is difficult for employees to negotiate long-term housing loans and any other credit facility since banks do not have the guarantee of a steady income flow,
- usually, such working arrangements involve less fringe benefits for employees.

Slovenia is known for an extensive one-year period of leave for giving the birth and later to care for the infant. Although the social security system is taking care of the financial aspects of this leave, such a period could, in case of complicated pregnancy or further sick leaves to care for the baby, produce an adverse effect on the working career of mothers. Although illegal, there are many cases of implicit pressures on young women to postpone births or to choose a less ambitious career path. There are currently some campaigns to support women- and family-friendly companies, however these existing problems in the private sector could hardly be solved by campaigns.

On the other side, opinion polls are showing the changes in the value system: in the 1997 Slovenian public opinion survey, 77.1% of the respondents agreed that work is the most important activity and only 66.4% of younger people, less than 30 years old, agreed. There is now more freedom for young generations to create a valuable life-style, but also an increased challenge for young people not having already made up their mind about their career. While young people want to be productive, to express themselves in a creative job and having an exciting life and career, the opportunities to get such a job are not ample.

Although quite a small country in terms of its territory of 20,273 sq. km, Slovenia is characterized by large regional differences in the level of economic development, extending also to unemployment. It provides therefore a highly diverse picture also for young people searching for employment in different regions.

4. Youth entrepreneurship in Slovenia

One of the main characteristics of the SME development in transition countries is the relative maturity of owner-managers in the first wave of entrepreneurship. A large number of enterprising people have waited for their chance to start private businesses during the socialist period. Slovenia provided some opportunities during the 1980s by its lax policy towards crafts, enabling a number of firms in trade, catering, and transportation other than crafts to start even before 1989. Still, the majority used the Enterprise Law of 1988 to start. As a result, mostly adults started new ventures and not so much young people that joined the process.

4.1 The early 1990s

A survey of dynamic entrepreneurs in five CEE countries by the EFER (European Foundation of Entrepreneurship Research) revealed that Slovenian entrepreneurs as adults aged an average 43 years, only Hungarian entrepreneurs being older with 44.4 years. Also, 95% companies in Slovenia were founded by the entrepreneur him-/herself while in other countries many of them were bought from the state or privatized (up to 20% in Slovakia). Slovenian companies were owned only for 4% by an entrepreneur aged up to 30 years, a further 36% in the age group of 30-39 years and even 26% older than 50 years. Few dynamic entrepreneurs started with no previous working experience (only 5%) and 83% have more than 5 years of experience, and 62% more than ten years. Only 5% experienced their business as their first job. Even 76% of Slovenian entrepreneurs came from the middle and top managerial ranks (46-59% in other four countries) and one should consider that it takes years to occupy these ranks; only 5% came from white-collar workers (16-40% in other countries). Slovenian entrepreneurs started a company mostly alone (30%)

or with their family members (33%) while 5% inherited the company. Slovenians, although from the country with the highest per capita income in the survey, started in 57% with less than 1,000 EUR (19-42% in other countries) of own equity, but also 13% of them with more than 100,000 EUR (second after Hungarians).

Another survey in late 1990s, comparing Croatian and Slovenian entrepreneurs, has found that Slovenians are somewhat younger (on the average 42 years), most of them again founders (87.9%) and 6.8% inheriting the business. In this survey, 10.8% of entrepreneurs started their active working life by establishing their own business and the majority started from the managerial and professional ranks.

In 2002, in a sample of 222 entrepreneurs, 58.6% of them owner-managers of family businesses and 17.6% being female, 87% started the business on their own (only Polish family businesses had a higher share of founders with 88%, while 15 other countries, including developed market economies, have more businesses run by descendants), and only 19% having started their own business or joined the family businesses immediately after finishing their formal education. The majority, 81%, started their own businesses or joined the family businesses only after a certain period of working elsewhere (higher shares of these respondents could be found only in Finland and Poland). Again, among these entrepreneurs 55% of them had more than 10 years of previous working experience and 27% less than 5 years.

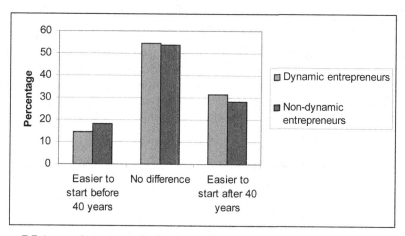

Figure 7.7 Age and start-up of a business, dynamic and other entrepreneurs, 2005
Source: Kotar 2006, 129.

Kotar (2006) analyzed 184 entrepreneurs. Only 7.7% of firms were founded before 1989 and the majority, 55.7% firms, in the period of 1989-1994. The average age of entrepreneurs was 43 years, while only 39 years among dynamic entrepreneurs (having sales and employment figures 20% above the average). Less than 10% of entrepreneurs were below 30 years, while 22.5% were 50 years and older. Dynamic entrepreneurs proved to be the high-end of the entrepreneurial stratum judged by their entrepreneurial characteristics (see Glas and Kotar 2006) and 85.7% of them have shown their entrepreneurial intentions even before starting their own business and a third tried to earn some money on their own while still in the childhood. Again, 80% of dynamic and 70% of other entrepreneurs have started the business on their own. Kotar asked entrepreneurs whether it is easier to start younger than 40 years or older.

Dynamic entrepreneurs, starting younger, probably remember the problems they faced at the start even more, but having more experience seems to help. Entrepreneurs also agree that it is easier to start business for men, since 32% consider it more difficult for women and only 3% for men.

4.2 Entrepreneurial activity among young people in early 2000

The GEM (Global Entrepreneurship Monitor) research is analyzing entrepreneurial activity looking at the proportion of the adult population between 18-64 years who are either in the process of setting up a business or are owner-managers of a young firm, active for no more than 42 months (Total Entrepreneurial Activity (TEA) index). Slovenia is participating since 2002. Entrepreneurial activity was by far the strongest in 2002, while really disappointing in 2004 and recovering in 2005, probably related to a more pro-business government.

For the year 2002, we are presenting in Table 7.4 the main findings about the age-specific TEA index. There are two dominating features: (a) the entrepreneurial process in Slovenia is mostly run by men, the ratio of male to female entrepreneurs was 2.2:1 (in all GEM countries 1.8:1 in 2002), although the general attitude towards female entrepreneurs should be quite favorable according to expert opinion (Rebernik et al. 2004, 18) and starting a business is a socially acceptable career choice for women; (b) the most entrepreneurially active groups are those aged between 25 and 34 years. Younger people are mostly attracted by the opportunity and less by the necessity (e.g. being unemployed). However, there is almost no difference in necessity-driven entrepreneurship in terms of gender, while opportunity is a stronger drive for men.

Table 7.4 Age- and gender-specific Total Entrepreneurial Activity index for Slovenia, 2002

	Gender	Age groups (years)				
		18-24	25-34	35-44	45-54	55-64
General TEA index	Men	13.2	19.7	14.6	11.2	6.8
	Women	7.7	12.8	10.2	6.2	5.0
TEA-opportunity	Men	10.8	13.3	9.8	7.1	3.7
	Women	5.6	7.6	5.2	3.2	2.5
TEA-necessity	Men	1.8	6.0	4.3	4.1	2.8
	Women	1.9	5.0	4.8	3.0	2.4

Source: Rebernik et al. 2004, 14.

The subsequent years of research have confirmed these structural features while on the whole entrepreneurial activity was at a substantially lower level, hard to explain besides by reference to the impact of recession, some disincentives created by the changes in the tax system, discontinuing support for SMEs, among other aspects.

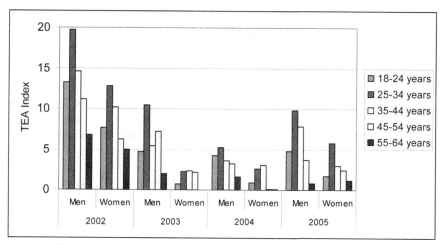

Figure 7.8 Age- and gender-specific TEA index for Slovenia, 2002-2005
Source: GEM Slovenia, 2002-2005.

While the level of the TEA index has changed substantially over the years, the pattern of age-specific TEA index remains virtually the same – entrepreneurial activity for the age group of 18-24 years lags behind the groups, aged 25-44 years. This fact, besides the doubts among young people due to their lack of business experience, could also be attributed to the weaknesses of the business environment in Slovenia. Considering the entrepreneurial conditions as assessed by experts in the GEM research, Slovenia has been weak on the following issues:

- financial support, despite the Slovenian Enterprise Fund, some municipal funds for micro credits and an elaborated network of commercial banks,
- the R&D transfer from the university and research facilities to business,
- commercial professional infrastructure offering services with quite an unsatisfactory "value for price" relationship according to the opinion of entrepreneurs,
- government policies and programs that lacked coherency and long-term determination.

On the other side, SME experts have praised Slovenia for:

- the level of entrepreneurship education and training for the variety of programs, training institutions and experiments undertaken,

- the open internal market and the simplicity to start a new business having discovered a promising market opportunity; however the access to location and marshalling proper resources has not been that easy,
- the level of available skills, and
- the protection of intellectual property rights.

While research has not explicitly focus on youth entrepreneurship, by looking at the low level of conditions and real barriers, the following observations can be made:

- it might be even harder for young people to get access to finance, although a number of service businesses do not depend on high capital investment;
- the disappointing R&D transfer points to the fact that proper incentives have not been developed for the academic community to work with business; young researchers also lack the incentives to either work part-time in companies or to engage in entrepreneurial activities in order to commercialize their research findings;
- the lack of professional infrastructure makes it difficult to compensate for one's own weaknesses in business skills and the deficiency in managerial know-how by engaging in professional support and,
- government policies and programs lack a focus on young people, although young graduates have been identified as a focal group in both strategic documents on SME and entrepreneurship development of 1996 and 2001.

4.3 Students and entrepreneurship

The graduates from vocational and professional secondary schools as well as students are interesting groups of young people to consider as having potentiality for the start-up of a business. We will briefly summarize some surveys among university students to present the picture of entrepreneurial intentions.

In 2001, we sent a questionnaire to all students in the graduate M.Sc. Entrepreneurship Program run since 1992 at the Faculty of Economics, University of Ljubljana. 46% of students participated, 58% being female. The respondents had an average of 8.2 years of working experience, but 20% had none prior to the program. The sample is interesting since 42% had no prior business education. The hierarchical cluster method divided 77 students into three groups by their characteristics: 30 of them were "entrepreneurs", competitive, ambitious, self-confident, very much oriented towards SMEs after graduating; 34 were "opportunists", students with no typical entrepreneurial personal traits, seeking a secure and life-long job (mostly coming from marketing as core orientation), and 13 were "career makers", they enrolled for perceived future benefits, a larger share being women. A large proportion of students had prior entrepreneurial experience and 40% have already started up a company. Among others, 21% planned to start up a company in the near future and 51% might start up a company in the future, while only 11% firmly opted against starting up their own business: the most important reason to start was independence, followed by opportunity, profit and additional income. These students came from an entrepreneurial social environment with 52% having parents running a private business and 10% other relatives doing so; 49% already helped their relatives in managing their private ventures. Students intending to start their businesses (47%) were quoting the following obstacles: for 24% there was the scarcity of resources (finance, people, own experience) and further 20% were still seeking the right business opportunity. 43% of the graduates from the program were regularly consulting other businesses and 34% only sporadically. Entrepreneurial studies have been beneficial: 41% of graduates were promoted or expected to be promoted soon, 31% have been offered a new career related to entrepreneurship, while 43% have changed their job or planned to do it very soon.

Consultants for the PHARE project evaluating strategic possibilities for the development of university spin-off incubators in Slovenia conducted over 200 interviews among students and researchers during the spring 2002 concluding:

- students show generally a positive approach to entrepreneurship, with 54% saying they would consider starting their own company as a career alternative, however, they were not well aware of the possibilities and benefits from a spin-off incubator;
- students understanding the concept of incubation would use such a facility for faster and cheaper development of their business ideas;
- students would mostly appreciate financial support and assistance in commercializing their business idea as the support from the incubator;
- further services demanded from the incubator would include training, coaching, mentoring and counseling as well as promoting business contacts with the private sector (Zizek and von Liechtenstein 1994, 9).

As a result of the provision of government support for the incubation concept at universities, three projects have started since late 2002, among them the project at the University of Ljubljana. The project group provided a broad analysis among students as an important target group, questioning 933 students at three science and technology departments and Faculty of Economics, 42% being female, most of them 21-24 years old (graduate students being older). Most students (44%) still intend to look for a job in a large company and 14.3% intend to work in a smaller private business, 5.5% only in the business of their own. However, 18% of undergraduate students and 32% of graduate students intend to start their own business in less than 5 years, while 13.6% graduate students already own one. Even 80% of undergraduate students said they would start their own business if having external support, while 65.5% of graduate students would do the same.

It is very important to note that many students intended to start their own business as part of an entrepreneurial team, while the prevalent pattern among Slovenian entrepreneurs is single or family ownership (see Figure 7.9). The team-oriented students have really been prevalent among the first 12 students projects since 10 of them started with at least two students in the team (Glas 2004). It is interesting that University of Ljubljana has its departments spread through the city of Ljubljana but students still find contacts with colleagues from other departments. Ninety percent of undergraduate and even 98% of graduate students consider participating in any entrepreneurial project as beneficial for their further career and most of them would welcome the introduction of a course on entrepreneurship, either as a compulsory (prevalently) or an optional course.

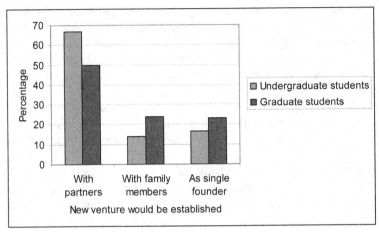

Figure 7.9 The pattern of new venture creation among students, 2002
Source: Drnovsek et al. 2003, IV-V.

More than half of students are contemplating a business idea for a product or service, 16.4% of graduate students already have an idea; 32% undergraduates and 46% of graduates would enter the university incubator. Most of them would prefer soft financial sources, followed by information support, counseling on business planning, opportunity to develop the business idea within the incubator and later the possibility to find a location in a business zone. Students already understand the need to consider the market for their product/service besides the technical aspects. Students are still wary about creating their own business and many would rather participate as team members or professional partners.

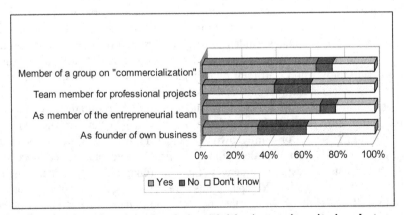

Figure 7.10 Students' options for their activities in a university incubator
Source: Drnovsek et al. 2003.

The research has shown that there is a strong potential for student entrepreneurship and the recent interview with the manager of the Ljubljana University Incubator (LUI) proved that 70-80 students are participating in the workshops introducing key aspects of the entrepreneurial process (marketing, finance, intellectual property rights, business planning) and also the same number joined the meetings of entrepreneurial clubs at the university. However, the real proof will follow after LUI will start operations on new premises in early 2007, as it is still a kind of "virtual" incubator since its establishment in 2003.

4.4 Family businesses as an option for young people

Relevant research has shown that 55-65% of SMEs in Slovenia could be considered family businesses. We already provided some information on their status from the point of view of the first of succeeding generations. Important is that family businesses differ in some aspects from other businesses opening alternative ways to some young people:

- family businesses have less educated managers; although the education of the younger generation is higher, they still fall behind the education of other, particularly dynamic entrepreneurs – they offer more space to heirs with secondary education as well;
- share of women managing family businesses is significantly higher as found by Lovsin Kozina (2006) (28.7% of businesses) and Kotar (2006); family businesses offer to women a different career path and many of them have decided for a family business in order to coordinate family and business in a better way than in large companies that lack the appreciation for such a behavior;
- they offer the job to family members and 47% of businesses strive for that.

It is important that a large share of family businesses established in the period of 1990-1994 will experience the transfer into the next generation in the next 5-10 years. The weakness of these businesses for the young generation is the fact that they live under the pressure to become the heirs of the family business and to choose education according to the needs of the family business. The problem is that few family businesses are ready to develop strategic plans including also a plan for succession: according to Lovsin Kozina (2006) 65% think of succession plans as not necessary (true, the average age of these owner-managers is 42.3 years only), 27% are in the phase of developing a plan (average age of 48.3 years) and only 8% already have the plan (aged 52 years). Herle (2003) has found a more encouraging picture with 25% of family firms having a written plan for management and ownership transfer, but her sample included larger, more mature businesses. On the other side, many family businesses are rather fast in transferring (at least a part of) the ownership to the younger generations before they really prove their determination and loyalty.

A further problem with family firms is that founders are late in transferring control (a managing position, ownership, power) to successors and they continue to play an important role in the business even after retiring in the absence of a plan for the post-retirement activities, somehow undermining the authority of successors. Slovenian family firms are fairly closed to outsiders, which is a problem for marital partners that could become alienated by this attitude.

These weaknesses of family businesses apart, continuing the family business tradition is an option a number of young people will face in the future since most family businesses (92% according to Herle 2003) intend to keep the business through the next generation.

5. Problems encountered by young entrepreneurs

From 1990 onwards, researchers have often tried to identify obstacles faced by Slovenian entrepreneurs. While financial barriers prevailed in the early post-independency period resulting from the macro-economic financial imbalances, weaknesses of the financial system and the weak financial strength of would-be entrepreneurs, further development revealed the real problems of the limited competitive strength of SMEs on the market, further enhanced by the lack of skilled workforce. Glas et al. (2001) identified the nine most important problems of SMEs in terms of finance and marketing.

Table 7.5 The nine most important problems of Slovenian SMEs, late 1990s

Rating	Problem / barrier
4.00	Collecting payments (lack of regulation)
3.83	High interest rates for loans at commercial banks (including other costs)
3.54	Increased competition on the domestic market (already small by its size)
3.39	Advertising costs (SMEs not used to pay for high quality promotion)
3.31	Lack of tax incentives for research and development (R&D)
3.22	Access to market information
3.21	Absence of tax incentives for investments
3.19	Lack of sales personnel (lack of high quality training)
3.12	Difficulties to provide loan guarantees (collaterals)

Source: Glas et al. 2001.

In the survey in 2002, backing the research on the support organizations, a sample of 197 entrepreneurs, some of them also private SME consultants, evaluated the problems they face in different business areas.

From all 70 problems identified, entrepreneurs ranked highest the problems of the lack of tax incentives for R&D and investments (both for firms and private investors), relatively high income tax (inflating labor costs, particularly for managers and professional staff), different problems with the access to finance e.g. high interest rates and other costs of bank loans – insurance, guarantees, lack of "soft" loans, problems with payment collection, problems of competitive pressures, both from legal and illegal, "underground" competitors, also the volume of documentation demanded by banks and public funds. SMEs also complain about the regulatory demands of inspections and the complacent and self-willed officials at the local level.

Table 7.6 The intensity of problems of Slovenian SMEs, 2002

Rank	Business area	Issues identified	Intensity of problems*
1	Access to finance	14	2.652
2	Taxation, accounting, procedures compliance	12	2.777
3	Marketing and sales	10	3.153
4	Labor force	9	3.220
5	Production and research & development	16	3.302
6	Procurement and logistics	9	3.593
Total	Average	70	3.088

* Assessment on the 5-point Likert scale between 1 (very important) and 5 (no problem at all)
Source: Glas et al. 2002.

Considering these complaints, as justified as they might be, they are really a result of several factors:

1. There are well-known problems of bureaucracy and the complicated legal/ administrative procedures:
   - unnecessary strict demands by inspectors and officials considering problems of locations, premises;
   - difficulties to comply with ever-changing legislation, regulations, standards;
   - the bureaucratic attitudes expressed by the personnel of public institutions, financial organizations, insisting on rather formal documentation instead on their profound knowledge and understanding of business.
2. The hard way of financial organizations to extend their "pro-business" approach to SMEs: commercial banks while pretty handy with craftsmen, still need more time to develop a more friendly, emphatic attitude towards owner-managers that would need more financial advice, not only money.
3. Lack of know-how and skills among entrepreneurs: many complaints of entrepreneurs are rooted in their lack of appreciation for their gaps in many business fields – they think they lack mostly:
   - legal know-how where they should rely on the professional know-how and advice;

- foreign languages to back the need for internationalizing business as well as sourcing technology and know-how;
- know-how to expand the business to the EU centers;
- lack of a more structured approach to market research and analysis;
- financial and accounting know-how: understanding balance sheets, financial parameters, financial management;
- expertise in management information systems and;
- managerial know-how.

Looking at these problems, it is quite easy to identify difficulties as perceived by young entrepreneurs:

1. General difficulties of Slovenian entrepreneurs and owner-managers:
   - for younger people, the access to finance is further constrained by their lack of experience in managing finance, lack of collateral possibilities due to their weak financial position, lack of real-estate ownership;
   - they are less versatile in overcoming lengthy bureaucratic procedures and their power of lobbying local administration is significantly weaker;
   - compared to well-established craftsmen, young entrepreneurs do not possess premises to start their own businesses and equipment to be transferred to business use;
   - the support systems for young entrepreneurs depend on their parents and other relatives: entrepreneurial parents usually provide a lot of support while other parents often prefer children to apply for less riskier careers in large companies; students complain about the weak encouragement from their professors (in Drnovsek et al. 2003, only 7% of undergraduate and 18% of graduate students enjoyed strong incentives and support from professors, although 56% of professors claimed to be ready to extend professional support to students);
   - until recently, there was a general lack of business infrastructure to support young entrepreneurs.
2. Specific obstacles encountered by young entrepreneurs:
   - young people lack experience which often allows them to act in a more creative, unimpeded way but certainly expresses itself in increased uncertainty about entrepreneurial career;
   - even in family businesses, younger generations lack the credibility and adult persons often lack trust in their business ideas and actions;
   - while Kotar (2006) discovered a low importance of social networks for Slovenian entrepreneurs, these networks could become more important for young people that prefer to act in supporting teams; it is why so many young people prefer to act in less riskier professional roles as employees, supporters, not entrepreneurs;
   - lack of education on entrepreneurship: only some curricula already systematically promote entrepreneurship as one of the key competencies for modern employees.

Young people lack also the targeted support from the state and local governments and a general lack of focus on the problems of young people. The Slovenian business culture does not really trust in young people to become entrepreneurs soon.

6. Government policies: past and future

Slovenian government lacked a consistent and diversified approach to the promotion of entrepreneurship. Young entrepreneurs have never been considered a target group to deserve special attention. Younger people lacked political power and other interest groups (pensioners, farmers) managed to push through their group interests in more effective ways. It was the Small Business Development Centre at the national level that experimented with some projects to promote entrepreneurship and creativity among young people, in cooperation with Employment Services. These projects included:

- support for entrepreneurship education in grammar and high schools, either as an introductory course in vocational schools or extracurricular activities, workshops elsewhere; some programs were transferred from the international practice (Junior Achievement, Enterprise in School) and some were originally created by Slovenian experts – however, the lack of resources limited these efforts;
- support for the cooperative movement to start social or commercial activities in some areas – never reached beyond the pilot stage;
- support for training for young start-up owners through a network of training organizations, in cooperation with the Chamber of Economy and local Chambers of Crafts;
- entrepreneurial clubs at the local level.

Slovenian Enterprise Fund tried to develop a special micro-finance scheme for young entrepreneurs but only attracted few applicants due to the cumbersome application procedure.

The lack of these efforts at the local level has been partly due to the highly centralized system of public finance that did not allow municipalities to allocate substantial resources beyond the support for education, training and some promotional events.

The future looks currently more promising. Along with the national strategy to support the Lisbon Strategy Goals, the national government recently recognized the need to support entrepreneurship and to devise some measures specifically aimed at young people. Development Strategy of Slovenia (June 2005), the Program of Reforms (October 2005) and most recently the Program of Measures to Support Competitiveness (2006) strongly support entrepreneurship education at all levels of formal education which should create entrepreneurship culture and provide specific skills to start and grow new businesses. The draft of the strategy for entrepreneurship education is under review. Recent initiatives include:

- introduction of entrepreneurship contents as part of curricula and extracurricular activities at all levels of formal education;
- integration of education and work through scholarships, practical training;
- supporting the first employment of young people with a university or postgraduate education within six months after the completion of their studies;
- sponsoring the transfer of young researchers from academic institutions to businesses either through spin-offs or jobs in established companies;
- supporting a period of studying abroad linked also to the practice in companies located at most creative world regions e.g. Boston, Silicon Valley, London, Singapore (a pilot group of 100 students envisaged);
- support for a network of university spin-off incubators, as the first phase to science and technology parks;
- support for new regional colleges offering study programs better adapted to the regional economic structure, ensuring better employability of graduates.

The recent period of stronger economic growth has encouraged entrepreneurial activity in Slovenia and young people are increasingly sharing this process. However, Slovenian social values are not unequivocally aligned to the entrepreneurial spirit and entrepreneurship as career option has to be further promoted.

Conclusion

The Slovenian entrepreneurial wave started in the early 1990s mostly through the activities of seasoned, experienced people who had been awaiting the chance to develop their own private business for a long time. Young people, although identified as having a strong potential in many programmes, have not been the focus of targeted support, at least not for a sustained period. While some ministries experimented with different programs for young people, several pilot programs were never upgraded into more long-term measures.

After the first wave of SMEs mostly exhausted the potential of adult persons, young people started to figure as an important source of new ventures or as heirs to existing family firms that await succession. Also, the government is currently developing more projects to establish proper business infrastructure and some recent strategic documents firmly declare the stimulation of the development of entrepreneurial skills and intentions of young people among their priorities.

Bibliography

Beibst, M. et al. (eds.) (2005), 'Proceedings of the 3rd International GET UP Workshop' (Jena: University of Applied Sciences).

Drnovšek, M. et al. (2003), *Poslovni Načrt – Ljubljanski Univerzitetni Inkubator* (Ljubljana: Univerza v Ljubljani).

Drnovšek, M. and Glas, M. (2006), 'Women Entrepreneurs in Slovenia: By Fits and Starts', in Welter et al. (eds.).

Duh, M. and Tominc, P. (2006), 'Primerjalna Analiza Druzinskih in Nedruzinskih Podjetij v Sloveniji', in Rebernik et al. (eds.).

Glas, M. and Cerar, M. (1997), 'The Self-Employment Programme in Slovenia: Evaluation of Results and an Agenda for Improvement' (Babson College – Kauffman Foundation Entrepreneurship Research Conference).

Glas, M. (1998), 'Eastern Europe: Slovenia', in Morrison (ed.).

Glas, M. (1999), *Slovenski podjetniki* (Ljubljana: Univerza v Ljubljani - Ekonomska Fakulteta).

Glas, M. (2004), 'Supporting University Based Start-Ups Within an Environment With a Low Culture of Entrepreneurship', in Beibst et al. (eds.).

Glas, M. and Petrin, T. (1998), *Entrepreneurship: New Challenges for Slovene Women* (Ljubljana: Faculty of Economics).

Glas, M. and Drnovsek, M. (2000), 'Small Business in Slovenia: Expectations and Accomplishments' (London: RENT XIII Conference).

Glas, M. and Lovsin, F. (2000), *Druzinsko Podjetnistvo v Sloveniji: Vkljucevanje Mlajse Generacije* (Ljubljana: Univerza v Ljubljani - Ekonomska Fakulteta).

Glas, M. and Drnovsek, M. (2001), 'Support for Graduate Students with Entrepreneurial Intentions: the Case of Slovenia' (Dublin: 31st ESBS 2001 – An Enterprise Odyssey).

Glas, M. et al. (2001), 'Problems Faced by New Entrepreneurs: Slovenia and Croatia – a Comparison' (Gent: 30th ESBS seminar – EFMD – Vlerick Leuven Gent Management School).

Glas, M. et al. (2002), *Projekt Izgradnje Celovitega Sistema Ugodnejsega Financiranja Malih in Srednjih Podjetij po Sistemu Drzav Evropske Unije* (Ljubljana: Univerza v Ljubljani).

Glas, M. et al. (2002a), *Spodbujanje Podjetnistva* (Piran: Visoka Sola za Podjetnistvo).

Glas, M. and Drnovsek, M. (2003), 'Does the Entrepreneurship Programme Matter?' (Tampere: 2002 IntEnt Conference).

Glas, M. and Vadnjal, J. (2005), *Transition of Businesses Into the Next Generation in Slovenia* (Ljubljana: University of Ljubljana – Small Business Development Centre).

Glas, M. and Kotar, S. (2006), 'Entrepreneurs in a Transition Country: How Different Are They?' (Brussels: RENT XX Conference).

Herle, J. (2003), *Stratesko Planiranje kot Dejavnik Uspeha Druzinskega Podjetja* (Ljubljana: Univerza v Ljubljani – Ekonomska Fakulteta).

Kotar, S. (2006), *Slovenski Podjetniki in Njihove Zmoznosti* (Ljubljana: Univerza v Ekonomska fakulteta).

Lovsin Kozina, F. (2006), *Kriticne Tocke Uspesnega Medgeneracijskega Prehoda v Slovenskih Druzinskih Podjetjih* (Ljubljana: Univerza v Ljubljani – Ekonomska Fakulteta).

Morrison, A. (ed.) (1998), *Entrepreneurship: An International Perspective* (Oxford: Butterworth-Heinemann).

OECD (1998), *Fostering Entrepreneurship* (Paris: OECD).

Rebernik, M. et al. (2004), *GEM 2002: The Winding Road to Entrepreneurial Society* (Maribor: Univerza v Mariboru – Ekonomsko Poslovna Fakulteta).

Rebernik, M. et al. (2004), GEM 2003: Spodbujati in Ohraniti Razvojne Ambicije (Maribor: Univerza v Mariboru – Ekonomsko Poslovna Fakulteta).

Rebernik, M. et al. (2005), *GEM 2004: Podjetnistvo na Prehodu* (Maribor: Univerza v Mariboru – Ekonomsko Poslovna Fakulteta).

Rebernik, M. et al. (2006), *GEM 2005: Podjetnistvo med Zeljami in Stvarnostjo* (Maribor: Univerza v Mariboru – Ekonomsko Poslovna Fakulteta).

Rebernik, M. et al. (eds.) (2006), *Slovenski Podjetniski Observatorij 2005* (Maribor: Univerza v Mariboru – Ekonomsko Poslovna Fakulteta).

Slovene Public Opinion Survey 1997/3: ISSP 1997 Work Orientations and Environment (Ljubljana: Center za Raziskovanje Javnega Mnenja in Množičnih Komunikacij).

Strategic Possibilities for the Development of Science/Technology and University Spin-off Incubators in Slovenia – Final Report (Ljubljana).

Vadnjal, J. (2005), *Razvojna naravnanost druzinskih podjetij v Sloveniji* (Ljubljana: Univerza v Ljubljani– Ekonomska fakulteta).

Welter, F., Smallbone, D., and Isakova, N., (eds.) (2006), *Enterprising Women in Transition Economies* (Aldershot: Ashgate).

Zizek, J. and von Liechtenstein, H. (1994), *750 CEE Dynamic Entrepreneurs Database Survey – Final Report* (Brussels – Schiphol: EFER – Phare – Evca).

Sources

Employment Services of RS, Annual Reports (different volumes).

GEM Slovenia <http://www.gemslovenia.org/> 2005 IPMMP, All rights reserved; (home page) accessed 31 January 2007.

Statistical Yearbook of Slovenia (different volumes) (Ljubljana: Statistical Office of RS).

Chapter 8

The Development of Youth Entrepreneurship in Bulgaria

Rossitsa Rangelova

Introduction

There is a lack of research on youth entrepreneurship in Bulgaria. Until recently, youth entrepreneurship had been the object of study only in analyses on the presence of young people on the labour market, i.e., as part of the total work force but not as a specific target group. The lack of knowledge on youth entrepreneurship does not allow for a more comprehensive idea and a serious analysis of the phenomenon, which hampers the elaboration of an effective policy towards this activity.

As a rule, studies are lacking when a given phenomenon is not yet well known, has not strongly demanded research attention, or when the issue is simply disregarded. In our case, the following reasons can be pointed out:

- Throughout the period 1945-90, which means during the period of central planning, and as a result of the nature of the social and economic system, including the lack of private property, a specific type of individual value-system was cultivated in Bulgaria much like in the other former socialist countries of Central and Eastern Europe (CEE). This value-system emphasized diligence, willingness, a sense of collectivism, but without encouraging the model of entrepreneurial behaviour with its typical spirit of enterprise, risk-taking, working in a team, and creating business relationships. Thus, the perception of entrepreneurship was blocked for at least two generations, and after 1989, when the new economic environment demanded developed entrepreneurial skills, young people did not have any relevant experience in terms of knowledge transmitted by their parents or relatives, but had to develop this kind of skill themselves in the unstable transition period.[1]
- The hard and long-lasting transition to a market economy did not create a favourable environment for the emergence and development of youth

---

1 Looking back at the history of Bulgaria, it seems that entrepreneurship and risk-taking are not amongst the most typical features of the national entrepreneurs, which refers to young people too. It is a well-known fact, for example, that from the end of the 19th century to the beginning of the 1930s, the state had a very protective policy of promoting industrial development. It turned out that the middle class as a whole felt more comfortable working under the conditions of very strong state protectionism without facing competition (see Rangelova 2006a, 34-44).

entrepreneurship in Bulgaria. It appeared more or less spontaneously and, initially, on the basis of the so-called 'trial-and-error' method.

It is very important, both theoretically and empirically, to be able to study the possibilities and barriers for youth entrepreneurship. Such an analysis is very useful for elaborating and implementing an effective economic policy, because:

- In general, young people are not well represented among the entrepreneurs in spite of their high potential.
- Youth is regarded as a strategic resource for business and macroeconomic development of any country. This means that national policy should give priority to youth education, employment and, in particular, entrepreneurship.
- In the case of the CEE countries, Bulgaria included, young people should adapt their economic and social attitudes, behaviour and skills to market economy requirements in a very short time and become active participants in the process of transformation and integration into the EU. This is, to date, an unknown experience.

The present study aims at the analysis of the development of youth entrepreneurship in the transition period in Bulgaria. The definition of the target group is as follows: The youth group considered covers people from 15 to 29 years of age, subdivided into three groups: 15-19, 20-24 and 25-29. This grouping aims to outline the specific traits of the different subgroups, predetermined by their role in current and future youth entrepreneurship. Young people between 15 and 19 years of age should be in secondary school and this is of crucial importance for their future quality as part of the labour force. These individuals have to be strongly encouraged to complete their education. The increase of economic activity has to be considered as a primary task for the group between 19 and 24 years of age. This age relates mainly to obtaining a university (higher) education required as a fundamental prerequisite of human capital for creating a knowledge-based economy, and gradual inclusion in the labour market. The typical enterprise activity is to be expected from the people aged up to 29 years and in a broader sense up to 34 years.

The study is organized as follows. First of all, it is important to know what was the macroeconomic environment for the development of youth entrepreneurship. For this reason, in the first section, the transition process in Bulgaria is presented briefly, showing the very hard and long-lasting reforms but also a tendency to some improvement. Considering the environment of youth entrepreneurship, demographic and social phenomena should also be taken into account. Like other countries in Europe, Bulgaria is subject to a steady process of depopulation and ageing. The demographic processes greatly concern young people, including would-be entrepreneurs, as far as their potential number decreases both relatively and absolutely. The severe demographic crisis was accompanied by the consequences of large-scale emigration of primarily young and active people. The two issues are briefly described in the second and third section respectively. In the period of transition, employment and unemployment became the most serious economic and social problems. Young people were among the most vulnerable. The fourth section presents youth on the labour market, including active labour market policy. In the fifth section, basic problems of the development of youth entrepreneurship in Bulgaria are discussed, in particular the current experience, existing barriers and challenges, as well as emerging positive trends.

1. Macroeconomic development in Bulgaria, 1990-2006

In early 1991, Bulgaria undertook a very hard and painful transition to a market economy. It was a difficult period, including a process of price, trade and foreign exchange liberalization, restitution of land and urban property, privatization and the de-monopolization of segments of the large enterprise sector. Stabilization policies were initially successful in containing the budget deficit and inflation. The newly created environment for private small business fostered entry by new private firms, mainly in trade and services. Debt reduction agreements improved the external debt situation to a certain extent. It was, however, insufficient for economic recovery. GDP declined for five years, and growth did not resume until 1994, and two years later, in 1996, it dropped again by over 10 per cent in comparison with 1995 (Table 8.1). The cumulative decline in output was followed by a rapid increase in unemployment.[2] The political instability and the very slow implementation of reforms were instrumental in causing the severe downturn and lack of progress. In the period 1990-97, there were seven successive governments in Bulgaria, each one supported by different political forces. These changes led to an inconsistency in economic policy and reforms, and provoked much disputed criticism in society. The lack of structural reforms began to have harmful repercussions on monetary reform and economic stabilization. This led to a weakening of the balance of payments and decline in foreign reserves. In addition, impending external debt service obligations helped to create an exchange rate crisis. The banking system collapsed. Both high inflation and large exchange rate movements undermined credibility in economic management.

The political and economic changes in the first half of 1997 aimed at stabilizing the economy and at restoring confidence. The programme, agreed with the IMF, entailed the introduction of a currency board regime, price liberalization and an acceleration of privatization. In general, the programme had a strong emphasis on structural reforms. As a result of the implemented programme, Bulgaria achieved a relatively good economic performance in the following years (Table 8.1). Under the conditions of good financial stabilization, the main challenge for Bulgaria now is to make the growth faster and sustained.

The Bulgarian governments are strongly committed to integration of the country into the EU. Judging by the level of the economic development, however, Bulgaria is one of the lowest per capita income countries amongst those newly integrated

---

2 The decline in Bulgaria's output was much more pronounced than in the other CEE countries (Hungary, the Czech Republic, Poland, Slovakia), as the country was more affected by the break-up of the former CMEA and by the price increases in energy imports from the former Soviet Union. Bulgaria also suffered from the conflicts in the former Yugoslavia and loss of market in some Arab countries.

into the EU. The country's GDP per capita based on PPPs is about one-third of the average for the EU members. The described macroeconomic performance in the transition period in Bulgaria implies that conditions for youth entrepreneurship were not favourable. The outlook for future economic performance and the question whether it will be friendly for entrepreneurship activity could be outlined by the following tendencies:

• Theoretically, positive changes in entrepreneurship depend on economic growth and its potential to create new activities and jobs. The GDP growth rates in recent years are moderate (from 4 to 5.5 per cent) and are not sufficient to experience any accelerating power in the economy. Growth is expected to accelerate in the near future after utilization of the assets coming from the EU Structural Funds as well as other global or international funds. Until now, however, this practice is quite sobering in Bulgaria, mainly because of low administrative capacity.

• Investment increased substantially throughout the most recent years but it is not connected to large-scale economic restructuring and technological changes.[3]

• In the coming years we can assume a more widespread introduction of modern technologies, information and telecommunication technologies. The entrepreneurs and branches that will succeed in attracting foreign investments, in adopting Structural Funds, and in renovating their equipment will be in a competitive position. In a parallel direction, low effective activities will continue to attract people in branches such as services, civil construction works and agriculture. This implies that changes in employment will involve both qualified labour and labour requiring a low level of education and skills.

• According to the report of the Agency for Small and Medium-sized Enterprises (ASME), small enterprises particularly are the generator for employment and entrepreneurship in Bulgaria.[4] The main problems of the SMEs are: low labour efficiency, slight integration of high technologies in the production process, and the insufficient use of personnel. SMEs in Bulgaria have a two to seven times lower rate of labour efficiency in comparison with the new member states and 15-30 times lower than the EU-15.[5]

• The SME sector covers mainly trade, the processing industry, hotels and restaurants (catering). In most cases they are not sub-contractors of big companies and part of their chains. The development of the SMEs faces the restrictions of consumer demand of the population, while a significant

---

3 There are serious grounds to consider as to whether the investment growth is due to credit expansion, the efforts of businesses to meet the European standards of quality and of work safety conditions or the work to restore the damages caused by the severe flooding in the country in 2005 (Loukanova 2005, 67-89).

4 According to the ASME report, the distribution of the total number of employed in 2003 is the following: 31.5 per cent are engaged in micro firms, 23.8 per cent in small-sized firms, and 23.6 per cent in medium-sized firms, which means that 79 per cent of the total number are employed in SMEs (see Report of the ASME 2004, 16).

5 See Council of Ministers 2006, 36.

change in its level cannot be expected (except for the seasonal months in the tourism sector). At the same time, in predominant cases, the SME sector applies to simple (routine) labour functions and does not imply a qualitative development of the work force.

• A positive development on the production (supply) side consists of an increase in economic potential of the private sector in agriculture. The eventual stabilization of the sector could boost entrepreneurship in the near future. However, this implies that this tendency will lead to an increase in labour productivity in agriculture, keeping its relatively lower rates of employment than in industry and services.

• The increase of the indicator for gross value added (GVA) gives strong evidence for the fast growing and prevailing private sector in the economy – nearly 80 per cent in 2005 as compared to 9.5 per cent in 1990 (Table 8.1).

• The NSI survey on the business climate in 2006 shows that the economy continues to develop. This is due mainly to the development of industry, but also due to construction works and retail trade.

2. The ageing of the Bulgarian population

The worsening of the demographic situation under the conditions of economic and social crisis in the transition period may be the most alarming phenomenon in Bulgaria (Table 8.2).[6]

The tendency of a dropping mortality rate until 1960 (when it reached its minimum of 8.1 per 1,000 population) gradually increased again afterwards. In 2005, it was close to 15 per 1,000 population. At present, the total life expectancy at birth (about 72 years) is among the lowest in Europe, not only when compared with many developed countries but also with other CEE countries. A growing gap between a male's life expectancy and that of a female can be observed in favour of women, from only a year and a half in 1935-39, to three and a half years in the mid-1950s, to nearly seven years at present.

The described demographic trends lead to depopulation and changes in the age structure, respectively to an ageing population in Bulgaria. This means that the share of young people declines and that that of old people increases. In 1989, the share of young people (0-14) was 20.6 per cent and that of old people (65 and over) was 13.6 per cent. At the beginning of the 21st century, the share of old people is already higher than that of young people. At the same time, the share of the working age population (15-64) has increased only by approximately two percentage points for the period

---

6 During the second half of the 20th century the rate of natural increase was continuously dropping: by official data of the National Statistical Institute (NSI) from 7.2 per 1000 population in 1970 to 3.4 in 1980, -0.4 in 1990, -7.7 in 1997 and -5.4 in 2005. Thus the country faces a marked depopulation: from 8.9 million in 1989 to 7.7 million in 2005. As a result, at the beginning of the 21st century the size of the Bulgarian population is at the level of 1960. There are differences among the countries of the CEE, but most of them have experienced deterioration of demographic and health indicators in the 1990s (see Rangelova 2006b).

Table 8.1 Bulgaria: macroeconomic indicators, 1990-2005 (% change over previous year unless indicated otherwise)

	1990	1991	1992	1993	1994	1995	1996	1997	2000	2005
Real GDP	-9.1	-16.7	-7.3	-1.5	1.8	2.1	-10.9	-7.4	5.4	5.5
GDP per capita (USD)	769	943	1,008	1,276	1,147	1,559	1,189	1,227	1,542	3,443
Industrial output	-17.5	-22.2	-15.9	-10.9	8.5	4.7	0.1	-7.5	15.8	10.7
Agricultural output	-5.1	-0.3	-12.0	-30.2	10.7	16.4	-11.8	12.0	-4.6	-6.9
Structure of GVA, incl.	100.0	100.0	100.0	100.0	100.0	100.0	100.0	100.0	100.0	100.0
Agriculture, forestry, fishing	17.7	14.5	12.0	10.6	12.3	13.9	11.7	18.0	13.9	9.3
Industry	51.3	37.4	40.5	35.0	32.1	33.6	32.6	36.0	29.1	30.4
Services	31.0	48.1	47.5	54.4	55.6	52.5	55.7	64.0	57.0	60.3
CPI (December to December previous year)	–	573.7	179.5	163.9	222.0	133.0	411.0	678.6	111.4	105.7
Real wages, indices	100	61.0	68.8	69.6	57.1	54.0	44.5	36.1	53.9	74.7
Employment rate, %	-6.2	-13.1	-8.2	-1.6	0.6	2.1	-0.1	-2.7	-4.7	1.5
Unemployment rate, %	1.5	6.7	13.2	15.7	14.1	10.7	12.5	13.6	17.9	10.7
Share of private sector in GVA, %, incl.	9.5	11.9	15.6	35.4	39.4	48.0	52.5	58.8	69.6	79.4
Agriculture, forestry, fishing	6.7	5.5	4.5	7.2	9.5	10.1	13.6	22.7	13.7	9.1
Industry	1.7	3.9	6.1	6.0	6.6	8.7	7.1	11.2	20.3	25.9
Services	1.7	2.5	5.0	22.2	23.3	29.2	31.8	24.9	35.6	44.4

Source: Statistical Reference Book of the Republic of Bulgaria, Sofia: National Statistical Institute, various years.

Table 8.2 Demographic statistics for Bulgaria, 1989-2005, per 1,000 (unless indicated otherwise)

Indicator	1989	1995	2005
Population – to 31.12 (thousand)	8993.4	8384.7	7718.7
Birth rate	12.6	8.6	9.2
Mortality rate	11.8	13.6	14.6
Rate of natural increase	0.8	-5.0	-5.4
Total fertility rate	1.81 (1990)	1.23	1.31
Life expectancy at birth (years)	71.2 (1989-91)	70.6	72.4 (2004)
Including			
Men	68.0	67.1	69.1
Women	74.7	74.9	76.2
Average age (years)	37.3	38.9	41.2
Age structure (years), incl.			
0-14	20.6	17.7	13.6
15-64	66.8	67.1	69.2
65+	12.6	15.2	17.2

Source: Statistical Yearbook of Republic Bulgaria, Sofia: National Statistical Institute, various issues.

under consideration.[7] The ageing population leads to an increase in the average age, which in the 1990s changed faster than in the previous decades. In 2005, the average age of the population was 41.2 years: 39.5 years in the towns and 45.2 years in the villages.

Since 1989, a dynamic process of an ageing population and depopulation has been observed in Bulgaria. This process will be even stronger in the next decades of the 21st century when the size and proportion of young people will continue decreasing both absolutely and relatively. However, the target group of the young people under review in this study, in particular those 19 years of age and over, were born before 1989 and they do not reflect the worsened demographic situation after 1990. The consequences of the latter will be observed in the next decades.

3. Youth migration from Bulgaria

To get a better idea of current migration from Bulgaria, one has to bear in mind that during the 40 years until the end of the 1980s, the population could not move abroad freely. Since 1989, the Bulgarian transition to a market economy has been accompanied by a massive external migration of primarily young and active people. The emigration wave was a result of the lifting of those administrative barriers and

---

7 The ageing of the population is a distinct trend in the rural areas (where about 30 per cent of the Bulgarians live), see Table 8.2, and less so in urban areas.

restrictions which were a legacy of the reticence of the regime of the period 1945-89, and the very big difference of living standards between Bulgaria and the developed countries. According to official data of the NSI, from 1989 to 2005, the migrants constituted nearly 750,000 persons, that is, nearly one in every ten Bulgarians. Migrants from Bulgaria continue to be mainly young people, as the prevailing part of the total potential migrants has a secondary education.[8]

A very important indication of the existing family climate forming the inclination of the youth to emigrate emerges from the following data. According to the 2001 NSI study, the percentage of parents encouraging their children to study or work abroad is very high: nearly 90 per cent. The percentage of people encouraging their children to resettle abroad is also very high: nearly 55 per cent. According to the 2001 IOM study, 72 per cent of respondents would stimulate their children to work abroad for shorter or longer periods of time (Rangelova and Vladimirova 2004, 7-30).

The two sources on migration data show that Germany and the USA are the first two country destinations, which is relevant to some extent for the expected influence on the young migrants' professional skills and enterprise feeling.

The social and economic consequences of emigration for the country should be considered, both from the positive and negative side. Among the well known positive consequences are the following: remittances to relatives in the country of origin, moderation of labour market problems (migration mitigates the pressure on the domestic labour market), obtaining higher professional qualifications and labour market participation abroad, and so on. Among the negative consequences could count, first of all, the loss of people of a fertile age (which has very strongly influenced the level of de-population in the country), decline in the work force (according to NSI projections due to the deteriorating demographic situation, Bulgaria will be forced to import a labour force after 2012), decline in the skilled work force, lower return on investment in public education (if many young people migrate and live abroad, the social return from such investment is reduced and taxpayers in fact subsidize the human capital and productivity growth in the host countries).

Concerning youth entrepreneurship in a narrower sense, we can specify the following negative consequences of migration (Rangelova 2006c, 50-73):

• Reduced rents from innovation. If the most talented scientists, and present or future entrepreneurs go abroad, host countries will come to own more patents and will take advantage of this. For the country of origin, this means a likely reduction in the proportion of good jobs in the economy in the future.

---

8 "The average potential migrant is a highly mobile, well-educated young person, more often male than female, rather single than married, and inhabiting the capital or other larger towns in Bulgaria. This reflects a significant shift in the social profile of the potential migrant since, during the last decade of transition, it was the poorly-educated people who prevailed in the group of potential migrants. The average potential Bulgarian migrant is a temporary labour migrant. He is most likely to stay abroad for a shorter period of time than is usually thought. The survey showed that the majority of Bulgarians who plan to migrate would not wish to spend more than 3 years in a foreign country and would rather work there for a while than to settle permanently" (IOM study 2001 on potential migrants from Bulgaria, 3).

- Undesirable specialization of economic activity in the country of origin. Due to the absence of highly skilled specialists or entrepreneurs in the home country, economic activity is predetermined and must adjust to the available human capital.
- Negative effects on entrepreneurship and business development. The absence of active and highly skilled people limits the chance of creating and developing business. In the Bulgarian case, this means a decisive lack of entrepreneurial potentiality during the very important period of economic transformation and necessity of progress, including entrepreneurship development.
- Migration practice and economic de-motivation. The people remaining in the country of origin could be de-motivated from developing entrepreneurial behaviour. In many cases they are strongly influenced by the successful examples of fellow countrymen (countrywomen), believing that the only correct way of achieving personal success is emigration.

Experiences at the global level show that, as a rule, a given country is abandoned mainly by young people, who are more adventurous and ready to take risks; these young people are among the most creative, ready to try various opportunities and willing to work hard, and to rely on their own capacities more so than the people remaining in the country of origin. In this sense, large-scale emigration from Bulgaria hits the country considerably. Bulgaria is likely to continue to experience an outflow of skilled and young people when it joins the EU (1 January 2007) and current member countries open their labour markets.[9] Younger and better-educated individuals are more likely to move. Very well paid workers are less likely to emigrate and, in contrast, the youngest and most educated emigrants are the least likely to return. Given the economic situation in Bulgaria as a country with the lowest income per capita among the other EU countries, it is not realistic to expect that most of these young people who are in a very adaptive age and who are living in a better economic and social environment will come back and start (or continue) their own business. Experiences on the global level show that many people who did not intend to do so, in fact stay in their host country forever. The ongoing global processes accelerate this tendency.

The reasons for migration from Bulgaria show the way in which it may be limited. There are two basic reasons: (a) the crisis wrought by the transition to a market economy, and (b) the lack of an adequate national policy towards Bulgarians abroad. Until now, the official Bulgarian policy has been as if to encourage emigration, i.e., as a forcing push factor, rather than attracting people to live in their own country. In reality, what Bulgaria needs is to achieve further marked economic progress. The outflow of young people would be more limited if the economic catching-up with current EU member states were to happen more quickly than expected.

---

9 The latest study of the NSI shows that the tendency to migrate exists mainly amongst young people (see Kalchev 2002 and 2005).

4. Youth on the labour market

4.1 The youth proportion in the adult population

In order to study the realization of youth labour, including youth entrepreneurship in Bulgaria, we have to take into account the proportion of these people in the total number of the population aged 15 years and over (Table 8.3). The following tendencies can be outlined:

- The total number of the population, including the young population, decreased absolutely from 7.1 million in 1990 to 6.7 million in 2005;
- The proportion of young people is nearly one-quarter of the total population aged 15 years and over;
- The present number and the proportion of young people, in particular those aged 19 years and over, reflect the period before the demographic crisis, which means that the generation from the higher birth-rate period still enters the working-age group. This is why the proportion of those young people aged 25-29 increases over time and that of young people aged 20-24 years fluctuates and begins declining from 2000 onwards, while the proportion of the youngest group (15-19) decreases during the entire period under review. Thus the structure of the young population gradually changes in favour of the groups of people at the higher age (25-29);[10]
- As a result of the above-described demographic changes young people in the three age groups will continue to decrease.

Table 8.3 Population aged over 15 years at the end of the year and proportion of the young people by age group, 1990-2005

Year	Total number of population aged 15 and over years	Including population aged 15-29				
		Number	% of total	Of which proportion of the young people by age group, %		
				15-19	20-24	25-29
1990	7,168,683	1,871,026	26.1	9.3	8.5	8.3
1995	6,903,368	1,794,876	26.0	9.0	8.8	8.2
2000	6,883,053	1,775,828	25.8	8.0	9.0	8.8
2005	6,671,699	1,622,416	24.2	7.6	8.0	8.6

Source: Statistical Reference of Republic of Bulgaria, Sofia: National Statistical Institute, various years.

---

10 This tendency could be related also to the intensive migration of young people going to study abroad.

An important feature of young people is their educational attainment level (Figure 8.1). Several positive tendencies can be observed in the period 1998-2001, which continue to develop at the present time. The first one is the increased proportion of young people with higher education. The second tendency is the better professional orientation of young people resulting in the decreased proportion of people with secondary/high school education from 27 per cent in 1998 to 19.5 per cent in 2001. The third tendency is the decreased proportion of young people with basic and primary education.

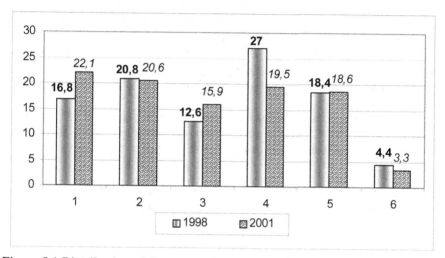

Figure 8.1 Distribution of the population aged 25-29 by level of education (1998 and 2001), %

Legend:
1 - Higher education
2 - Secondary specialized/college
3 - Secondary vocational
4 - Secondary/high school
5 - Basic
6 - Primary
Source: Employment Agency in Bulgaria.

A very important precondition for development of competitive economic agents, including young entrepreneurs, is the possibility of easy movement of young people from school/university to employment. This objective has been formulated as one of the priorities in labour market policy in Bulgaria.[11]

---

11 This is one of the aims in the "Strategy for National Youth Policies" worked out by the National Agency for Youth and Sports for the period 2003-07. Since its publication, however, no data has become available regarding the results achieved so far. For the full text of the Strategy, see: http://youthsport.bg.

4.2. Youth employment – main trends

The young employed people in Bulgaria were about one-fifth of the total of employed people in the 1990s and the first years of the current decade. While the coefficient of economic activity of the total population was a little over 51 per cent, for the age group 15-19 it was 13 per cent, for the age group 20-24, over 53 per cent, and for the age group 25-29 it is over 77 per cent. This means that the economic activity of the people aged 20-24 is higher than that of the total population, and the economic activity of the people aged 25-29 goes considerably beyond that of the total population.

Concerning the youth employment rate, the situation follows the pattern of economic activity but with lower magnitudes. The employment coefficient of the total population for the period under review was about 43 per cent (reaching 44.7 per cent in 2005); for people aged 15-19 it was 5.4 per cent; for people aged 20-24, about 40 per cent; and for the highest young age 25-29, nearly 62 per cent. This proves that the latter group of young people is most successful in finding a job on the labour market.

Bulgaria, however, is lagging behind in terms of average employment levels when compared to the EU (25) countries. This unfavourable position concerning young people at the start of their professional carriers is outlined by the data in Table 8.4.[12]

Table 8.4 Employment rates of young people aged between 15-24 years in Bulgaria and the EU member countries, %

	2001	2002	2003	2004	2005
EU - 25	38.1	37.5	36.9	36.8	36.8
EU - 15	40.9	40.9	39.9	40.0	39.8
NMS – 10*	27.1	25.3	24.4	23.9	24.2
Bulgaria	18.3	18.9	20.7	21.5	21.6

* NMS – new member states
Source: Indicators for monitoring the 2004 Employment Guidelines, 2005 Compendium, EC, 11.07.2005; http://www.nsi.bg and www.employment_strategy/indic/compendium_jer2005_en.pdf.

The data in Table 8.5 show the increasing educational level of employed young people for the period 1998-2001. As a result, the proportion of the employed young people with basic and primary education decreased.[13]

---

12 It has to be added that young women are in a more vulnerable position than men. At the same time, the encouraging fact is that the share of unemployed youth in the respective age category is lower than the registered levels in EU. In relation to unemployment, Bulgaria does not lag behind European levels.

13 A special issue with regard to young people is the so-called dropout of school problem in Bulgaria, and the effective measures to overcome this problem.

Table 8.5 Distribution of employed young people by educational level, June 1998 and June 2001, %

Level of education	Total employed	Total employed young people (15-29)	Including		
			15-19	20-24	25-29
June 1998					
Higher*	21.7	13.9	..	7.5	19.8
Secondary specialized/college	22.1	22.7	13.1	23.1	23.7
Secondary vocational	ND***	14.9	10.2	15.8	14.9
Secondary/ high school	22.1	27.1	28.5	30.1	24.9
Basic	32.1**	17.9	35.6	19.7	14.4
Primary and lower	–	3.3	12.2	3.4	–
Total	100.0	100.0	100.0	100.0	100.0
June 2001					
Higher*	26.4	20.7	–	12.3	27.4
Secondary specialized/college	22.6	24.5	21.1	26.9	23.4
Secondary vocational	16.2	18.2	15.7	20.4	17.1
Secondary/ high school	16.4	21.0	28.4	25.8	17.5
Basic	16.3	13.4	26.5	12.5	12.9
Primary and lower	1.8	1.8	7.6	1.8	1.3
Total	100.0	100.0	100.0	100.0	100.0

* For 1998 this higher and college education
** Including primary
*** Not defined
Source: Beleva 2001, 113-135.

Judging by professional groups, employed young people are concentrated in services, followed by skilled workers in the production sector, operators of machines, equipment, means of transportation, and so on. The share of management personnel is lower than that of low skilled workers. It is positive, however, that the latter decreases in favour of the former (Table 8.6).

Table 8.6 Distribution of the employed young people by professional group, June 2001, %

Professional group	Age group 15-19	Age group 25-34
Employed in the service sector	29.2	16.9
Skilled workers in the production sector	15.9	15.1
Operators of machines, equipment, means of transportation	14.6	13.4
Analytical specialists	5.2	13.0
Applied specialists	8.6	12.8
Low skilled workers	12.1	8.8
Management personnel	2.7	8.0
Supporting personnel	5.7	6.4
Producers in agriculture, forestry and fishing	4.5	3.8
Not indicated	1.5	1.8
Total	100.0	100.0

Source: National Employment Office 2001, 57.

In Bulgaria, like in other countries, most of the young people start their professional careers from positions at the low administrative/technical level. Within the structure of the employed by class of profession, the highest share of youth belongs to the "Personnel employed in services, security and trade" category (nearly 30 per cent). The majority of them have secondary or higher than secondary education. They are followed by young people who have an incomplete secondary education and low vocational qualifications, which is the category of the so-called unqualified workers (18 per cent). Like in many other countries, seasonal and part-time employment is popular among the youth in Bulgaria. As a rule, young people are concentrated in large towns where the opportunities to find work are highest.

For youth entrepreneurship development, it is interesting to analyse the structure of employed young people in terms of professional status. They are engaged predominantly as hired workers (employees) and this is explainable by taking into account their age (Table 8.7). The second important status for youth is self-employment, but the number of young people engaged in this kind of activity is nearly 10 times less than those employed.[14]

---

14 According to a UNDP survey in Sofia (February 2001), the main reasons for the low participation of the young people in self-employed businesses are difficult access to credit and the considerable bureaucratic barriers to starting a business.

Table 8.7 Distribution of the employed young people by status of employment, September 1993 and June 2001, %

Age group	Total	Employer	Self-employed	Employed	Unpaid family worker	Not indicated
September 1993						
Total	100.0	9.8		88.7	1.4	0.1
15-24	100.0	6.7		88.8	4.4	0.1
25-34	100.0	8.6		90.1	1.1	0.2
June 2001						
Total	100.0	3.6	10.0	84.2	1.6	0.6
15-24	100.0	1.0	4.9	89.5	3.8	0.8
25-34	100.0	3.9	8.0	86.3	1.3	0.5

Source: Survey on Employment and Unemployment, National Employment Office, September 1993, June 2001.

According to their status, about 88-90 per cent of young people are employed, 70 per cent of whom in companies in the private sector. The branches where young people find employment are the processing industry; trade and repairs; services; hotels and restaurants. The share of the hired employed with secondary education is the highest in the "hotels and restaurants" branch (74 per cent). The same share is also relatively high for "trade and repairs" (68 per cent) and for the processing industry (68 per cent).[15] This distribution hints at the fact that the highest number of youth with secondary or higher education will also find employment within the same branches. On the other hand, technological innovation in Bulgarian enterprises has not been strongly promoted, and there is not much evidence that young people start to work under high-tech conditions.

The private sector was the main generator of jobs. It constituted over 70 per cent of the total number of the vacancies offered by employment services in Bulgaria, including jobs created as a result of the measures to encourage employers to hire unemployed people. For the time being, no drastic changes have been observed in the demand for labour. Supply and demand are largely determined by and for the unemployed with low levels of education and skills (Vladimirova and Rangelova 2006, 6-9).

There is strong evidence of a decreasing scope of the grey economy in Bulgaria and a respective increase of the employment rates. This concerns young people engaged in the grey economy in branches such as tourism, hotels and restaurants,

---

15 According to the Employment Agency data, the biggest number of job openings is observed in textiles, food and tobacco goods, trade, agriculture and construction sectors, as well as in the processing industry.

and civil construction. One positive consequence of this fact is connected with the higher opportunity for improving the quality of the labour force.[16]

A main reason for the unfavourable position of young people at the start of their professional career – relatively low levels of payment, and a high possibility of further long-term unemployment – is their low educational level. One of the main issues of vocational training and education is the mismatch between the demand for and the supply of professions (skills). In 2005, a special study on the needs of employers for particular vocations was carried out. The results were taken into account in the preparation of the employment promotion plan in 2005 and for vocational education. After 2003, growth in youth employment became more intensive. This was achieved because of the overall expansion of labour market policies and measures, and because of an increase in the employers' demand. The changes are parallel to those of the total population and do not exceed them. The rates of employment and unemployment of young people are constantly double the level of that of the total population – lower in employment and higher in unemployment. The utilization of the now existing reserves from the side of the labour supply will add to the labour force and employ mainly low skilled and insufficiently educated people in their mid-ages or older. An improvement in the quality of labour resources is highly necessary. There are indications of the development of a better coordination between the needs of employers and vocational education and training, but it is still not proactive in its nature.[17]

4.3 Youth unemployment

The unemployment rate in Bulgaria was high in the past 17 years. Its statistical registration started from the beginning of the 1990s and the rate of unemployment showed a tendency to increase over time, reaching the highest rate of 18.1 per cent in 2001, and declining afterwards to about 8.5 per cent for 2006. It was on a par with that of other CEE countries, new members of the EU, with high unemployment. According to Eurostat data, the situation was as follows in 2004: Poland (18.2 per cent), Slovakia (16.2 per cent), Lithuania (12.0 per cent), and Latvia (10.8 per cent). At present it is about the average level of the EU countries.

According to annually reported data by the Employment Agency in Bulgaria both the number of the registered unemployed and the proportion of the young unemployed (15-34) in the total number decreased from 2000 to 2005.[18] Youth unemployment decreased both absolutely and relatively from about 30 per cent in 2000 to nearly 25 per cent in 2005.

As a rule, the high and persistent rate of total unemployment is accompanied by a higher rate of youth unemployment, a high rate of long-term unemployed and

---

16 The employed in the grey sector as a rule do not have access to regular vocational training and practically do not have career development. Such a perspective is totally unacceptable keeping in mind the requirements connected with the EU membership of the country and the Lisbon strategy.

17 For further details, see Loukanova (2005), 67-89.

18 The number of unemployed decreased from 693,483 in 2000 to 424,381 in 2005.

slow labour force mobility from unemployment to employment. Almost half of the unemployed young people stay in the labour market for more than 12 months, which means they are so-called long-term unemployed. This is caused mainly by the high starting level of youth unemployment. In addition, nearly two-thirds of the long term unemployed young people remain in the labour market for more than 24 months. This leads to increases in the number of discouraged young workers (Loukanova 2005, 67-89).

Another specific feature of unemployment in Bulgaria is that it is static and unchangeable, which means that the inflow-outflow process is insignificant. More often than not, the inflow exceeds the outflow; if the opposite takes place, it is mainly because of the high numbers of 'de-motivated' people abandoning the labour market. Although the officially reported unemployment figures show a decrease, the growing number of de-motivated persons who are leaving the labour market, of inactive people at working age, of those eligible for social assistance, and of those socially excluded, are evidence that the active population is being transformed into an inactive one (Vladimirova and Rangelova 2006, 6-9).[19]

During the last 15 years, young people in Bulgaria were amongst the most hit by unemployment. This explains the traditionally highest proportion of young people among the trained unemployed people aged up to 29 (47.9 per cent of the total number in 2005). The major youth employment indicators are improving, while unemployment is decreasing. Despite these trends youth remains a risk group on the labour market. In the last five years, the unemployment rate of young people was twice as high as the average rate for the total population. About 40 per cent of unemployed youth remains on the labour market for longer than 12 months and about two-thirds of them for more than 24 months (Employment Agency 2005). This is a quite unfavourable starting point for young people, and results in a growing number of discouraged young people. The lack of education and work experience are the main obstacles to the entry of young unemployed into the labour market. People, including young people, who have no vocational qualifications or skills in terms of their employability, are the most vulnerable in face of economic changes. This explains why the unemployed with a low education make up the majority of the unemployed and why the trend is so persistent.[20] The decrease in unemployment in

---

19 The persons described as 'de-motivated' are those wishing to work but not actively looking for a job over a four-week period, including the week in which the survey takes place, as they no longer believe they will find one. Although it is true that such persons are outside the active working population, they make up the so-called labour reserve and most of them would start work if sustained economic growth is achieved. So far, employment policy in Bulgaria has ignored this fact. This fact, however, can explain the low activity and employment rates in the mainstream (official) economy and the high percentage in the informal (shadow) economy.

20 According to data of the Employment Agency, while young people aged 15-24 with basic and lower education or secondary comprehensive education are not preferred on the labour market, the opposite situation exists for those with higher or secondary specialized education. In 2001, the number of unemployed *young* people with higher education was half the total number of unemployed persons with higher education (3.4 per cent against 6.6 per cent).

Bulgaria, reported from 2002 onwards, is to be attributed, first of all, to the slowing down of the privatization process, fewer closures of loss-making firms, and an active policy leading to the creation of a large portion of available jobs. Concerning the development of youth entrepreneurship, the possibility to look for young people among the unemployed is limited. The biggest share of them should, first and foremost, increase their education and professional qualification.

4.4. Active labour market policy towards youth unemployment and entrepreneurship

Throughout the 1990s, a passive type of employment policy dominated in Bulgaria. Since the end of the decade, a shift from passive to active employment policies could be observed, along with the promotion and expansion of the state employment services' mediating role. There are two basic forms of active policy towards youth: (a) subsidizing employers to hire young people and (b) the promotion of young business start-ups through training or ensuring access to money credit. The national regulations since 1998 have included participation of young people in all kinds of active policy as well as in specially designed programmes.[21]

At present, youth employment measures are mainly for subsidizing jobs or training unemployed for a 6 to 12 months duration and in-house vocational training. There are different measures: for typical apprenticeships and internships, for hiring youngsters up to 29 years, and for hiring those who are handicapped. A positive indication is that the number of young people covered by measures and programmes has been increasing over the last four years. It seems that the measures become more focused on the specific needs of youth, who represented nearly one quarter of all participants in 2005. The share of unemployed young people included in these programmes is also increasing in the total number of unemployed at the same age (from 1 per cent in 2002 to 3.5 per cent in 2005), but it remains very low.

The employers' interest in hiring of young people is of varying intensity. The total number of those who have remained employed upon completion of the subsidized employment period is decreasing slightly. The highest employers' demand is however for youths with low vocational qualifications.[22]

In 2003-05, youth formed 20 to 23 per cent of the total number of persons covered by the national programmes "From Social Assistance to Employment", "Beautiful Bulgaria" and "Programme for Overcoming Poverty", programmes for a new start for women after maternity leave and for single mothers. The programmes combine modules of vocational training with further employment. About 30 per cent of those who have received loans from the National Trust Fund for Micro Credits for the first

---

21 Large-scale national employment programmes include modules for subsidized training and vocational education, subsidies for employment, specialized grant schemes, additional services for finding of employment, including lifelong learning schemes.

22 According to data of the Employment Agency, the number of young people who have found a job was increasing in 2004-05. Half of them were hired in positions that do not require any particular vocational qualification. In 2005, 43 per cent of the hired young people did not have a vocational qualification.

9 months of 2005 are young people.[23] Nearly half of the newly included persons in literacy, vocational qualification and employment programmes are also young people.

During recent years, different programmes targeted at a decrease in youth unemployment were applied. For example, the programme "Employment Promotion Project[24] "is of particular interest for youth entrepreneurship. It promotes youth employment and entrepreneurship at the local level as well as provides other initiatives for the employment of youth, such as internships, vocational education, subsidized employment, self-employment and the provision of employment. It provides training opportunities in vocation and skills that are needed in order to start one's own business, as well as subsidized employment.

The national Programme for student internships aims at reducing the mismatches between the skills and knowledge taught at universities and the competencies demanded by the employers. It also acts towards the improvement of business-university relations. The Programme offering computer skills training aims at improving the access of young people to information and communication technologies through acquiring knowledge on their usage and application.[25]

Numerous labour market policies and measures are being applied for the promotion of youth employment and entrepreneurship. Wide-scale changes aiming at enhancing general and vocational training are implemented. Efforts to decentralize the management of vocational training have been made so that it is in line with the demand of employers. However, employers' demand regards primarily a labour force with low qualifications, which discourages youth to increase their level of education.

The measures taken so far cover a limited number of unemployed young people and have not yet led to a significant increase in the employment rate and, moreover, to the promotion of entrepreneurial skills. This brings to the fore the need for special care of young people, improvement of the efficiency of all measures through their permanent examination, and the revision of their goals and targets.

5. Developing youth entrepreneurship in Bulgaria

The most widespread motives amongst the youth to start up a business are to use the opportunity to achieve a good personal professional realization, to enjoy a higher income, or to avoid unemployment. In general, youth entrepreneurship concerns mainly two basic groups of economic actors: (a) those who create jobs and mostly self-employment and (b) those who represent so-called innovative entrepreneurship. Young entrepreneurs create, in most cases, micro-firms (often they are family firms) or even one-person firms in the following sectors and activities: self-employment in the service sector (hairdressers, beauty parlours or gyms), retail trade and catering (small shops or cafeterias), different kinds of repair works, cable TV service,

---

23 They are 86 in number, and up to 29 years of age (Loukanova 2005, 67-89).

24 Project BG 0202.01 financed by PHARE.

25 In 2005, nearly 1,950 young people participated in this Programme, which is over eight times higher than in 2003.

construction works, agriculture, printing and publishing, and so on. Innovative entrepreneurship can be observed mainly in information and communication technologies (assembling, trade and repair of computer equipment, but in a wider sense one can also include internet clubs).

Sources of initial capital for the young entrepreneurs, in particular in the early years of transition, were more often than not their own or family funds (inheritance, savings or loans by mortgage of their own or parents' property, loans from relatives or friends, funds received under different national or international projects and programmes, etc.), while in a number of cases they resorted to bank-credits.[26]

Up till now youth entrepreneurship in Bulgaria faced the following main challenges:

- An unstable business environment from the point of view of macroeconomic performance (insufficient economic activity, legislative omissions and imperfections, incorrectly carried out privatizations, wide-spread illegal practices in the shadow economy and corruption, insufficient social tolerance towards domestic entrepreneurs and so on), as well as from the point of view of development of the business sector which as a whole has not yet proved to be sufficiently stable and reliably creative.
- A lack of experience of youth because of age and the lack of continuity in the experience of previous generations, because of the specificity of Bulgarian historical development described above.
- A lack of those effective links between school, university and the business sector, which should awake interest and render business start-ups for young people easier.
- Due to an underdeveloped banking sector in the 1990s, favourable conditions for financing of private entrepreneurship for young people were unavailable.
- The unavailability of the above mentioned large share of migrants from Bulgaria, amongst whom are enterprising and smart young people who would have been capable of developing their own business in their country of origin.
- The lack of a special attitude towards and the promotion of youth enterprise activity both on the part of the State[27] and on the part of the business sector. The State's concern with some forms of active labour market policy (discussed in the previous section) is limited and should not be overstated because of

---

26 According to a survey on small firms in Bulgaria carried out in 1993, the share of own capital in starting-up business was 63 per cent, while the rest of 37 per cent is distributed as follows: bank credits – 16 per cent, family funds – 8 per cent, loans from friends – 5 per cent, from state funds – 3 per cent, loans from other firms – 3 per cent, other sources – 2 per cent (see in Bartlett and Rangelova 1997, 231-248).

27 A comprehensive Strategy for National Youth Policies was accepted for the period 2003-07 by the Ministry of Youth and Sport in Bulgaria. It is based on the principle of well-coordinated actions of all institutions that work with young people and follows recommendations of the Council of Europe, the White Book of the EU (2001), and the European charter for youth participation at a regional and local level. Until now, however, there is no information available regarding its implementation.

its nature and because it concerns unemployed young people, who have a relatively low level of education which predetermines the difficulties for them to start-up a business and (if they decide to do so) the nature of the business they will establish.

Conclusions

The perspective for further development of youth entrepreneurship in Bulgaria seems to be more favourable than in the recent past. The relevant aspects include the following:

- The further stabilization of the economic environment for business in the country, including the introduction of an institutional context for a modern market economy and the development of a successful economic policy.
- A very important incentive in this direction is full membership for Bulgaria in the EU from 1 January 2007, which is likely to involve a fuller consideration of those economic agents who have the capabilities to develop business in the context of the EU.
- Youth has gained some experience with the conditions of a market-type economy. Throughout the past 17 years young persons have lived, studied, and worked in an adequate market economy environment. Apart from education, young people benefit from the support of different national and international organizations, including NGOs.[28] This favourable environment sustains the idea that entrepreneurs are not born as such but are created and that the best type of entrepreneurial education is combined with practice.
- The observed increase in the educational level of young people and the encouraging policy by the state are indicators of the best type of policy a given country can implement.

---

28 Such an organization is the Junior Achievement Bulgaria (JAB), which is a branch of Junior Achievement (JA), the world's oldest, largest and fastest-growing non-profit economic education organization (founded in the U.S. in 1919). It was created 10 years ago to educate young Bulgarians to value free enterprise, understand business and prepare themselves as a workforce ready for the challenges of the future. JAB offers programs for elementary, middle, and secondary (high) school students. While elementary students learn about their roles as individuals, workers, and consumers, middle and high school students study the fundamentals of economics, create and operate their own student companies, and compete locally, nationally, and internationally in trade fairs and computer based competitions. JAB realizes its activity through many programmes, events and projects. JA's most popular program is the Student Company. This allows students to take part in creation and operation of an actual company that will produce and market its own product. In the process, students share in the decision-making, record-keeping, marketing, and other experiences that are crucial for the operation of successful businesses. In this setting, they can make mistakes, and gain experience and knowledge in a protected environment. This activity has become very popular as the number of students included in such firms increased nearly 3 times within a period of only three years: from about 5,000 in 2003 to 1,150 in 2005. See: www.jabulgaria.com.

- A vocational type of education has replaced the more hierarchical and comprehensive type of education, and this is a useful approach to prepare young people to start-up their own business.
- An initial process of the creation of necessary links between the university and the business sector can be observed. Different forms are envisaged: the set-up of technological centres, organized contacts, and training. There are indications that this activity will turn into an effective form of partnership for the development of young people's potential and their preparation for the real competitive business world.
- Young people tend to innovate and to take part in competitions more than adults. This is why business-oriented university centres focus on the mobility between teaching and research work based on competitive projects. It is furthermore very important to increase private business sector participation significantly; investment in this type of activity is in accordance with the Lisbon strategy. This means that the business sector should have enough incentive to invest in science and the improvement of the quality of human capital, in particular that of young people. Such an activity would have the positive effect of activating and stimulating the educational system in order to prepare a more adequate training for the market economy.[29]
- There are indications that a national policy for creating of stronger relationships between companies, on the one hand, and between companies and public sector research bodies, including universities, on the other, is in elaboration. This policy entails the idea that studying the industrial implications of university research projects and facilitating both relationships with companies and the development of start-ups is of great importance.[30]

---

29 The Innovation Strategy of Bulgaria related to youth entrepreneurship (2004) goes 'in tandem' with the National Strategy for Scientific Research and complements it in practice. It has been developed for industrial R&D and SMEs, and aims to strengthen the relationship between public and private research, technology and innovation, and to build up a system for entrepreneurship training. The measures related with the 'non-financial instruments' of the Innovation Strategy also demonstrate particular care for young and highly qualified professionals, by means of: training in entrepreneurship and the establishment of centers for entrepreneurship at high schools. The Innovation Strategy, in particular Measure No. 10, recommends high schools to offer specialized programs or modules in entrepreneurship as an additional (optional) qualification to their undergraduates. High schools should encourage entrepreneurial activities through: informing students about the possibility of starting a private business; supporting students in estimating the possibility for the implementation of their own ideas; supporting students in the assessment of the marketability of a product which is supposed to be the result of the implementation of a relevant idea; supporting start-up enterprises founded by students; training of teams for submitting project proposals in the context of the EU framework programmes; directing the start-up of firms to already existing incubators.

30 Since 1993, the Bulgarian-American Investment Fund (BAIF) has organized a competition for young entrepreneurs aimed at encouraging Bulgarians aged from 18 to 29 to develop a private business. In the last 10 years, about 40,000 young people took part and about 1,000 business-plans were evaluated. Until now, two-thirds of the projects evaluated continue

- The more stable and friendly economic environment is expected to attract emigrated young people who have already obtained an education and have acquired initial funds abroad to return home and start-up their own business.
- A good indicator of a more favourable economic environment is the development of bank credit in the last couple of years, also aimed at young entrepreneurs, which allows young people to apply for preferential credits for venture capital.
- The Structural Funds, and other external and internal programmes, raise expectations for the financing of youth entrepreneurship.
- The marked increase in the number of educated and trained young people is a positive tendency for the future development of business and the wider economy. The increasing proportion of vocationally trained young people would contribute to overcome the observed current discrepancy between, on the one hand, the professional skills of young people, gained in high school and the university, and, on the other hand, labour market demand.
- Youth entrepreneurship is gradually developing, both through the creation of a friendly business infrastructure and an active labour market policy.
- Different international projects and many, mainly bilateral, agreements between Bulgaria and different European countries play a significant role in the creation of entrepreneurial spirit and skills amongst the youth in Bulgaria. Youth entrepreneurship is still in an early stage, but is expected to achieve more perceptible results in the near future.
- In the transition of youth from school to labour, youth entrepreneurship should become particularly important and a permanently monitored process. This life-phase should become a subject of research and studies, and standardized indicators should be published periodically.

References

Agency for Small and Medium-sized Enterprises (2004), *Small and Medium-sized Enterprises in Bulgaria, 2002-2003*, Report of the ASME, Sofia.

Bartlett, W. and R. Rangelova (1997), 'Nature and Role of Small Firms in Bulgaria', in *The Bulgarian Economy: Lessons from Reform during Early Transition*, D.C. Jones and J. Miller (eds.), (Ashgate), 231-248.

Beleva, I. *et al.* (2001), 'Targeting Youth Employment Policy in Bulgaria', *Economic and Business Review for Central and South-Eastern Europe*, 3, June, 113-135.

Council of Ministers of the Republic of Bulgaria (2006), *National Development Plan of Bulgaria, 2007-2013*.

Employment Agency Labour Market, *Annual Survey, Republic of Bulgaria*, various years, http://www.az.government.bg.

Government of Bulgaria (2004), *Innovation Strategy of Republic of Bulgaria* (Sofia: Ministry of Education and Science), http://www.government.bg.

---

to function successfully. There are three money rewards for the best young entrepreneurs selected by an international jury.

IOM (2001), *Profile and Motives of Potential Migrants from Bulgaria* (Geneva/ Sofia: International Organization for Migration).

Kalchev, J. (2002), *Sample Survey of Mobility of Population. Population Census in Bulgaria 2001*, Vol. 6, Book 3 "Territorial Mobility of Population" (Sofia: National Statistical Institute).

Kalchev, J. (2005), 'External Migration of Bulgaria's Population', in *Demographic Development of Republic of Bulgaria* (Sofia: National Statistical Institute). Labour Market, Annual Survey, Republic of Bulgaria, various years, http://www. az.government.bg.

Loukanova, P. (2005), 'Youth Employment in Bulgaria', *European Employment Observatory, Review:* Autumn 2005, EU, Directorate General for Employment, Social Affairs and Equal Opportunities, December, 67-89.

National Employment Office (2001), *Survey on Employment and Unemployment*, June (Sofia: Ministry of Labour and Social Policy).

NSI, Statistical Reference of the Republic of Bulgaria (Sofia: National Statistical Institute), various years.

Rangelova, R. (2006a), 'Bulgaria in Europe: Economic Growth in the 20th Century', (Sofia: Publishing House of the Bulgarian Academy of Sciences "Prof. M. Drinov").

Rangelova, R. (2006b), 'Ageing Population in Central and Eastern European Countries. Proceedings of the conference "Ageing Population: Reality and Consequences, Policies and Practices" (Sofia: Centre for Population Studies at the Bulgarian Academy of Sciences and National Insurance Institute), 304-315.

Rangelova, R. (2006c), 'New Bulgaria's Emigration: Scale, Socio-demographic Profile, Economic Consequences', in G. Fóti and T. Novak (eds.), *Facing Challenges: Selected Key Issues of Economic Transformation and European Cooperation*, Proceedings of the Hungarian-Bulgarian Bilateral Workshop, 16 September 2005 (Budapest: Institute for World Economics, Hungarian Academy of Sciences), 50-73.

Rangelova, R. and K. Vladimirova (2004), 'Migration from Central and Eastern Europe: The Case of Bulgaria', *South-East Europe Review for Labour and Social Affairs*, Vol. 7, No. 3, 7-30.

Vladimirova, K. and R. Rangelova (2006), 'Human Factor and the Unused Possibilities for Growth and Competitiveness', *Economics*, No. 3, 6-9.

Chapter 9

Promoting Youth Enterprise and Self-employment: The Case of Croatia[1]

Ivo Bićanić and Marina Lang-Perica

1. Introduction

Quite justifiably and not necessarily for similar reasons youth entrepreneurship (YE) and self-employment (SE) have a special place in economics. This special concern is primarily a result of two important common features. First, both YE and SE are seen as especially important engines of dynamic change. This is because YE and SE are considered different with regard to: (i) factor mobility that leads to dynamic changes, and the exploitation of hitherto unperceived market niches and, (ii) innovative activities involving quick development and acceptance of new technologies and products. They are also viewed as economic agents with an above average propensity for risk taking and they very often constitute the first step from which larger firms developed. Finally, and no less important, they are seen as those parts of the economy from where future captains of industry are recruited and trained.

Their second common characteristic is no less important. It concerns capital market imperfections and the economic and social barriers faced by YE and SE. This market-generated suboptimal level of YE and SE results from important information asymmetries leading to imperfect credit distribution and credit market imperfections, their higher entry costs and their lack of networks and social capital that additionally hinders entry. The joint consequence of these two features is the suboptimal development of YE and SE, and the consequent social losses. Jointly these two features have often led to them being labeled as 'strategically important' and as 'untapped sources of growth, change and innovation' that face barriers that justify a special consideration in industrial policies.

This special position and concern for YE and SE is true for 'mature economies', i.e. economies that are institutionally and spectrally stable or slow-changing, which face no major internally generated shocks, and where levels of secondary uncertainty are low. EU policy is a clear manifestation of this. However, it is very likely even more true for 'transformation economies', i.e. economies that started dismantling socialism in 1989 or 1990, and replacing it with a capitalist economy, and which after 15 years of 'transformation' certainly do not fit the above description of 'mature

---

1 The authors would especially like to thank Mr. Marko Karan for help with the data.

economies'. These economies are still facing ongoing accelerated institutional and structural change, and experiencing the instability and various forms of deficits, both intentional and unintentional, the process generates.

For the European transformation economies, this transformation-engineered instability is further increased by the engineered instability resulting from EU integration, also with intended and unintended consequences. All three types of European transformation economies, i.e., the recently accepted EU members, EU candidate countries, and those involved in the stability and accession pacts, face this EU integration-engineered instability. Because of this accelerated change and instability for all these three types of economies, YE and SE are even more important than in 'mature economies'. This is because of the ability of YE and SE to be more dynamic, adaptive, mobile, flexible and generally technologically above average. Furthermore, in these economies YE and SE are very likely an untapped source not only of growth but also of accelerated change as well.

Croatia, a small (population 4.4 million, 2005 GDP of 38.5 billion dollars and an income per head in ppp of 13.185 international dollars, see EBRD 2006) Western Balkan economy, provides an interesting 'case study' for YE and SE in a transformation and integration setting. Its justification as a case study is a result of three things. First, it is a transformation economy facing both of the mentioned sources of instability. Probably its transformation generated instability is decreasing but definitely EU generated instability is increasing (a result of prospective EU membership and currently undergoing membership negotiations). Second, Croatia is a transformation laggard. As such, it has some important similarities both with other transformation laggards generally, and with other Western Balkan economies specifically (which are all laggards). Third, because since 2000 Croatia has been implementing YE and SE promoting policies and designing an institutional framework supporting them, the effects of which can be seen. This makes it an interesting case study, relevant for others.

The chapter proposes to deal with the Croatian case-study of YE and SE in four sections. The first briefly describes the entrepreneurial deficit in Croatia and thus defines the setting in which YE and SE operate. The second concentrates on YE, first by discussing the demography as a supply of YE, and then by studying the institutional and policy framework it faces. The third section deals with SE, by first determining its scope, and then studying policy support. The fourth and last section discusses the central aspects of YE and SE: namely some political economy aspects that determine their size and future development.

2. The entrepreneurial deficit and general entrepreneurship promoting measures

The 'entrepreneurial deficit' is still present in Croatia and has a dominant influence on YE and SE. This deficit defines the general framework for entrepreneurship and provides for the framework in which YE and SE operate. By implication, to understand the YE and SE-related issues, the general characteristics of Croatia's entrepreneurial deficit have to be described first.

In spite of relatively favorable initial conditions in 1989, Croatia started the transformation with an 'entrepreneurial deficit'. This deficit could be seen with respect to the number of entrepreneurs and their innovative behavior and, even more importantly, with respect to the social capital relevant for entrepreneurship. This 'deficit' can be interpreted as the lag of Croatian entrepreneurship indicators behind those of similar economies, indicating a relatively low level of entrepreneurship activity. As the transformation unfolded in Croatia, either all aspects of the entrepreneurial deficit were maintained or, more likely, have expanded. Furthermore, the deficit's relative size has unquestionably increased in relation to the transformation frontrunners (and the subsequent new EU members). The lag expanded in spite of pro-active policies aimed at promoting entrepreneurship implemented before 2000 and, much more vigorously, after 2000. Circumstantial and anecdotal evidence (more reliable analysis does not exist due to the lack of accessible data and a marked lack of interest) indicates the size of the deficit, and lag behind the frontrunners, which was even more pronounced regarding YE and SE (for an extensive discussion, see Franičević and Bićanić 2005).

The first aspect mentioned above, the 'entrepreneurial deficit', concerns the supply of entrepreneurs and their innovative behavior (the second aspect concerns social capital and is largely a question of political economy that will be dealt with in the fifth section of the chapter). The size of the deficit can be measured by actual entrepreneurial activity and its allocation, the innovative behavior of entrepreneurs and by the relevant features of the institutional framework supporting and promoting entrepreneurship. In spite of almost a decade of implementing pro-active policies, the data clearly indicate a low level of entrepreneurship (hence the existence of the deficit), and the continued existence of an unfavorable climate for entrepreneurial activity and investment. Some recent studies, however, indicate a possible mild improvement in entrepreneurial activity and dynamics in recent years.

2.1 Entrepreneurial activity

Three indices are used to measure the intensity of entrepreneurial activity. The first is the Gross Firm Formation Rate (the ratio of gross firm formation to the number of registered firms), the second indicator is the Total Enterprise Activity or TEA Index (the ratio of newly established companies to the adult population over a 42-month period), and the third is Firm Density (the number of firms per capita). The first and third can be derived from official statistics, while the second is calculated as part of the Global Enterprise Monitoring (GEM) Project (for comprehensive results see Reynolds 2004, while GEM the results for Croatia in 2003 and 2005 are in Singer et al. 2003 and Singer et al. 2006). National surveys such as FEM 2006; also seek to measure entrepreneurial activities. These empirical results form the backbone of entrepreneurship related research (see Franičević 2005; Bartlett and Čučković 2005; and Singer 2003).

The values of all three indicators clearly indicate a below average enterprise performance in the nineties, which stretched into the early part of the twenty-first century. The Total Entrepreneurial Activity (TEA) (the index measures the dynamics of new entry and is derived from official statistics), index in 2002 was 3.6 (the

Slovene, Hungarian and Irish one were 4.6, 6.6 and 9.1 respectively), giving Croatia the last place among the 41 countries included in the 2003 GEM project.

Another index is Firm Entrepreneurial Activity (FEA) (this index measures the established firms that expect to have an innovative activity on the market and grow; it is derived from survey data and because of its 'soft' basis is used more rarely and with caution). Its value for Croatia in 2003 was 1.12 (the average was 2.0 and the Slovene value was 2.7), ranking Croatia as 36th out of 41 countries. With a value of 37 in 2003, the Firm density index in Croatia is also relatively low, e.g., Slovene firm density is 57. The Gross firm formation rate is also low; Croatia's 2000-2003 average was 2.2. In all these cases, the values of the indices clearly indicate that in the early part of the first decade of the 21st century Croatia has a relatively low level of entrepreneurial activity. They are lower than most other similar economies (e.g., Slovakia), lower than in transformation frontrunners (e.g., neighboring Slovenia or the Czech Republic) and similar to transformation laggards (e.g., Russia and Poland, in many respects including this one, Poland is a transformation laggard).

On the one hand, this clearly indicates a low level of entrepreneurial interest and, if one assumes talent to be non-discriminatory, significant entry barriers. However, when taking a more positive view, these low levels show a great potential for development and an untapped resource.

The most recent data on entrepreneurial activity is ambiguous. While the Gross firm formation rate and Firm density have not changed significantly, the Total Enterprise Activity calculated by Global Enterprise Monitoring Project (GEM) for 2005 (published in Singer et al. 2006) shows a major improvement. Comparing the GEM calculated TEA index for 2002 (see Singer 2003, and 2005, see Singer 2006) shows a 70% increase from 3.6 to 6.1, and an improvement in the ranking from 41st to 18th. This result, while showing a major increase in firm start-ups and in dynamics, does not say much about levels, which have remained relatively low. In addition, the explanation of the increase may be in the business cycle.

The first results pertain to the start-ups in 1999 and 2000, while Croatia was in a recession (the 1999 growth rate was negative and in 2000 a political regime change took place), the second refer to an upswing in 2003 and 2005. There may be other explanations for the increase (some institutional changes gave incentives to ghost companies) as well as in a structural improvement and effects of pro-active policies (which set up a pro-entrepreneurship policy framework in 2000 and supported SMEs as described). The values of one index (TEA) does not necessarily show a reversal and an upward trend, but certainly does indicate more research is required to explain the unquestionable improvement in the TEA index and the stagnation of other indices.

There are other aspects of the entrepreneurial deficit, which are more difficult to quantify, but which are no less important. The first concerns innovative activities. When measuring the innovating activities of entrepreneurs by the number of registered patents and R&D expenditures, one finds that Croatian values are low (see Franičević 2005). The second regards the goals of entrepreneurial activity. It seems that most entrepreneurial talent and effort is dedicated to 'unproductive activities' (rent seeking and protection). Results from extensive interviews (reported in Čengić 2005) seem to show this.

Table 9.1 The entrepreneurial deficit

	Croatia GEM 2003	Croatia GEM 2005
Total Enterprise Activity (TEA)	3.6 rank: 41 (out of 41)	5.6 rank: 19 (out of 50)
Firm Density	21.5	20.6*
Gross Firm Formation Rate	1.80	4.4*
Active firms as % of total	39.5	44.8*

TEA: ratio of newly established firms over a 42-month period to adult population
Firm density: number of firms per capita
Gross Firm Formation Rate: ratio of gross firm formation and number of registered firms
* data for 2004
Source: Singer (2003) and Singer (2006), *Statistical Yearbook of the Republic of Croatia* (various years).

Research shows the main characteristics of the 'typical' Croatian entrepreneur (for results on the national level, see Čengić 2005 and for a case study of one town (Osijek), see Šišljagić 2005). Usually he is male, middle aged (35 to 45 years), with prior work experience (usually over 10 years with more than one employer, usually in the private sector) and above averagely educated (often with a university degree). Furthermore, the 'typical entrepreneurs' his driving motive is independence and a relatively short time horizon. It must be added that due to the peculiarities of Croatian law so-called 'crafts' are a separate category, therefore, those entrepreneurs registered as craftsmen are not included among entrepreneurs.

2.2 The general framework of entrepreneurial activity promotion

YE and SE operate in a general framework, which defines entrepreneurial activity and provides specific measures regulating YE and SE. Since the latter are derived from the former an understanding of YE and SE is impossible without a discussion of the general framework defining entrepreneurial activity. This framework determines the entrepreneurial climate and is defined by regulations, policies and their applications. While data on laws, regulations and policy statements is available (not always easily), data on applications and policy efficiency is not easily accessible. This is because of the administration's lack of interest in issues related to policy monitoring and analyses regarding policy efficiency (both regarding implementation and its effects). However, international institutions showed an interest in these questions and, as a result, most of the available data is in publications from international organizations (see World Bank 2005 or OECD 2004), or international projects (see Reynolds 2003 or Singer et al. 2003 and Singer et al. 2006). There are only two domestically generated data sets. One is national (see Čengić 2005), and the other a regional one (see Šišljagić 2005). These provide a snapshot view of the investment and business environment but do not yet allow for comparisons over time. Perhaps additional research will enable a comparative analysis based on the GEM results for 2002 and 2005.

The data regarding the investment environment clearly indicates that starting a business in Croatia is not easy. As the data in Table 9.2 shows, the formal costs are high and if administrative foot-dragging is added they increase further. Certainly, the notorious widespread corruption provides more sand than grease. Especially important is the time required to start a business; for YE or SE, which start with relatively low amounts of capital, this is especially important. The national rate of savings (around 20%) and investment (around 22%) are low in comparative terms, especially when compared to fast growing economies (whose investment rate is over 25% and for some Asian fast-growing economies with investment rates around 30%). Šišljagić (2005) notes that 52% of entrepreneurs included in his study estimated that the conditions and environment for business were very bad or bad. Even though 'hard' data does not exist, anecdotal evidence shows that the inherited 'bias to bigness' remains (a tendency of the state and banks to operate with large firms and their over representation in the size distribution of firms), as does the bias to large investment projects. In addition, the state's share in investment is high (state led growth through financing large infrastructure projects, e.g., motorways and railways). This puts YE and SE at a further disadvantage because they involve small projects, which as a rule are not dependent on the state.

Another aspect of the unfavorable institutional framework for entrepreneurship concerns start-up costs expressed in time and money. As Table 9.2 shows both are high. Again, they should put YE and SE at a relative disadvantage because of their lack of capital, time and experience. In May 2005, the government attempted to reduce them through an ambitious project simplifying start up called 'HITRO.HR'. This service is a one-stop shop where potential entrepreneurs, including YE and SE, can get all start-up information at one address, at which they can register new firms. The service that operates from 22 regional centers has reduced the registration time to, on average, 14 days for firms, and 2 days for crafts. Between May 2005 and February 2006, the service was used to establish 1.100 firms. Other institutional changes aimed at making the business environment more favorable concerned 'e-PDV' (electronic payment of VAT)' and 'e-zamljišne knjige (electronic land register)'. While these services are an improvement, their effect on the business climate still has not been determined, because the number of permits and approvals has not changed.

Data on the state's direct influence on the business environment point to similar conclusions about the business climate. This is seen in the state dominance in the economy (reflected in high levels of subsidies, a 'large' state with regard to the budget and ownership of assets and state-led growth), the level of corruption (see below), administrative barriers, (e.g., the number of permits for start-up or days required for registering a property), and the low accountability and reliability of some important institutions (the notorious slowness of courts and outdated land books). Even though the World Bank's *'Doing business with...'* series indicates Croatia is not the worst case with regard to all these indicators, it is always at the bottom end of the ranking and firmly behind the front-runners (see World Bank 2004).

Table 9.2 Time and permits required for start-up

	Croatia
Days required to register company	49
Number of procedures for registration	12
Days required to register a property	956

Source: World Bank (2004).

Table 9.3 General entrepreneurial activity promoting institutions

Government ministries	Ministry for the economy, labour and entrepreneurship Ministry of finance Ministry for Youth, Veterans and Intergenerational solidarity Ministry of Agriculture
Government Agencies	Croatian Agency for Small Firms (HAMAG)
Local government institutions	Department for Economy/Development in each of the 22 counties and additional ones in large towns
National lobbying institutions	Croatian Chamber of commerce Croatian Chamber for Crafts Croatian Association of Cooperatives Croatian Association of employers
Specialized state owned banks	Croatian Bank for Reconstruction and Development (HBOR)
Local institutions	Entrepreneurship zones/Technological parks Incubators

Source: Internal MELE communication.

The described unfavorable environment exists in spite of a pro-active government policy regarding entrepreneurship. The first relevant policy was indirect and aimed at reducing interest rates through subsidies. It started in 1997, and reduced commercial interest rates from the range of 18-35% to 9-11% by 1998. The program worked by establishing a fund with money from the central and local government and banks. During 1998 and 1999, it approved 2.275 loans at an average interest of 7-9%. When commercial interest rates fell in 2000, the program was terminated. The price of capital can no longer be viewed as a major barrier to entrepreneurial activity (banking practices in loan approval are another matter).

The first government document explicitly promoting SMEs was dated December 9, 1999. Among the pilot projects it involved, there was one for young professionals (this experimental pilot policy was conducted in the capital, Zagreb, and through it students in their final year worked with chosen entrepreneurs; its efficiency was never monitored and it was not extended to other regions), training the trainers for entrepreneurship, and an entrepreneurship promoting program.

For YE, the program aimed at young professionals was the most important. After the elections a new coalition came to power on a wide popular mandate to dismantle crony capitalism (see Bićanić and Franičević 2005, for the efforts they made and their subsequent failure). An important part of its program was a very pro-active policy supporting entrepreneurship and the formation and development of small and medium sized firms. A new Ministry for Small and Medium Sized Firms and Entrepreneurship (MSMEP) reflected this new interest. The ministry had its own budget, a discrete but effective minister and was to a great degree staffed by enthusiasts. Its activities were based on an analysis and a program for developing small firms in the period 2001-2004 (see Vlada 2001). The program was accepted by the government on June 14, 2001, and in 2002, a law promoting small firms was passed (see Zakon 2002). The policy mostly included 'soft' measures' (involving education, consultation and local infrastructure) and a few 'hard' measures (subsidies). After the 2003 elections, the new government's reorganization of early 2004 abolished the MSMEP and its activities were divided. Most of them came to the new Ministry of the Economy Labour and Entrepreneurship (MELE), that is now the principal actor in entrepreneurship related activities. The new policy framework is based on the Program for promoting small and medium sized entrepreneurship for the period 2004 to 2008. This program was accepted by the government on May 5, 2004. The policy framework follows EU policy guidelines and recommendations in this area.

The program involves three goals. The first concerns general policy guidelines (e.g., raising competitiveness, increasing exports, supporting manufacturing, improving the business climate, supporting clusters). The second 'soft' policy measures (e.g., zones, reducing barriers, education, and tax policy). The third includes quantifiable targets (e.g., a TEA of 10, average employment in crafts of 2). The program also gives mention to 'special target groups'. The four groups deserving special attention are the young (those below 30 in the case of Croatia), women, invalids and war veterans. This document forms the basis for the current policy towards entrepreneurship generally, and thus for YE and SE.

MELE defines the government's policy framework with regard to entrepreneurship, including YE and SE, but it is not the main actor implementing it. The main policy implementation is in the 21 counties (20 regional administrative units and the City of Zagreb that has the status of a county) and some larger towns while the lowest level of local government, i.e., the communes, is not very relevant. Each of them has a Department for the economy/development that deals with entrepreneurship-related issues. Through these local government offices central policies are implemented and, rarely, local policies added.

Among the general entrepreneurship promoting activities, those of special importance for YE and SE are subsidized premises in entrepreneurship centers (entrepreneurship zones are primarily aimed at entrepreneurs with high growth rates, or larger business ventures and hence not suitable for YE and SE), or business incubators. Both centers and incubators are established by local government (counties or towns), and thus subject to local initiative but also partly financed by central government. Not infrequently these central funds are used for administrative and management purposes or for financing office space and premises instead of maximizing entrepreneurship promotion. There are many such zones (255) (communes establish them as well) in Croatia. The 2006 MELE budget allocated about 11.5 million € for the zones and about 1.65 mil € for infrastructure in these zones. Currently in Croatia, there are 13 incubators (or institutions, which under a different name, e.g., technological parks, perform the same task). These incubators subsidize entrepreneurs generally by providing space for three years (the first year is rent free, in the second year only 25% of the rent is paid, and in the third 75%), bookkeeping and office assistance (for a limited period), and help them to prepare loan applications and find financial support from commercial banks.

Another general entrepreneurship promoting activity open to YE and SE concerns bank loans. They come in three forms. First are the subsidized loans and financial facilities offered by the Croatian bank for Development and Reconstruction (HBOR). This bank offers loans for export activities, some sectors and for some targeted groups (e.g., family hotels in tourism and rural environments). Second are the loans offered by commercial banks with guarantees given by the Croatian Agency for Small Firms (HAMAG). This independent government agency has its budget and can guarantee up to 80% of the value of loans (the entrepreneur approaches the bank, the bank approves the loan and then it seeks the guarantee). Usually these are loans for ten years with a two years grace period. The third are loans for two kinds of targeted groups. The first are first time entrepreneurs. The second are special groups, in the case of Croatia these are women and young entrepreneurs, invalids and war veterans. Even though these subsidized loans have low interest rates in Croatia till 2006, there are no funds for seed or venture capital loans, and these kinds of loans and funds are not included in the laws. Policy-makers intend to develop the system in the direction of establishing public funds for seed and venture capital and give incentives to private capital to provide more seed and venture capital. Another direction of future development of the promoting system will go along the lines of the Lisbon declaration by providing incentives for a greater involvement of universities in R&D firms.

The efficiency of these programs is unknown since there is no monitoring or analysis (internal or published). This complete lack of interest among policy makers for monitoring their policies and analyzing their efficiency and impact will be a recurrent theme in the chapter. In addition, arguably, it is the central deficiency of the whole policy framework. The only data that sheds some light comes from a regional study of 214 respondents to a questionnaire that shows that entrepreneurs consulted entrepreneurship promoting agencies, the ministry and the employment office in 12%, 7% and 10% respectively. The main support came from family, friends and other entrepreneurs, in 76%, 57% and 45% respectively (for the data see Šišljagić 2005).

3. Youth entrepreneurship

Young entrepreneurs form one of the specially targeted groups in the pro-active government policy towards entrepreneurship (women, veterans and invalids are the other groups). Before discussing the actual policies supporting and promoting YE its supply must first be discussed.

3.1 The demographic framework for 'youth entrepreneurship'

The demographic statistics concerning youth provide a framework for the supply of YE. Three sets of data stand out because of their importance in this respect. The first is the composition, the second human capital, and the third employment.

The first supply-side aspect of YE concerns the number of eligible young people. The data from the most recent population census for 2001 shows that the share of the age group 20-24 and 25-29 in the total population of 4.4 million was 6.8% and 6.6% respectively (see Statistical Yearbook of Croatia 2005). The latter value is included since in Croatia youth statistically, and with regard to benefits and various policy targets, lasts until 30 and not until 25 as in the EU. Thus the aggregate supply for YE eligible for support is 13.4% of the population or almost 600.000 inhabitants. However, the data also indicate an aging population (this is not unusual for a Central European society) indicating this share will decrease over time. However, this is not the only reason for an increasing dependency rate going beyond the share of the old age retirement. This is a result of two things. The first is that in the early nineties the main labour shedding policy was through early retirement. The policy has created a large number of retired people who are now in their late middle ages. The second is that after the Homeland war (which ended in 1995) force reductions that was largely managed through early and beneficial retirement for veterans (sentence is not clear). As a result the present ratio of dependent to employed is almost 1:1 and Croatia has the youngest retired population (the average age is 50 years).

The second supply-side aspect of YE concerns education and the level of human capital of the under 25 and under 30 population. The basic data can be found in Table 9.4. In Croatia, secondary school coverage varies around 90%, with about 70% of secondary school leavers continuing in some form of higher education (in recent years many private non-university higher education schools have been established). The education system thus yearly produces 18-year-old labour market entrants with vocational training, and almost 10.000 labour market entrants with a university degree. For many social and historical reasons the average duration of university studies in Croatia is above 6 years so most labour market entrants with a university degree will be more than 25 years old when entering the labour market, and high number will drop out of university education in order to find employment. This would not make them young by EU standards, but by Croatian standards it would, as a cut-off point is put at 30. Among the population of under 30 over 3% have a university degree, which is below the EU level. However, there is another important aspect to the statistics indirectly linked to YE. The number of paying students (i.e., those whose tuition fee is not covered by the Ministry) is increasing. Partly this shows a 'quiet privatization in education' and a mismatch but partly also an increased interest in investing in education. Regardless of the reasons, it is clear that an increasing number of young are investing in their education. Their study costs are covered by their families (credit facilities are only now becoming available but are still far from the rule) and they have limited subsidies (health insurance and canteen). Infrequently they also have lower academic standards because in entrance exams they did (suggestion: do) not pass the threshold for the Ministry quota. This interest in investing in education should not come as a surprise if one considers the results calculated by Šošić (2004), which showed a significant increase in the return on education.

Table 9.4 Education attainment of youth/youth human capital

	2000	2001	2002	2003	2004
Secondary school 'coverage', % of 15 year olds entering secondary school	91.1	90.9	88.1	91.9	90.3
Number of secondary school leavers	49 081	48 203	48 057	47 092	48 548
Number of higher education entrants (% of secondary school leavers)	84.6	91.3	98.2	96.6	94.8
Number of university entrants (% of secondary school leavers)	58.0	63.0	67.0	69.3	70.1
% of higher education students paying for their education	11.2	13.4	15.3	16.7	17.2
% of university students paying for their education	12.3	13.9	16.1	17.2	17.9
Tuition cost for one academic year at university	670€	670€	670€	670€	670€
Number of university graduates	8 884	8 387	9 415	9 243	9 362
% of university graduates in population under 30 years	3.01	2.84	3.19	3.13	3.17

Group 24-29 in population census 2001. There were 294 497
Source: *Statistical Yearbook of the Republic of Croatia* (various years).

In addition to the numbers of secondary and higher education students, the quality of education is important for YE. Numerous results seem to indicate low quality and plenty of room for restructuring. Lowther (2004) shows that the educational system is not well adapted to the needs of the 'knowledge-based economy'. Šošić (2004) shows that the enrolment rate and its structure are unfavorable since enrolment rates in age groups of 15-24, 25-34 and 35-59 are lower than in the EU-15 and the share of technical education is low. The same author (see Šošić 2004, 35) shows a low level of efficiency in the educational system with only 1/3 of graduates completing their courses and only 1/5 of young completing college and university education, placing Croatia at the bottom of the range observed in developed countries. Other recognized inefficiencies in the educational system (see Lowther 2004) concern the average years of education, which in Croatia is significantly above the four-year average for an OECD student. He also notes that both teaching and learning methods, and the organization of the curriculum (on all levels), '[are] not conducive to developing high-level technical, technological and social competencies needed by a competitive economy' (Lowther 2004: 20). With such education indicators 'it is hard to expect catch-up to the level of human capital that exists in countries with developed economies' (Šošić 2004, 35). No doubt, fundamental educational reforms are needed as well as an increase in education's share in GDP (currently below the EU-15 level). They may prove to be far more important for future growth than any highly publicized explicit pro-entrepreneurship policy considered by the government.

Table 9.5 Youth employment and unemployment

	2004
Youth employment age group 15-24	
Working age pop. 15-24	545.000
Labour force 15-24	215.000
Employment 15-24	144.000
Employment rate*	26.0%
Share in agg employment**	9.1%
Activity rate***	39.5%
Employment/population ratio	44.0%
Youth unemployment group 15-24	
Registered unemployed 15-24	71.000
Unemployment rate#	32.9%
Share in total unemployed##	23.1%

*Employment rate: ratio of 15-24 employment to 15-24 labour force
** Share of employed 15-24 in aggregate employment
*** Share of labour force 15-24 in working age population 15-24
# ratio of registered unemployed 15-24 and labour force
Share of unemployed 15-24 in aggregate unemployment
Source: *Statistical Yearbook of the Republic of Croatia 2005* Central Bureau of Statistics, Zagreb, 2005.

The third aspect of YE supply concerns the employment and unemployment record of the under 25. The most recent basic statistics are shown in Table 9.5. The data shows that there is 71.000 registered unemployed youth and 144.000 employed youths. Regarding unemployment, almost a third (32.9%, the total registered unemployment rate is 13.8%) of all youth is unemployed, and that almost a quarter

(23.1%) of all unemployed are under 25 years. Concerning employment data, the youth activity rate is 39.5% (the total activity rate is 51.1%) and less than a tenth (9.1%) of all is employed. The 71.000 unemployed and 144.000 employed youth together with the 330.000 inactive provide the demographic supply eligible for YE. Space prevents a more detailed study of the supply here.

3.2 The institutional framework of 'youth entrepreneurship' promotion

YE face the general entrepreneurship-promoting framework discussed above. In addition to this, there are special targeted policies promoting YE. The first program, targeted at YE, which started in 1998, was a secondary school educational program (Junior Achievement Education), which was offered as an elective workshop to secondary schools. However, since it did not get the sincere support from the Ministry of Education it did not have any lasting impact. The same year and with similar effects, the Training the trainers program for Entrepreneurship, which included a topic on YE, was set up. The interest in YE got under way more seriously after 2000.

After the 2000 election, a new coalition came to power on a wide popular mandate to dismantle crony capitalism (see Bićanić and Franičević 2005 for a survey of these efforts and their subsequent failure). This government had a special interest in promoting small and medium term enterprise formation (the interest was reflected in a new Ministry for Small and Medium Sized Firms and Entrepreneurship, MSMEP) which included YE. Within the policy framework described above, the first targeted YE program was formulated in the MSMEP in 2002 and its implementation started in 2003 (for its impact, see Izvješće 2003). This program defined a general approach to YE that later became the basis for all subsequent efforts but also included a major flaw because it left out agriculture (still 30% of the population are rural). This was not only due to the lack of interministerial communication and turf war but also a result of institutional reasons (with the land books being outdated, in agriculture YE could not get the financial support envisaged by the program).

With the 2004 reorganization of public administration (following the electoral defeat of the Social Democrat Party and its coalition partners, and the return to power of the Croatian Democratic Union with its coalition partners, the latter party was in power during the whole nineties), there was a reduction of the number of ministries and a reshuffling of their mandate. In the process, 'youth'-related issues ended up in the care of a number of ministries whose YE activities were mutually uncoordinated.

First, the Ministry of Youth, Veterans and Intergenerational Solidarity drew up a National Youth Policy. This was a framework document intended to provide a coherent strategic policy for all youth-related policies but ended as a document of very generalized and rather vague policy statement. YE was declared as one of its priorities. This Ministry, however, had neither the mandate nor the funds to implement policies promoting YE (by 2005 even the youngest veterans were not under 30). The task of actually designing, implementing and partially financially supporting YE promoting policies became part of the mandate of numerous government institutions. The ministries involved were the Ministry of the Economy,

Labour and Entrepreneurship (MELE) and its Department for entrepreneurship, the Ministry of Finance (MF), which regulates tax incentives and the Ministry of Agriculture, Forestry and Water, which had programs for YE in rural development and agriculture. Various development and entrepreneurship supporting agencies were also involved; the most important among them was The Croatian Agency for Small Business, HAMAG (established in 2002) and the Croatian Bank for Reconstruction and Development (HBOR). All these institutions designed a policy conglomerate and their activities are not mutually coordinated. In addition to this, there was an overlapping mandate of central and various levels of local government (county, cities and commune) that did not add to clarity. Certainly, the multitude of policy agents provided an entry barrier that the government tried to reduce by instituting a one-stop Croatia program in May 2005. The current (2006) actual policies for YE in place have five aspects: (i) education, (ii) financial subsidy, (iii) soft loans, (iv) start-up support and (v) craft oriented measures. Of course, many other programs for entrepreneurs and crafts are also very important for YE but these are not targeted specially at the young and were dealt with above.

The educational policy is the main YE task of MELE and part of their general policy package for educating entrepreneurs targeted at young 'first' experience entrepreneurs. The main policy forms are workshops financed, but only partly organized, by central government, and that are usually held locally, i.e., on the premises of chambers of commerce or other business institutions, and rarely in educational institutions (schools or universities). Since the start of the program in 2000 until December 2005 there are no statistics regarding the number of such programs or the number of participants, and no follow-up studies to show how efficient they were in mobilizing YE and provided later useful advice (suggestion: 'after-care'). The current workshops are usually 3-day workshops with up to 30 participants, organized 2 or 3 times in a given region a year. The actual teaching is outsourced to the private sector. In secondary schools, especially business and commercial ones, YE are largely covered by the curricula of other subjects even though depending on the interest of the local headmaster, while workshops are organized on a demand-driven basis. However, the MELE is not satisfied with the interest for such capacity-building activities.

The second kind of policies for YE are interest-rate subsidies for YE and first entry entrepreneurs. Assuming that they do not have financial resources, in Croatia YE can currently get a subsidized loan with a 2% interest rate. Until 2003 the program reduced the commercial interest rate by 2 percentage points but with the general fall in interest rates it now offers a fixed interest rate. The difference between 2% and the commercial interest rates is financed out of a special fund. The procedure for getting these loans takes place at the local level and is organized by the County Department for the Economy (Croatia is divided into 21 countries plus the City of Zagreb). In the first step each county allocates funds for subsidized loans. These local funds are then automatically matched by central government funds (i.e., from the state budget), and then commercial banks add their share. Local authorities choose the banks, in the beginning only one was chosen but now increasingly more than one are included. Then the local authorities set up a committee to approve loan applications. There is no fixed formula for membership in these committees but they aim to include all local stakeholders. As a rule, they include representatives from civil society (e.g., youth organizations), the local financial community (the local government determines which banks' local branch is represented, initially only one bank was chosen but now the number of banks is increasing), local government, local Chamber of Commerce and the Chamber of Crafts and appointees of central government (MELE).

This committee makes a list of recommended loans, after a public call for applications (the call determines a list of all required documents), which are usually for 7 years with a 2 year grace period and a minimum threshold of 35.000 Kuna's (about 5000€) and no maximum. The final decisions are made by the banks (due to the size of the loan usually not the local branch but the head office that, as a rule, is not in the region). For example, in 2005, the committee approved 423 loans but banks eventually approved only 228 of them. The two main shortcomings of the procedure are if loans are below the minimum threshold and that the final decision taken by the head office of the bank and not locally (sentence not clear). The procedure checks moral hazard and adverse selection problems that can result from local power relations and networks (corruption?) both by the representation of MELE and banks' head offices. Its actual performance is difficult to determine due to bank secrecy (regarding selection and default) and lack of interest in follow up studies by the local government or MELE.

The public only has access to the aggregated credit subsidies in the MELE budget. More complete data exists only for 2003 (see Izvještaj 2003), which shows that in Croatia 227 young entrepreneurs applications were accepted whose aggregate value was almost 25 million HRK (about 3.4 mil €) and 47% were in the service sector (the remainder of the report aggregates data for credits to women and youths). In addition to the credit subsidy, HAMAG offers YE guarantees for up to 80% of an approved commercial loan. Since this facility is offered to all SMEs, the share going to YE is unknown. Occasional anecdotal evidence in the press indicates that there are cases where YE subsidies and loans have been abused by otherwise ineligible firms, using them as soft loans through dummy firms, but this anecdotal evidence also seems to indicate abuses are very much the exception.

The third policy is another kind of subsidy but this time aimed at reducing overhead start-up costs for YE (as well as for other targeted groups and first time entrepreneurs). Four kinds of costs are included (program compilation, IT costs, loan application and transaction costs that are up to 0.98% of the loan value and office equipment). There is a minimum amount offered in this support program but there is no maximum. The 2006 MELE budget has earmarked 5 mil HRK (around 650.000€). This is an increase from the 4 mil. in the 2005 budget which was used for dealing with the 1.200 applications. Again, follow up studies to determine the efficiency and use of this kind of subsidy are not available, so one cannot claim Croatia has a coherent start-up support program.

Table 9.6 Interest rate subsidies for youth entrepreneurship

	2003	2004	2005	2003-05
Number of subsidized loans	227	423	212	862
Size of interest rate subsidy (mil HRK, mil €)	1.5 (0.2)	3.51 (0.5)	5.33 0.7)	10.34
Interest rate subsidy as % of aggregate support for entrepreneurship	0.54	0.78	0.83	0.72
Interest rate subsidy as % of central government budget	0.002	0.004	0.005	0.004

Source: Internal MELE communication.

Table 9.7 Start-up subsidies for youth entrepreneurship

	2003	2004	2005	2004-05
Number of subsidized youth entrepreneurs	n.a.	72	285	357
Av. Size of start up subsidy (HRK, €, thousands)	n.a.	11.1 (1.5)	8.8 (1.2)	9.2 (1.3)
Aggr start-up subsidies (mil HRK, mil €)	n.a.	0.85 (1.1)	2.5 (3.4)	3.3 (0.52)

Source: Internal MELE communication.

The only available study about the efficiency of support program is Šišljagić (2005). His results are based on 214 respondents to a questionnaire in one town (Osijek). They show that 10% of respondents were entrepreneurs who started their business after secondary school and that 25% started young (18-30 years). The most frequent start-up is in consumer services or trade.

4 Self-employment

The SE are recruited from the whole adult population. In the case of Croatia, according to the 2001 population census, out of a population of 4.27 million the share of the active population is 43%. Among the active population 1.27 million or 69% are employed and around 300.000 or 16.4% are registered unemployed (the Survey unemployment rate is 13%). Studies show that the employed do not have a special interest in SE or any kind of entrepreneurship (see Pološki-Vokić and Frajlić 2004). The average employee is in his/her 40s, undereducated, not mobile and has no additional training. This description does not fit an entrepreneurially minded active population but does support the entrepreneurial deficit discussed above.

4.1 The importance of self-employment in the economy

Determining the size of SE in Croatia is not easy. Due to peculiarities of the Croatian economy the SE appear in two kinds of business establishments: firms and crafts. The SE in firms has the standard meaning. Crafts are an important peculiarity. Crafts in Croatia relates to a long tradition of artisanship and small firms that has far-reaching historical roots (going back to Austro-Hungary and before 1918), persisted in socialism (as the only domain of the private sector) and has continued during the transformation. Crafts face no sectoral constraints (they operate in almost every sector of the economy) and face no employment constraint (even though SE firms dominate, and on average they employ 1.6 persons, there are some that employ over 100 workers). The difference is that firms are registered in courts while crafts in the local government offices, and firms pay taxes based on performance while crafts pay lump sum taxes determined by local tax authorities (this opens room for flexibility, perhaps corruption). Another difference is that for registering a craft one needs some proof of expertise or education in the area of registration while this is not a requirement when registering a firm. The latter is an important feature that has kept crafts alive and attracted many newcomers, especially in the knowledge-intensive sectors.

The basic data on SE is in Table 9.8. The number of SE (i.e., the number of firms not employing anyone) in 2004 was over 42,000, which is 44% of all active firms. Since 2000 and the introduction of a Ministry for small and Medium sized Firms and for Entrepreneurship and a more pro-active entrepreneurship-promoting policy these numbers have increased, the number of firms by 17,000 and their share by 12 percentage points. Regarding the sectoral distribution of SE, not unexpectedly, the majority of them are in consumer services.

Table 9.8 Number of self-employed firms

	2001	2002	2003	2004
Self-employed	25498	33889	35680	42232
% of all firms	32.9	38.8	40.1	44.4
Y-onY index	–	132.91	105.28	118.36
Self-employed in consumer service	9143	12258	12099	13977
Self-employed in tourism and restaurants	2683	4222	4754	6674

* Number of self-employed firms (firms with no employees)
Source: Statistical Yearbook of the Republic of Croatia (various years).

4.2 Self-employment promoting policies

Policies promoting SE in firms and crafts differ. Concerning SE firms, they face all the mentioned policies designed to promote entrepreneurship. There are no special policies aimed particularly at the SE as a special category of entrepreneurs. The SE face the same policy package as other entrepreneurs: education, membership in incubators, business in enterprise zones, interest rate subsidies, start-up support, etc.

The policy towards crafts, and with it SE in crafts, is different. First, crafts are organized in special chambers and have a lot of lobbying power. Second, to a great extent policies are locally determined, especially regarding the taxing regime. Third, there are no special policies for SE crafts, indeed the policy tries to increase the employment so that they leave the SE arena (a policy subsidizing employment and apprenticeship).

5. The political economy of youth entrepreneurship and self-employment

A discussion of the formal institutional framework relevant for the promotion of YE and SE is incomplete without a discussion of the political economy framework. This framework is, in turn, determined by the type of capitalism that was generated during the transformation in Croatia.

Elsewhere (see Bićanić and Franičević 2005) the name 'crony capitalism' was suggested as the term best describing the type of capitalism that emerged in Croatia during the transformation. In the economic literature, this term is increasingly being used. The dominant feature of 'crony capitalism' as an economic system is that the allocation of capital through capital markets, however organized, has a second place, behind other types of allocation. Capital allocation is determined by mechanisms that rely heavily on informal and non-market considerations and above all on personal networks, i.e., 'cronyism'. This is also a system in which large rents persist and which generates extensive quasi rents. Rents or quasi rents are not distributed through markets and are not competed away. Instead, they are distributed through rent-seeking behavior and state capture. Entrepreneurs see the state as a generator and protector of profits and rents, and cronyism as a major way of achieving entrepreneurial goals. The state thus becomes important and large but weak. Corruption is widespread, the rule of law and security of contracts weak and public administration and governance ineffective. While this kind of system may have generated fortunes for the few it has excluded many and economic inequality and equity levels are high (see Bićanić and Franičević 2005).

The justification for using a special term, i.e., 'crony capitalism', for the type of capitalism prevalent in Croatia was twofold. The first was to stress the difference of capitalism practiced in Croatia and Modern Regulated Capitalism (and in this sense, it provides a measure of transformation failure with regard to its actual course and expectations). The second was to stress what was argued as its main feature, namely 'cronyism' (and with it the dominance of non-market and thus non-transparent decisions and networks).

The implications of 'crony capitalism' for YE and SE are fa-reaching and reflected in several barriers. In the case of YE and SE in Croatia, the three most important barriers to their development are arguably those resulting from a large and weak state, the tolerance of the unofficial economy, and widespread corruption.Each is briefly discussed below.

Three consequences of a large but weak state are especially important for YE and SE. The first and obvious one is a result of YE's and SE's small economic power and weak bargaining positions due to their size and influence. By definition, they are small and by tradition unorganized. While this permits YE and SE to coexist on the margins of the economy, it also precludes their full development and their role as a growth engine. The second and no less important consequence of the weak state implies a bad administration. With regard to YE and SE this is reflected in administrative incompetence and ignorance as well as in conservatism (here it is not intended in the political sense) and lack of flexibility. Neither is conducive to the development of YE and SE and shows a lack of understanding for their main features and advantages. In that kind of public administration there is also a bias to postpone decisions and an even more important bias to bigness. This leads to the third important consequence of crony capitalism for YE and SE in Croatia: The delegation of YE and SE related issues into the local government level. Apart from general policy guidelines the local level is the place where policies for YE and SE are actually implemented.

The implications of 'crony capitalism' on the local level are perhaps the greatest barrier for the development of YE and SE. Over time, and 'crony capitalism' has been developing in Croatia since the early nineties, the system has generated excessive predatory administrations and specific structures and social capital through pronounced clientism and paternalism (of course there are some counties in Croatia where this is less pronounced). At the local this very often involves the collusion of politicians and 'local' tycoons. Since at the local level even YE and SE-generated rents and quasi rents can become interesting, both YE and SE have become subject to crony capitalism practices. This brings us to the third mentioned consequence for YE and SE. It concerns the lack of will and, very likely, of knowledge and political power, to sincerely promote YE and SE at the local level. The required changes and improvements in local government that are fundamental for promoting YE and SE involve, of course, undermining the very basis of local crony capitalism and thereby imply its dismantling. Currently, in early 2006, there is no such internal pressure for change but there is hope in some quarters that external conditionality from the EU may provide the required pressure (but given past experiences of conditionality there may not be much room for optimism). The importance of 'crony capitalism' at the local level resulting from state failure is best reflected in the big regional variety of YE and SE in Croatia. The most outspoken understanding for them exists in the north coastal region and the northwest. These regions are not only the most developed ones but were also least influenced by war.

A discussion of the political economy of YE and SE in Croatia would not be complete without reference to corruption. The Croatian economy is considered both internally and externally a highly corrupt economy whose corruption levels are a major barrier to economic growth (and many other things not directly concerned here). The level of corruption is not only routinely discussed in World Bank reports but is also a subject of EU conditionality (which requires a credible anti-corruption strategy in place). In spite of notorious problems of measuring corruption there seems to be no doubt that Croatia is a highly corrupt economy. Both aspects of corruption, i.e., 'large scale' (as a form of accumulating wealth at places of public and private sector interfaces through siphoning and policy capture), and 'low level' (as a form of everyday survival, i.e., in health, administration, etc.) are high. All things considered, the Corruption Perception Index, CPI, is the most frequently used and its values provided in the Table 9.9 clearly indicate these high levels and no improvement in Croatia's ranking.

Given such high levels of corruption and a bad reputation regarding YE and SE, efforts to reduce the scope for corrupt practices must be mentioned. This primarily concerns the financing of YE and SE. The YE and SE promoting system (and that for SMEs) has included safeguards aimed at reducing corruption. Thus, in developing procedures special care is given to transparency, both that of the administration (accessible public information about procedures, application deadlines and the results of loans awarded) and banks (they must register all subsidized loans to the antimonopoly agency and approve loans with adequate collateral and repayment guarantees, the involvement of central offices, etc.). The banking system itself is, arguably, one of the most advanced sectors of the economy (having gone through a costly rehabilitation scheme, periods of numerous bankruptcies which cleansed the financial sector of banks with dubious practices and it is now over 90% owned by foreign banks). This does mean that as far as central government involvement in the YE and SE promoting system has shown a concern and reduced the possible scope for corrupt practices (sentence not clear). This does not mean there is no corruption elsewhere but it does indicate where anticorruption efforts with regard to YE and SE should be directed to in the future.

Table 9.9 Corruption indicator

	2000	2001	2002	2003	2004	2005	2006
Corruption indicator*	3.7	3.9	3.8	3.7	3.5	3.4	3.4
Croatia's ranking**	51 (of 90)	47 (of 91)	52 (of 102)	59 (of 133)	67 (of 145)	70 (of 160)	69 (of 163)

* value of 1 indicates no corruption, value of 5 indicates complete corruption
** number of countries included in brackets
Source: Transparency International.

There is another important feature of the Croatian economy that is extremely relevant for SE. This is the unofficial economy. From socialism, Croatia inherited a dynamic and entrepreneurially-oriented tradition of second jobs in the unofficial economy and in unofficial economic activities in general (see Bićanić 1990). In the late 80s, the estimated size of the unofficial economy was around 30% of the Gross Material Product. The importance of unofficial SE further increased in the early days of the transition. This was due to not only the institutional deficit but also to the transformation and war-generated crises (Croatian production fell by about a half). Authorities turned a blind eye towards it and saw it as a kind of 'social safety net' (see Franičević 1997 and Bićanić and Ott 1997). In the mid 90s, its size was estimated around 25% of GDP, but in some sectors (construction, tourism), it was much larger and in one (retail) it was larger than the official sector (see Bićanić 1997). The most recently reliable estimates estimated the size of the unofficial economy around 15% of GDP (see Ott 2002), while less reliable ones continue to offer much higher estimates.

However, the nature of the unofficial economy has changed with the transformation. Now, arguably, Croatia's unofficial economy is much more like that in other middle-income capitalist economies. Even though second jobs remain important unofficial activities related to unregistered employment and tax evasion have probably increased. For SE the unofficial economy remains extremely important.

This is true for at least two reasons. First, because the official statistics undervalue true SE, to what extent is, however, unknown. Second, and arguably more important, is because the unofficial economy can be considered as a training and testing ground for potential 'open' SE. Before registering, potential SE reduce the risk of failure by trying their ideas in the unofficial economy. Croatia's policy makers still turn a blind eye on unofficial activities of SEs, part-time or full-time. Furthermore, YE and SE can straddle the divide with some activates involving official and some unofficial activities. The external influences pushing YE and SE into the unofficial economy are high taxes, numerous government regulations and a slow and inflexible administration. Together the two incentives provide 'push' factors. To these one must add the prevailing business culture with a high tolerance for the unofficial economy (this bias towards the unofficial economy predates the transformation). All the YE and SE promoting policies give rise to an opposite incentive system. All the benefits provided by these policies depend on that part of YE and SE activities conducted in the official economy.

Finally, two empirical results from different questionnaires may indicate two more relevant aspects of the political economy of YE and SE. The first is from Šišljagić (2005) where the main motive for entrepreneurship is freedom and the main barrier the business climate and support (52% of respondents estimate them as bad and very bad). This would probably make YE and SE firms less prone to 'crony capitalist' activities. In this sense they could not only provide an engine for growth and change but also an active agent for reducing 'crony capitalism'. The second result does not provide such ground for optimism. Štulhofer (2002) inquired into, among other important youth related topics, the value system of the young. He notes a high level of conformity and opportunism with respect to their values. If that is true then YE may not be able to fulfil some of the expectations placed upon it. In either case, both results are important indicators regarding the social capital that is a precondition for major path switching and possible discontent with crony capitalism.

5. Conclusions

The chapter tried to show that YE and SE in Croatia provides an interesting case study for youth entrepreneurship (YE) and self-employment (SE) promoting policies in transforming economies facing an entrepreneurial deficit, i.e., a relatively low level of entrepreneurial activity. The Croatian experience is especially relevant for Western Balkan economies that share many similarities with Croatia.

A more serious interest for designing promoting policies regarding YE started after 2000 when YE were first identified as a target group. Since then the government has been implementing various policy packages. The current policy package for YE has four pillars. It is focussed on education programs, support for start-ups, interest rate subsidies and a program for crafts. The program is defined by the central government but implemented locally (on the town, commune or county level) through procedures that try to involve all stakeholders. The main drawback is the lack of knowledge on policy efficiency that could act as a feedback for policy improvements (it shares this deficiency with all economic policies in Croatia). In addition to policies specially targeted at YE, the latter also have access to a wide variety of general entrepreneurial promoting policies.

SE does not have any special policy package but enjoys the benefits afforded to first time entrepreneurs, small and medium sized enterprise, and pro-active policies for some sectors. Due to institutional specifics SE includes two different types of establishments, firms and crafts. SE in crafts seem to be in a far better position as is shown by the large number of SE in crafts. Crafts have a well-organized and influential lobby which seeks benefits for all crafts, including SE. For both types of establishments the main policy guidelines are centrally designed, but the policy implementation level is that of the local government. As in the case of YE there are no comprehensive studies of the success of these policies but interviews and anecdotal evidence seem to suggest that the policy package is not the main barrier.

The main barrier for the efficiency of YE and SE promoting policies is on the implementation level and a result of the specific form of capitalism generated in Croatia by the transformation, which is best referred to as crony capitalism. The most relevant aspects of crony capitalism for YE and SE concern the large but weak state, policy inflexibility, and the high tolerance for unofficial economic activities and to a lesser degree high levels of corruption. This in turn implies that the main barriers for the development of YE and SE are in the political economy. As a result, and in spite of policies promoting them YE and SE, both remain an untapped important source for future growth and, no less importantly, an important agent of social change.

References

Baumol William (1990): 'Entrepreneurship: Productive, Unproductive and Destructive' *Journal of Political Economy*, 98, 193-201.

Bićanić Ivo (1997) 'Measuring the size of the unofficial economy' *Financijska teorija i praksa*, 21:1-2, 15-29.

Bićanić Ivo (1990) 'The Role of the Unofficial Economy in Yugoslavia' in Los Maria, editor *The Second Economy in Marxist States* (London: Macmillan).

Bićanić Ivo and Franičević Vojmir (2005): 'EU Accession and Croatia's Two Economic Goals: Modern Regulated Capitalism and Modern Economic Growth' *UACES 39th Annual Conference,* mimeo.

Bićanić Ivo and Katarina Ott (1997): 'Neslužbeno gospodarstvo u Hrvatskoj – uzroci, veličina i poslijedice' (The unofficial economy in Croatia: causes, size and consequences) *Financijska teorija i praksa,* 21:5-6, 765-784.

Čengić Drago (ed.) (2005) *Menadžersko-poduzetnička elita i mdornizacija: razvojna ili rentijerska elita* (Managerial entrepreneurial elite and modernization: developmental or rent seeking), (Zagreb, Institute Ivo Pilar).

Čučković Nevenka and Bartlett Will (2005): 'Entrepreneurship and Competitiveness: Europeanization of SME Policy in Croatia' UACES 39th Annual Conference, mimeo.

Franičević Vojmir (1997): 'Politička ekonomija neslužbenog gospodarstva - Država i regulacija' (The political economy of the unofficial economy: State and Regulation), *Financijska teorija i praksa,* 21:1-2.

Franičević Vojmir (2005): 'Poduzetništvo I ekonomski rast u hrvatskom postsocijalističkom kontekstu' (Entrepreneurship and economic growth in the Croatian post socialist context) in Čengić Drago, editor (2005): *Menadžersko-poduzetnička elita i mdornizacija: razvojna ili rentijerska elita* (Managerial entrepreneurial elite and modernization: developmental or rent seeking), (Zagreb, Institute Ivo Pilar).

Franičević Vojmir and Bićanić Ivo (2005), 'Challenges of Growth and Europeization: The Case of Croatia', in *Enterprise in Transition, Proceedings of the Sixth International Conference on "Enterprise in Transition",* Split-Bol, May, 26-28, 2005, Faculty of Economics: Split, pp. 328-331 (Book of extended abstract) and pp. 1539-1555 (CD Rom with full papers).

Izvješće (2003): '*Izvješće o provedbi programa poticanja i promicanja poduzetništva mladih za 2003 godinu*' (Report on the implementation of the program for stimulating and furthering youth entrepreneurship) (Zagreb Vlada RH).

Lowther Joseph (2004), 'The Quality of Croatia's Formal Education System', in Bejaković, Predrag and Lowther, Joseph (eds) (2004), *Croatian Human Resource Competitiveness Study,* Zagreb: Institute of Public Finance.

OECD (2004): *Croatia: Enterprise Policy Performance Assessment* (Paris, OECD, mimeo, October 2004).

Ott Katarina (2002): 'Neslužbeno gospodarstvo u republici Hrvatskoj 1990-2000' (The unofficial economy in the Republic of Croatia 1880-2000), *Financijska teorija i praksa,* 26:1, 1-30.

Pološki Vokić Nina and Frajlić Dubravka (2004), 'Croatian Labor Force Competitiveness Indicators: Results of Empirical Research', in Bejaković, Predrag and Lowther, Joseph (eds) (2004), *Croatian Human Resource Competitiveness Study* (Zagreb: Institute of Public Finance).

Reynolds Paul D., Bygrave William, D. and Autio Erkko (2003), *Global Entrepreneurship Monitor: 2003 Executive Report,* Wesley, MA: Babson College; London, London Business School and Kansas City, MO: Kauffman Foundation).

Singer Slavica, Pfeifer Sanja, Borozan Đula, Šarlija Nataša Šarlija and Oberman Sunčica (2003), *Što Hrvatsku čini (ne)poduzetničkom zemljom: Rezultati GEM 2002 za Hrvatsku* (What makes Croatia an (non)enterprising country, Results of the GEM 2002 report GEM for Croatia), (Zagreb: CEPOR).

Singer Slavica, Pfeifer Sanja, Borozan Đula, Šarlija Nataša Šarlija, and Oberman Sunčica (2006): *Hrvatska I poduzetništvo – ima nade Rezultati GEM 2002 za Hrvatsku* (Croatia and entrepreneurship – there is hope: Results of the GEM 2005 report GEM for Croatia), (Zagreb: CEPOR).

Šišljagić Vladimir (2005): *Prvi korak u podezewtništvo* (The first step into entrepreneurship), (Osijek BIOS).

Statistical Yearbook of the Republic of Croatia, various years.

Štulhofer Aleksandar (2000), *Nevidljiva ruka tranzicije: Ogledi iz ekonomske sociologije* (The invisible hand of transition: Essays in economic sociology), (Zagreb: Hrvatsko sociološko društvo).

Štulhofer Aleksandar (2002), 'Dinamika društvenog kapitala', Workshop on Social Capital in Croatia, Zagreb, March 6-7 (on www.vle.worldbank.org/gdln/Courses/Course47/Introduction2.htm?11000034).

Vlada Republike Hrvatske (2001) *Program razvoja malog gospodarstva 2001-2004* (Development program for small enterprises 2001-2004) Vlada Republike Hrvatske, Zagreb.

World Bank (2004): *Doing business in Croatia 2005: Removal of Administrative Barriers to Growth* (Washington: World Bank).

Zakon o poticanju razvoja malog gospodarstva (2002) (Law for promoting small firms), (Zagreb: Narodne Novine N.N. 29/02).

Index

Printed in the United States
by Baker & Taylor Publisher Services